Milton's Spenser

ALSO BY MAUREEN QUILLIGAN

The Language of Allegory

Milton's Spenser

THE POLITICS OF READING

By

MAUREEN QUILLIGAN

Cornell University Press

ITHACA AND LONDON

PR
3562
.Q54
1983

International Standard Book Number 0-8014-1590-X
Library of Congress Catalog Card Number 83-45149

Printed in the United States of America

*Librarians: Library of Congress cataloging information
appears on the last page of the book.*

*The paper in this book is acid-free and meets the guidelines
for permanence and durability of the Committee on Production
Guidelines for Book Longevity of the Council on Library Resources.*

TO MICHAEL MALONE

Slayer of dragons,
messenger of God,
and—what is rarer—
partner in true conversation.

Contents

Acknowledgments

The Cleopolis where I learned to read is a city of many houses. Among the principal residences are those mansions inhabited by Paul Alpers, Stanley Fish, Isabel MacCaffrey and Christopher Ricks. For their teaching, I thank them. In the long cultivation of my own garden outside these city limits, the seeds of fellow workers have borne much fruit. In particular, I wish to thank John Guillory and Lauren Silberman. For the care and humanity of their readings, I express my deep gratitude to Leslie Brisman, G. K. Hunter, and Thomas Whitaker. For the continuing generosity of their support, I thank John Hollander, and—yet once more—Calvin Edwards. For another extremely useful reading, I am indebted to Balachandra Rajan.

I thank as well all the people involved in the interdisciplinary conference "Renaissance Woman / Renaissance Man," Yale University, March 12–14, 1982, especially A. Bartlett Giamatti, president of Yale University, and Laura Bornholdt, vice-president for education of the Lilly Endowment, for their valuable support, and most particularly Nancy Vickers and Margaret Ferguson, my co-organizers, for their heroic endurance. The participants at the conference, both speakers and audience, made the recasting of some of the arguments in this book both absolutely necessary and a real joy.

Finally, I acknowledge with profound gratitude the John Simon

Guggenheim Memorial Foundation, whose grant made the completion of this book possible.

MAUREEN QUILLIGAN

New Haven, Connecticut

Preface

The origin of this book lies in historical accident, for I first happened to read *Areopagitica* the night of December 2, 1964—the night before the first large student "bust" of the 1960s, when the Oakland police forcibly removed eight hundred students who were sitting in at Sproul Hall, the main administration building of the University of California, Berkeley. I had decided not to take part in the demonstration earlier that night, but the next morning I changed my mind and joined the general strike called by the Free Speech Movement. Two things had happened to cause this difference: first, I had read Milton's tract, which had convinced me that in order to have freedom of speech a society had to allow its citizens not only all the materials for making a choice, but also the right to make one, actively. And second, I saw the Oakland police. I saw therefore what most middle-class American (particularly Californian) children are not usually in a position to see, the physical reality of social class and the official violence of the state. Newspapers had been taped over the large glass windows of Sproul Hall so that no one could see what was happening inside. But every once in a while the windows shook, the glass glinting in the sun.

I mention this historical accident because it has had a great impact on my interest in Milton in particular and in Renaissance literature in general. Because of it I cannot convince myself that literary studies do not have immediate and immediately political bearing on a citizen's daily behavior. Reading is not academic. It is a protopolitical act. Renaissance theorists had always said that literature, like rhetoric, has power within the polis—and oratory, as I had personal experience of it in those days, need not serve any particular politics to persuade individuals within a massed body of people that the times required active choice. (The spectrum of political opinion within the Free Speech Movement stretched from far right to far left, for *all* political activity had been banned: no one on campus could sell Goldwater bumper stickers—in autumn of an election year—*or* copies of Mao's Little Red Book; the students in the coalition objecting to this new and admirably evenhanded rule were united only by their desire to exercise their often diametrically opposite political persuasions.)

Milton's and Spenser's politics could hardly be more different. As public apologist for colonial violence of the most extreme order in Ireland, Spenser was no stranger to the state's necessary mayhem; secretary to Lord Grey, Spenser was present at the massacre at Smerwick (in which Sir Walter Ralegh was one of the two commanding officers directly in charge); two hundred English soldiers butchered six hundred men—unarmed Italian and Spanish mercenaries and Irish rebels—and hanged a few pregnant Irish women. Much of the pressure behind the events of Book V of *The Faerie Queene* is Spenser's analysis of the forces that make such force necessary. One senses too that all the conventional battles in *The Faerie Queene* where knights wade ankle-deep in blood are not mere rhetorical formulas for Lord Grey's secretary. Doubtless Spenser would have preferred a court appointment closer to the centers of power; yet like Swift, he was doomed to attempt the impossible, trying in his way to "save Ireland."

Milton's apology for regicide was to defend, of course, a violence considered much less defensible than the massacre at Smerwick— for those mercenaries, as Spenser argued, had unconditionally surrendered all their rights. To strike off the head of the head of state was far worse, if only because it struck at the entire structure of society. Should we see any incongruity in the high Renaissance art that Milton and Spenser create and their engagement with the sheer (violent) force of power in their societies? It is of course to stretch the case a bit, and perhaps to put too dangerously strong and literal an

image before my readers' eyes, but there is a certain represen-
tatively Renaissance congruous incongruity within the picture of
Federico of Montefeltro, duke of Urbino, reading with his armor
on. As for Federico, for the people of the English Renaissance reading was an activity congruent with the fullest exercise of secular
power.

Paradise Lost may seem a withdrawal into a paradise within, in
1667 the only retreat for a failed revolutionary. But it is not, and I
think we do it a disservice to read it without acknowledging its persuasive arguments for the necessary restructuring of society along
the lines laid down by the revolution's particular successes. If all
prior epics had traced the *translatio emperii* moving westward, from
Troy to Rome to Troynovant, Milton traces the empire as it moves
within. What is left after reformation and regicide is—to put it at its
most basic—the political unit of the individual nuclear family. Here
lodges Milton's empire, here he plies his subtlest political persuasions. That they may be termed private and sexual makes them no
less political.

In contemporary feminist theory, we are beginning to develop
terms for discussing the real political impact of such intimate sexual
arrangements. And recently in the current enrichment and qualifi-
cation of Marxist literary theory by its incorporation of post-
Saussurean developments in linguistically oriented interpretation
we have begun to have a critical vocabulary for defining the subtle
historical connections between literary texts and social power. At
certain points in the pages that follow, particularly Chapters 1 and
4, I have found it convenient to maneuver some of my arguments
with these useful tools. In the main, however, my terms for making
intra/extratextual bridgings in my readings rely less on trends in
current literary criticism than on the English Renaissance's own
assumptions about the action of language and literature within the
polis, and on the peculiarly political nature of sexual power. Thus
while the following arguments are inextricably bound up with the
concerns of current literary criticism, they are initially (and ultimately) historical.

The first chapter, "The Rhetoric of Reading," therefore focuses
its description of the problematic political effect of reading (fiction)

on contemporaneous Renaissance discussions (notably Sidney's *Apology for Poetry* and Spenser's Letter to Ralegh); it then reads selected passages of Book II of *The Faerie Queene* from the point of view of Milton's famous argument about them in *Areopagitica*. Guyon and the Palmer become for Milton paradigmatic readers who, in negotiating the linguistically dense landscape of fallen language in *The Faerie Queene*, reveal reading to be a process of making interpretive discriminations among verbal ambiguities, discriminations that simultaneously are also ethical and political choices.

The second chapter, "The Sin of Originality and the Problem of Fiction," deals with the problem of fictiveness which both poets confront in the very language they use when writing about the truth—the problem Spenser calls "Errour" and Milton "Sin"—and with the peculiar problems posed Milton by the residual allegory of his epic. Signaling his reader to be wary of the necessary mediating element of fictiveness by a distinctly Spenserian sort of wordplay, Milton makes the presence of *The Faerie Queene* felt within his text when he wishes to protect *Paradise Lost* against its place within a secular tradition of fiction. As Spenser's had before, Milton's reader learns to negotiate this fictiveness (which includes the tradition of Ovidian epic) by becoming self-conscious of its nearly seductive attractiveness and by learning to choose to remain free to change, not caught in the fixity of such fictions as Satan's metamorphoses in Book X of *Paradise Lost* or Malbecco's successive deformations in Book III of *The Faerie Queene*.

The third chapter, "Ineffability, Prophecy, and the Problem of Truth," broaches the obverse side of the issue of fiction: the intractable ineffability of sacred truth, essentially contrasting Milton's and Spenser's response to the divine authority of the scriptural text. Spenser's confrontation of divine ineffability ends in the writing of allegory parallel to that divine text, the interconnections between which are to be made by the sacral work of a community of readers. Specifically choosing not to write allegory, Milton wings past the barrier of ineffability into an astonishing inspiration of true oral prophecy, placing his remarkably literal narrative within the interstitial abysses of the divine text, all the while cautioning his readers to beware the fictive frame.

The final chapter, "The Gender of the Reader and the Problem of Sexuality," opens the issue of the poets' concern for the politics of sexuality—a concomitant issue to Milton's ideas about inspiration, which he often figures in sexual terms. To pose questions about the reader's gender is to probe further into issues of inspiration, for Spenser into his relationship with Elizabeth I, and for Milton into his relation with the sacred nurturing Muse. While the chapter begins from the widest disparity between the two poets (their historical audiences being so different), it ends in seeing one of the closest congruences. For entirely different political reasons, both poets saw sexual love as a proper heroic subject, fit for an epic. In the case of Spenser, who wrote under the authority of a single woman, the issue of the reader's gender goes immediately to the function of the epic's political effect. To pose the same question of Milton's epic is, surprisingly, to redefine the heroism and the empire he celebrates.

Milton wrote in *Areopagitica* that Spenser was a better teacher than Scotus or Aquinas because he made his reader experience the real strains of choice. I should perhaps at this juncture explain that the class to which I did not go during the student strike that fall day of 1964 was a Milton seminar taught by Stanley E. Fish, who was then writing the book that turned out to be *Surprised by Sin: The Reader in "Paradise Lost."* Being not so much a reader of that text as one of the readers within it, I confess that this particular dimension of the historical accident has had its indelible impact on these pages. Affective stylistics plus a profound belief in the political relevance of reading are like two twins cleaving together, forming the ideology that is the basis of my reading. I was a heretic then in that class, and trust that I am still one now—the strongest orthodoxies spawning the most enduring heresies. My heresy then was to argue that the presence of allegory in *Paradise Lost* posed interesting questions for Milton's poetic—and that is the enduring heresy firing the central thesis of this book: as an allegory, self-consciously interrogating its own status as fiction, *The Faerie Queene* intentionally offers strategies for interpretation which, when Milton incorporates them into his specifically nonallegorical *Paradise Lost*, form part of his text's self-consciousness about its necessary (intentional) interpretation by the reader's reading—not merely as a fictive but, revisionarily, as a true text.

My present heresy, in concretizing reading in a certain way, leaves the realm of critical abstractions and moves back into politics and history. Although to ask questions about the gender of the reader may seem merely the next logical question to pose in current theoretical concern over the reader, I in fact came upon it instructively enough not by way of querying reader theory (of any school), but actually by sitting down to read a Renaissance text, as I had been taught to read. In a sense, I simply took seriously for the first time Spenser's dedications and rededications to Elizabeth throughout *The Faerie Queene*. Attentive as I was being to "scenes of reading," I was struck by the concretization of the reading scene in the Proem to Book IV, where Spenser's invocation of Cupid, as I argue below, is not for inspiration for the poet to write, but for the queen to read, the text. Imagining a picture not unlike that of Federico of Montefeltro, I realized with a shock the very peculiar political implications of the scene: the reader, so pivotal within the historical context, was female.

The most attractive aspect of the critical issue of the reader's gender is very much bound up with the issue of the text's historical intentionality. To interrogate a specifically female reading of *The Faerie Queene* is to open the text to a potentially heretical (uncanonical) reading that need not be mounted against the text's intentionality. Manifestly, blatantly, with full and conscious political purpose, Spenser included at least one named female within his poem's addressed readership. And insofar as Milton grapples with the rhetoric of reading which he appropriates from Spenser, he grapples with the female experience within Spenser's (and his own) readership. To trace connections between the two poets in terms of their different address of the female reader is not merely to begin writing a history of the reader's gender; it is, I trust, to begin to assess in concrete terms the truly political implications of reading, whatever the century in which it takes place.

M. Q.

Milton's Spenser

CHAPTER *1*

The Rhetoric of Reading

JOHN DRYDEN announced in his *Preface to Fables Ancient and Modern* that Milton had confessed that he was Spenser's poetical son: He "has acknowledged to me that Spenser was his original."[1] While this ascription of Milton's filial respects could itself be one of Dryden's modern fables, it does have the ring of truth. "Original" sounds, after all, like a word Milton might have used—he was a poet manifestly interested in questions of origin. Obviously, it was convenient for Dryden to locate his grand rival's paternal seat in England and in the gothic, unneoclassical excesses of *The Faerie Queene,* reserving for himself a continental correctness. Yet even if Milton said no such thing, Dryden was right: "Milton was the poetical son of Spenser."

It is rather puzzling to think how long it has taken scholars to treat Dryden's theory with sustained critical interest. It is astonishing to realize how long the delay has been when we consider that we are talking about a lag in tracing connections between the two major Renaissance epic poets in English. While a number of recent books have given the question substantial consideration, and another is imminent and yet another promised, this flurry of activity is

1. John Dryden, *Essays,* ed. W. P. Ker, 2 vols. (1900; rpt. New York: Russell and Russell, 1961), II, 247.

quite new.[2] Such a cluster of recent critical interest is itself suggestive; if we take time to arm ourselves with some historical selfcon-
sciousness and ask not only when the relationship was not interesting
before, but why it has become so interesting now, we may the more
precisely fill in a bizarre hiatus in the genealogy of English literature.

Both the delay and the current interest in relations between
Milton and Spenser have something to do with our changing paradigms for the unfolding of literary tradition, and with the ways
these paradigms highlight or simply blot out whole chunks of the
literary landscape. To the eye of much nineteenth- and twentieth-
century criticism, Spenser's most typical procedures have been well
nigh invisible, and it is really not surprising that with an understanding of one crucial element in the equation essentially missing,
no one should have bothered to work the problem out. To name that
element "allegory" is to place under a now (and very recently)
privileged label a complicated rhetorical procedure for engaging the
reader in the production of meaning in narrative; it is also to point
to what is fast becoming the cynosure of most current critical under-
takings: the reader.[3] As an approach that places the reader (rather
than the author or the text) at the center of the critical enterprise,
criticism of allegory generally focuses on the consumer end of the
triangular process of literature, the other two angles of approach

2. Patrick Cullen, *Infernal Triad: The Flesh, the World, and the Devil in Spenser and
Milton* (Princeton: Princeton University Press, 1974); John Guillory, *Poetic Authority: Spenser, Milton, and Literary History* (New York: Columbia University Press,
1983); A. Kent Hieatt, *Chaucer, Spenser, Milton* (Montreal: McGill-Queen's University Press, 1975); Richard Mallette, *Spenser, Milton, and Renaissance Pastoral* (Lewis-
burg, Pa.: Bucknell University Press, 1981); Richard Neuse, "The Virgilian Triad
Revisited," *Journal of English Literary History* 45 (1978), 606–39; Joseph A. Wittreich, Jr., *Visionary Poetics: Milton's Tradition and His Legacy* (San Marino, Calif.:
Huntington Library, 1979).

3. For two convenient surveys of the vast array of critical approaches aiming
themselves at the reader, see Susan R. Suleiman and Inge Crosman, eds., *The
Reader in the Text: Essays on Audience and Interpretation* (Princeton: Princeton University
Press, 1980); and Jane P. Tompkins, ed., *Reader Response Criticism: From Formalism to
Post-Structuralism* (Baltimore: Johns Hopkins University Press, 1980).

being, in this economic metaphor, the producer (the author) and the product (the text). This metaphor is useful only insofar as it suggests that literature is not a static objet d'art but a set of transactions pressured by forces analogous to those that mark functioning economies, which are also forces that change over time—and which it is the business of criticism to describe. Now, as in the Renaissance, the reader is perceived to be an important element in any poetics; thus to spend time over the rhetoric of reading as practiced in the Renaissance may also be to illuminate it in our own time—an undertaking that has political implications.[4]

Critical approaches which have instead taken as their points of entry the author and the text—biographical and formalist criticism—have had little to say about Milton's debt to Spenser. Because criticism is now more interested in the rhetorical position of the reader with respect to the text, and so necessarily in the nature of allegory, it is in a much better position to gauge relations between these two authors and the two epic texts they produced.[5] This shift toward the reader is a recent development in literary criticism. Since the romantic period most theories of poetic tradition have focused on the author and the processes of lyric creation, on the way a poet generates a new work out of the bits and pieces of tradition he gathers by the labors of his own poetic procedures. In this poetical age, the critic's business has been to seek sources, to

4. For a discussion of the neglect of political considerations in recent critical theory see Tompkins, ed., *Reader Response*, pp. 201–11.

5. Patrick Cullen's *Infernal Triad,* approaching relations between Milton and Spenser in terms of an "allegorical lineage," is a case in point. However, in emphasizing the schematic nature of the allegorical procedures Milton and Spenser share, Cullen recognizes that he risks an "anachronistic" definition of allegory (p. ix) and he does not, in fact, concern himself with the reader's function. Yet his use of the term "allegory"—whatever his definition—is still germane. Joseph Wittreich's approach in *Visionary Poetics,* while it calls the reader's experiences "epiphanic" or "apocalyptic," rightly stresses the similarity of the reader's experiencing of the two poems. For a discussion of the difference between the reading process posited by structuralist (and poststructuralist, "deconstructive") methods of critical discourse and the process required in allegory, see my *Language of Allegory: Defining the Genre* (Ithaca, N.Y.: Cornell University Press, 1979), pp. 236–41.

find the pieces of the old facade in the new foundation. Thus, in the romantic sense of tradition, Spenser holds his place, insofar as he does, by providing in essence pretexts to Shakespeare's plays, producing those primitive plots that Shakespeare's genius expanded into *Lear* and *A Winter's Tale*. This approach does not illuminate relations between Spenser and Milton, which are in general even less visible than relations between Spenser and Shakespeare. Small pieces of *The Faerie Queene* do lie about the surface of Milton's texts; but they hardly betray the cornerstones or bracing struts that unobtrusively support Milton's major structures (and there are fewer and fewer in evidence as Milton's career progresses).

Recently Harold Bloom's much more self-consciously Freudian approach to romantic attitudes toward literary genesis has focused on the obstacles besetting the poet-producer of a text's meaning within a specific literary tradition of whole texts. He has very usefully suggested that *The Faerie Queene* is an essential text against which Milton wrote *Paradise Lost* and has also most usefully supplied us with a set of terms for describing links in poetic tradition more energized than "echo" or "allusion."[6] By establishing the currency of sexual metaphor for describing the dynamic of relations between poets and prior texts, Bloom has retrieved for poetry a power that had passed into a less personal and less intimately intense terminology since the Renaissance. However, at the same time that Bloom's approach translates the dynamics of a basically lyric intertextuality into the drama of family romance, it necessarily sacrifices our ability to appreciate a specifically narrative poetry's public and more corporate, political powers—powers poetry was assiduously argued to have during the Renaissance. Because Bloom needs to turn Milton into the first romantic poet rather than let him remain the last Renaissance man, he locates the influence of *The Faerie Queene* at the most subjective and least conscious id-level of Milton's private psyche; such criticism does not allow *Paradise Lost* to remain what it is, a Renaissance epic, one of the two most self-consciously public poems in the English language and therefore

6. Harold Bloom, *A Map of Misreading* (New York: Oxford University Press, 1975), pp. 50–51.

a poem supremely aware of the rhetorical, and so political, nature of its generic manipulations. Another general paradigm for conceiving of the order of tradition—best described by T. S. Eliot in "Tradition and the Individual Talent," where each successive work of literature changes the existing order—errs, I think, in the opposite direction. Out of such a conception grows Northrop Frye's sense of literature's ideal and impersonal hierarchies, the upwelling of archetypal forms in graded variations and permutations, which it is the business of criticism to perceive in their real order.[7] This second methodology does not allow room for the creative passion of a private reading performed within a specific range of public expectations, and while it equates meaning with generic form and translates reduplicated patterns of imagery into thematic contents, it tends to rest with the final application of a class label. In the generic view, *The Faerie Queene* is an exemplary romance and thus, presumably, not comparable to Milton's epic.[8]

Literature does not exist to be put on a shelf (or on a couch) by criticism, but to be read by readers. Neither does it seem entirely sensible to suppose that poetry is produced by a process of merely verbal parthenogenesis. This third paradigm, with its emphasis on abstractions of verbal process, either obedient to as yet undiscovered "laws" or itself utterly random is, I take it, the general attitude of deconstructive and related criticism toward the issue of intertextuality. Again, in the laudable interest of methodological rigor, it is an approach that tends to depersonalize if not entirely dehumanize the interactive dynamics of reading. Paul de Man may be held to speak for the deconstructive enterprise, an outgrowth of structuralism, when he asserts that "nothing, whether deed, word, thought or text, ever happens in relation, positive or negative, to anything that precedes, follows or exists elsewhere, but only as a random event whose power, like the power of death, is due to the random-

7. In *Anatomy of Criticism* (1957; rpt. New York: Atheneum, 1970), pp. 18–19, Frye describes his book as an "attempt to annotate" Eliot's approach.
8. Northrop Frye, *Secular Scripture: A Study of the Structure of Romance* (Cambridge, Mass.: Harvard University Press, 1976), pp. 187–88.

ness of its occurence."[9] Compelling in its extreme severity, de Man's argument also recognizes the need to have such random events "reintegrated in a historical and aesthetic system of recuperation that repeats itself regardless of the exposure of its fallacy." The need to recuperate, to reintegrate, to make connections is necessary even when one does not believe the fulfillment of the need will result in truth. How much more crucial is it, then, to trace the connecting threads of intertextuality when those slender roads and arteries may provide the only blueprint available to us for mapping how we, as a culture, have come to be where we are. Literature locates our culture for us, in the sense that the best texts tell their audiences where they are in relation to the rest of Western tradition. The Renaissance named itself specifically in terms of its historical imperial position; it had learned to see in the epic the locus of political power. *Troynovant* and the "paradise within" may be fictions, but they are fictions created to refigure otherwise intractable political facts.

Milton and Spenser are connected by a reader; what the two poets have in common is a very similar attitude toward this human being as he or she is embodied in their texts. Because notions of the "reader" are so fashionably current, I should quickly add that this particular character is the one posited by the main focus of English Renaissance poetics and not a construct of recent critical theory. It is the very particular reader posited, moreover, by the genre in which Spenser chose to write—by allegory—and it is by Milton's very decision not to write allegory (a decision he reenacts in the poem itself) that he will show his own most compelling connection to his precursor.

Because the issue of allegory and its reader has become so complicated in recent literary criticism, any use of the term needs careful

---

9. Paul de Man, "Shelley Disfigured," in *Deconstruction and Criticism* (New York: Seabury Press, 1979), p. 69; for a discussion of the differences between the procedures of deconstructive *allegoresis* and the reading of allegory, see my "Allegory, Allegoresis, and the De-allegorization of Language," in *Allegory, Myth, and Symbol,* ed. Morton Bloomfield, Harvard Studies in English, 9 (Cambridge, Mass.: Harvard University Press, 1981), 183–85.

explanation. As I understand it, there are in fact two "allegories" that may usefully be distinguished from each other. First, there is the allegory that refers to a technique of literary criticism that empowers the reader to find virtually any interpretation he or she wishes to find "hidden" within a text, whether that text purports to be allegorical or not. This is not the reader with whom I am concerned. Rather, the reader's reading I shall be interrogating is the activity addressed by narrative allegory itself, by which I mean that genre of narrative populated in the main by personified abstractions, such as *Piers Plowman, Pilgrim's Progress,* and, of course, *The Faerie Queene.* It is crucial to distinguish between these two "allegories" if we are to locate the two readers in relation to the historical intentionality of texts. While both allegories—both as a type of literary criticism *(allegoresis)* and as a type of narrative—have in common an interest in language, they have finally very different assumptions to make about the relationship of language to the world of referents and to the way the reader negotiates these relations. On the one hand, *allegoresis*—allegory as literary criticism—insists on the detachment or disjunction of the word from its referent (this is the traditional definition—*aliud verbum, aliud sensu*—of Quintilian, but also the effect of post-Saussurian linguistic theory). This assumed disjunction between sign and signified grants to the reader a huge and ahistorical interpretive freedom. (Thus Ovid's *Metamorphosis* is really "about" Christian virtues, Balzac's *Sarrasine* about castration, corrupt wealth, and the collapse of meaning in language.)[10] If the sign does not by some immutable law refer to its signified, then the reader is free to select the range of referents from which to produce the interpretation. As C. S. Lewis has recognized, the effect of this manner of reading is a blessed cultural conservatism—in the sense that texts that are in danger of being lost

10. For allegorizations of Ovid's *Metamorphoses,* see the list in J. de Ghellinck, *L'essor de la Littérature latine au XIIe siècle* (Paris: Desclée de Brouwer, 1946), I, 42n; *Ovid moralisé,* ed. C. De Boer, Martina G. de Boer, and Jeanette Th. Van 'T Sant, 5 vols. (Amsterdam, 1915–18). Roland Barthes reads Balzac's *Sarrasine* in terms of its interweaving of codes in *S/Z,* trans. Richard Miller (New York: Hill and Wang, 1974).

to a tradition can be saved, because they can be made to speak to the needs of a later (and very different) historical moment.[11] The freedom granted the reader in *allegoresis* is, then, culturally crucial.[12]

On the other hand, narrative allegory grants to the reader no such freedom. In narrative allegory language is disposed to call attention to its own signifying power, but not in a way that divorces the sign from its signified. While often words stand forth self-conscious of themselves as signs—and often what seems finally significant is their signifying power—still the word participates in the power of the things it names.[13] It may name a number of disparate things—as in a pun—but its multiple significations do not divorce its status from the realm of things. Thus a reading of an allegory (as opposed to a "critical" *allegoresis* of an expressive realist text) necessarily grapples with the complicated burdens of a self-querying interpretation, but the reading does so within the limits of the text's surface (generic) intentionality. And here, I think, is the largest difference between reading *as allegoresis* and the reading *of* allegory: in *allegoresis* where sign is severed from signified, reading enjoys a freedom to produce an interpretation that goes *against* the text's manifest intentions; in dealing with allegorical narrative, a reading cannot escape the text's historical intentionality. This limitation of the range of possible referents should not be construed, however, as a dogmatic chokehold on interpretation (although, instructively, it has been seen this way).[14] Rather, insofar as the text has named itself an allegory it may be said to intend its interpretations—however multiple they might be. The first signal of allegory is the initial steps taken by the text itself toward interpretation (a lady is

11. C. S. Lewis, *The Allegory of Love: A Study in Medieval Tradition* (New York: Oxford University Press, 1936), p. 62.

12. See Catherine Belsey, *Critical Practice* (London: Methuen, 1980), for a lucid argument about the dependence of a new critical practice on the assumption of a plurality of meaning (pp. 52–53).

13. The general argument derives from Michel Foucault's discussion of "resemblance" in *The Order of Things: An Archaeology of the Human Sciences* (1970; rpt. New York: Random House, 1973), p. 35. See also chap. 3 of my *Language of Allegory.*

14. See Northrop Frye's discussion of the commenting critic's irritable approach to narrative allegory in *Anatomy of Criticism,* pp. 90–91.

not called by a suitable realistic name: she is called "Philosophy"). If allegory's intent is interpretation, it produces its own— but it also intends the reader's active engagement in further interpretation. It intends the activity of interpretation. A realist narrative makes a contract that manifestly intends only the reader's passive "enjoyment" of the story. It is, of course, possible for a critic to "produce" the expressive realist text by deconstructing it—but this is not the initial, surface contract made with the reader. Narrative allegory makes this contract with all readers, whatever their professional involvement in reading: all readers must engage in the initiating generic activity of self-conscious interpretation. As a narrative allegory, then, Spenser's *Faerie Queene* offers an originating text for Milton's address of his reader in *Paradise Lost.* Insofar as Milton insists on the place of *The Faerie Queene* within his epic's generic background, he insists upon his reader's active engagement with interpreting the text of *Paradise Lost,* making choices.

Of course *The Faerie Queene* is not merely an allegory; it is also a Renaissance epic. And this genre has equally important weight in the impact of Spenser's text on Milton's. Inhabiting two generic categories, *The Faerie Queene* is, however, less of a hybrid genre than we might at first suppose. All sixteenth-century epic would have been read "allegorically": a text of Vergil came to Christian humanist readers as loaded with reader's commentaries as any action in Spenser's text comes qualified by its own self-commenting narrative exfoliations. Such commentary appears on the page with the text itself, crowding the margins. It is a continuous part of the text itself in a way that feels strange for a modern reader, for whom footnotes and marginalia are less privileged parts of a page of print.[15]

Yet Spenser's presentation of his text as epic asserts a specific dimension of the contract for the reader's reading: it must not be

---

15. An excellent example of a Renaissance *Aeneid* (Venice, 1544) is published in *Virgil: Opera,* 2 vols., in *The Renaissance and the Gods: A Comprehensive Collection of Renaissance Mythologies, Iconologies, and Iconographies,* ed. Stephen Orgel (New York: Garland Publishing, 1976).

merely moral, tending to the soul's salvation (which any medieval allegory would nurture), but political and therefore aimed at that obsessional concern of all Renaissance art—its reflection of (and on) the glittering magnetism of secular power.[16]

Because of its history, epic is generically interested in empire; its political concerns are therefore part of the text's intentionality. Unlike, say, a nineteenth-century (expressive-realist) short story that purports to offer only a vignette of an individual's private experience, a Renaissance epic—by virtue of its assertion of class membership—announces its intentions to deal with as large an area of political and economic power relations as is textually manageable. Epic manifestly intends its political contents. Thus we need not posit for the reading of allegorical epic quite so extreme a hermeneutic principle as that which Marxist Fredric Jameson, for instance, argues underlies all interpretation: that is, the existence of "some mechanism of mystification or repression" in the text, which legitimizes the critic's attempt "to seek a latent meaning behind a manifest one, or to rewrite the surface categories of a text in the stronger language of a more fundamental interpretive code."[17]

Developed for dealing with the political/economic material repressed off the surface of the expressive realist text, such Marxist argument is a strong critical tool, especially because it makes it possible for the same terminology to be used "to analyze and articulate two quite distinct types of objects or 'texts' "—and thus serves to reveal the fundamental unity of social life, "a single inconceivable and transindividual process, in which there is no need to invent ways of linking language events and social upheavals or economic contradictions because on that level they were never separate from

---

16. Michael Murrin, *The Allegorical Epic: Essays in Its Rise and Decline* (Chicago: University of Chicago Press, 1980), pp. 137–39, discusses *The Faerie Queene* in terms of its relations to contemporary politics, particularly English-Hapsburg conflicts about expanding American empires. See also Stephen Greenblatt's discussion of imperial colonialism in Book II of *The Faerie Queene* in *Renaissance Self-Fashioning* (Chicago: University of Chicago Press, 1980), chap. 4.

17. Fredric Jameson, *The Political Unconscious: Narrative as a Socially Symbolic Act* (Ithaca, N.Y.: Cornell University Press, 1981), p. 60.

one another."[18] Attempting to recreate this whole, the Marxist critic is, however, still left with his or her mediations—specifically with the need to posit the existence of the text's mystifications through which the analyst works to find the basic level—or that ultimate concentric framework surrounding the text (specifically, in the case of Marxist interpretation, the mode of production which the text takes pains to bury as deeply as possible).[19] Jameson specifically arranges this procedure to reveal the "deeper kinship" of the Marxist method with the fourfold method of biblical exegesis.[20]

Again, what seems fundamentally at odds between the two systems is that the fourfold method predicates its functions on the intentional interchangeability of the divinely authored levels, their sacred interconnectedness, while the modern approach to interpretation insists upon the repressive disjunction between the levels— the hiatus between word said and meaning meant. In Marxist theory, as in all strong modern theories of interpretation, the assumption necessarily is that the text does not, at the surface level, want said what the critic finds in it to say. The critic, by his or her interpretation, brings to light what was repressed from the text's surface. This sets up an odd balance of forces between the reader of a text and its manifest and latent contents; the reader is on the side of the latent content, struggling to get around, see through, or in some way demystify and dispense with the surface.

Self-announced allegories, by suggesting in their very generic labeling that the text is incomplete without the reader's active engagement in its interpretation, set up a different relationship between manifest and latent contents and therefore with the reader

18. Ibid., p. 40.
19. As Jameson observes in *Political Unconscious,* "The 'problematic' of modes of production is the most vital new area of Marxist theory in all the disciplines today; not paradoxically, it is also one of the most traditional" (p. 89); Jameson's proposition is of the "structural coexistence of several modes of production all at once" in a single society: "the temptation to classify texts according to the appropriate mode of production" hence fades, "since the texts emerge in a space in which we may expect them to be crisscrossed and intersected by a variety of impulses from contradictory modes of cultural production all at once" (p. 95).
20. Ibid., pp. 31–32.

who negotiates the connections between these two. Presumably, as in assumptions about meaning being fourfold, the latent content does not contradict (speak against) the manifest content, but rather augments it. A reading of an allegory then is not properly a deconstruction—that is, a reading that contradicts at many points the surface meaning (that seductive surface that would fool the critic into looking no further)—rather, such a reading extends, instead of undermines, the text's own commentary. In the reading of an allegory also announced as belonging to the genre of epic, such as *The Faerie Queene,* we may further understand that the political content is no more repressed than, say, the sexual content (and may in fact be the same). All the one-for-one correspondences between contemporaneous political figures and the dramatis personae of the last cantos of Book V—all the overt invitations to read the "historical allegory"—reveal just how manifest this latent content is. To invoke Marxist methods of *allegoresis* then is not to open up heretofore unrealized realms of the text, but to appropriate a vocabulary for crossing over that uncrossable critical boundary between the private and the public, the psychological and the social, the poetic and the political—for bridging the abyss between the "inside" of the text and its cultural, historical, "outside."

The reader whose activities are interrogated in the following pages is not then a critical tool for abstracting the text to a different level of discourse by turning a consumer of literature through critical fiat into a "producer" of the text. Rather he or she is a historically real and representative reader of allegory, for whom reading was assumed to be a protopolitical act. This assumption was a conscious and more or less fully articulated element in Renaissance poetics, as we shall see. But, nevertheless, insofar as the interdisciplinary methods of poststructuralist Marxist theory provide terms for articulating the political connections between some heretofore overlooked issues in these Renaissance epics (overlooked by readers, not repressed by authors), it places us in a better position to see how the private element of sexual identity and response addressed by each of these remarkable poems is only a further Renaissance exfoliation of the public realities of political power.

Epic narrative's ultimate purpose was to reach the will of the reader—to persuade (that is, to move) him or her to act for the public good. This Renaissance ideal of rhetorical poetics was not, however, a case of simple-minded and slavish imitation of a Ciceronian oratorical model—though that was the privileged paradigm; even had they wished to, sixteenth-century English humanists could not turn their realm into a society hospitable to that republican ideal of the *novus homo*. The realities of politics under Tudor imperialism would necessarily skew the oratorical process in complex ways, and the peculiar linguistic disposition of the age and its logocentric religion (so much a matter for contemporary political dispute) would put otherwise unaccountable pressures on any reader's sense of the powers of language.[21]

Unfortunately, we do not have the benefit of Spenser's own views on the subject of reading, once contained, perhaps, in his lost tract "The English Poet," but we do have what might well be that work's cousin, and we can usefully begin to define the Renaissance reader for whom Spenser wrote by glancing briefly at Sir Philip Sidney's discussion of the procedure for "right reading" in *An Apology for Poetry*. If we then place this kind of right reading, which Sidney specifically associates with allegory, next to the kind of right reading Milton defends in *Areopagitica,* we may be in a better position to see where the earlier and the later Renaissance rhetorics intersect.[22] Both the *Apology for Poetry* and *Areopagitica* are "orations" written to be read, the fictional frame of the text in each instance being oral delivery of a speech conceived as an exercise in forensic rhetoric. This simple fact not only underscores the constancy of the rhetorical emphasis in educational training throughout the Renaissance, it also insists forcefully on the remarkable persistence of an underlying tension between written and spoken, between the read and the

21. For a discussion of the impact of political reality on the humanist program, see G. K. Hunter, *John Lyly: The Humanist as Courtier* (Cambridge, Mass.: Harvard University Press, 1962), chap. 1, "Humanism and Courtship."

22. For a discussion of Milton's and Sidney's shared tenets, see S. K. Heninger, Jr., "Sidney and Milton," in *Milton and the Line of Vision*, ed. J. A. Wittreich, Jr. (Madison: University of Wisconsin Press, 1975), pp. 57–95.

heard, that marks the literature of the sixteenth and seventeenth centuries as "Renaissance." What was reborn in a literature manifestly changed by the technology of movable type was a set of standards abstracted from a dominantly oral culture.[23] *An Apology for Poetry* and *Areopagitica* describe what a reader does. The only apologia we do have from Spenser, the very brief "Letter to Ralegh," describes a poem (and that rather inaccurately), and is otherwise very different from the fictively "oral" texts of Sidney and Milton by insisting upon its own written status as much as the latter indicate their oratorical frames. Its fiction is that it is a private letter penned to a friend, though it is of course a poet's letter to another poet, made public, printed as a part of the most public of poems, an epic. The only description of a reader which we can extract from Spenser's brief letter is such an odd composite picture that we very much need Sidney's *Apology* to flesh out the letter's assumptions before we can put them beside Milton's rhetoric for comparison. Sidney's extremely tricky argument generously grants us a precision of detail lacking in Spenser's note to his neighbor, and his rhetoric of reading thus gives us a fuller sense of the intellectual contexts in which Spenser would have expected his reader to function.

An Apology for Poetry

For Sidney, poetry is crucially indistinguishable from rhetoric:

poets indeed do merely make to imitate, and imitate both to delight

---

23. Elizabeth Eisenstein, *The Printing Press as an Agent of Change: Communications and Cultural Transformations in Early-Modern Europe*, 2 vols. (Cambridge: Cambridge University Press, 1979), I, 173–75, 230, assesses the conflict: "Classical rhetorical conventions had allowed for the difference in tone between addressing a large assemblage in a public arena, where strong lungs and broad strokes were required, and pleading a case in a courtroom, which called for careful attention to detail. . . . But no precedent existed for addressing a large crowd of people who were not gathered together in one place but were scattered in separate dwellings and who, as solitary individuals with divergent interests, were more receptive to intimate interchanges than to broad-gauged rhetorical effects." Print technology places the experience of reading within a newly private, individual, and silent space, and serves the sense of the isolated, physically distinct subject.

and teach, and delight to move men to take that goodness in hand, which without delight they would fly as from a stranger, and teach, to make them know that goodness whereunto they are moved.[24]

Beyond poetry's use for teaching (and therefore beyond the power of mere didactic philosophy) is its power to persuade—its specifically rhetorical potency:

> And that moving is of a higher degree than teaching, it may by this appear, that it is well nigh the cause and the effect of teaching. For who will be taught, if he be not moved with desire to be taught? and what so much good doth that teaching bringeth forth ... as that it moveth one to do that which it doth teach? For, as Aristotle saith, it is not *gnosis* but *praxis* must be the fruit. [P. 112]

Repeatedly Sidney insists, "to be moved to do that which we know, or to be moved with desire to know, *hoc opus, hic labor est.*"

The famous pair of Renaissance purposes—to delight and to teach—is really for Sidney a triplet—to delight, to teach, and to move to action. This triplet was in the poetics of the Renaissance something necessarily more complicated and turned in upon itself than Horace's *aut prodesse aut delectare* or that production both *utile et dulce,* if only because Horace's notions of usefulness and sweetness were very different from any Renaissance Christian humanist's necessary sense of what was best for him in this life, and the next. Imitation being presumed a given, the ultimate value of poetry lay in its superior rhetorical power to move people to take that goodness in hand which without delight they might not merely overlook, but actively fear. By placing poetry above philosophy because it is more "moving," or more persuasive, and by placing it above history because it imitates a more idealized and golden goodness than mere fact (which may be tuned, moreover, "to the highest key of passion"), Sidney consistently praises poetry's power to move more effectively than its sister arts among the hard-hearted realities of man's fallen nature. Since "our erected wit maketh us to know what perfection is, and yet our infected will keepeth us from reach-

24. Sir Philip Sidney, *An Apology for Poetry,* ed. Geoffrey Shepherd (London: Thomas Nelson, 1965), p. 103; hereafter cited in the text.

ing unto it'' (p. 101), poetry's special power is to reach and seduce
that will so that readers "steal to see the form of goodness (which
seen they cannot but love) ere themselves be aware, as if they took a
medicine of cherries.''

So persuasive and powerful a medicine is poetry that its very
potency becomes one of the problems; Sidney's terms for describing poetry's virtues are strangely close kin to the complaints he
allows to be legitimately lodged against it by contemporaries. Poetry's appeal is alluring, nearly, in fact, erotic, and while Sidney
personifies poetry as male, the dynamics of desire it sets into motion
render it for him peculiarly seductive. "For as the image of each
action stirreth and instructeth the mind, so the lofty image of such
worthies most inflameth the mind with desire" (p. 119). That
Aeneas is the imaged worthy whom Sidney immediately names after this insistence on poetry's nearly erotic allure suggests the nature of the complications inherent in the dynamic interaction between inflaming by desire and informing by counsel. In the
speaking picture offered by Aeneas, an Odyssean feminine seduction is balanced against an Iliadic masculine resistance. The power
of such a speaking picture beyond the powers of masculine philosophy and history is a feminine charm no less seductive because male.

> Nay truly, though I yield that Poesy may not only be abused, but
> that being abused, by the reason of his sweet charming force, it can
> do more hurt than any other army of words, yet shall it be so far
> from concluding that the abuse should give reproach to the abused,
> that contrariwise it is a good reason, that whatsoever, being
> abused, doth most harm, being rightly used (and upon the right use
> each thing conceiveth his title), doth most good. [Pp. 125–26]

Sidney ultimately turns complaint into praise; by so easily and so
often seducing the reader into "wanton sinfulness and lustful
love," poetry proves its greater virtue. If when abused it has more
power to harm, then when rightly used it has more power to do
good.

The right use of poetry here lies not merely in the poet's responsibility. Most crucially a large portion of the burden falls upon the

reader, whose right use of the text as written is based upon his or her constant awareness of the fiction's fictiveness. The reader's self-consciousness then becomes the first step in the practical application of the fiction's moral usefulness to the reader's life. Here Sidney is defending poetry against the charge that it lies; his tactic is the same he uses to defend it against licentiousness: poetry is powerful to do good not despite the fact that it lies, but because it lies.

> If then a man can arrive . . . to know that the poet's persons and doings are but pictures what should be, and not stories what have been, they will never give the lie to things not affirmatively but allegorically and figuratively written. And therefore, as in History looking for truth, they go away full fraught with falsehood, so in Poesy looking but for fiction, they shall use the narration but as an imaginative groundplot of a profitable invention. [P. 124]

By associating allegory and "figure" with fictiveness (the opposite of that which is "affirmatively written"), Sidney begs complicated questions about lying and the reader's behavior in constructing his or her own profitable invention upon the poet's narrative groundplot. The recipe for right reading suggested here is not simple translation of literal story into figurative meaning; rather, Sidney's yoking of allegory, figure, and fiction with the profit to be gained by the reader from reading poetry rightly complicates a sense of poetry's rhetorical power over a reader (to "move" him/her) with the reader's awareness of the nonaffirmative nature of that power. The potential for having an impact on the reader's praxis within society—a more complicated issue than the reader's merely private gnosis—is a process quite different from the persuasions of simple demagoguery. Sidney predicates it on the sophisticated self-consciousness necessary for reading a thing "allegorically written," that is, written to provide a narration that may be resolved by the reader into "pictures what should be," which win the reader's active assent by insisting upon the idealization (passionately presented) of the fiction itself.

In Sidney's poetic, power shifts back and forth between text and reader; though the details of the process are obscure and seem to reside in a continuous fine-tuning and readjustment of response, the process ends, ideally, in the enrichment of the reader's nation and the world:[25]

> so far substantially it worketh, not only to make a Cyrus, which had been but a particular excellency as Nature might have done, but to bestow a Cyrus upon the world to make many Cyruses, if they will learn aright why and how that maker made him. [P. 101]

Here poetry seems to work by a method akin to contagious magic, rendering the reader an imitation of the hero depicted; yet Sidney predicates the success of this persuasion on a very undemagogic "if"—the reader must be allowed a wide and necessary freedom in order for the *imitatio* to have full effect. As Kenneth Burke reminds us, "persuasion involves choice, will; it is directed to a man only insofar as he is free."[26] Sidney's reader is free to be persuaded, to become inspired to imitate the hero; the freedom depends on a very active, specifically analytic reading. Readers must set out to "learn aright how and why that maker made" the hero as he did; readers do not merely second-guess the author's intention for the sake of some aesthetic analysis, but for their own "profit."

In using the author's story as the figurative basis for a profitable invention (that is, a newly found—different—interpretation), Sidney's reader appears almost to be producing (for profit?) an entirely new text. And finally, the process that Sidney describes has at its center an object rather more static than Spenser's reader has the leisure to analyze. But for each the "text" is one that produces the

25. For a subtle analysis of the dynamics of these shiftings throughout the *Apology*, see Margaret W. Ferguson, "Sidney's Defense: A Retrial," *Boundary 2* (1979), 61–96.

26. Kenneth Burke, *A Rhetoric of Motives* (Berkeley: University of California Press, 1969), p. 50; Burke also points out the connections between a magical and a rhetorical use of language: "Originally, the magical use of symbolism to affect natural processes by rituals and incantations was a mistaken transference of a proper linguistic function to an area for which it was not fit. The realistic use of addressed language *to induce action in people* became the magical use of addressed language *to induce motion in things* (things by nature alien to purely linguistic orders of motivation)" (p. 42). Sidney's argument appears to undo the confusion; Spenser, in Archimago's spells, recombines the two.

reader as social hero—someone who acts within society. Thus, while there are fundamental distinctions between the effective practices of the two poets, there are profound similarities of assumptions.[27]

Insofar as Spenser made extrapoetic pronouncements about his craft, what he shares with Sidney is the crucial sense of poetry's potential to shape its reader. Our one document from Spenser's hand directly connected to *The Faerie Queene,* the "Letter to Ralegh," is something of a puzzle and rather less immediately useful for reading the epic than one would have liked it to be. Spenser's assumptions about his reader as they are implied by his statements in the letter are strangely shaped by the letter's own rhetorical position. In it he defines as the poem's reader a man who is also a neighbor, another poet, and a would-be fellow courtier (out for real profit). In all of these particular, distinct relationships to Spenser, Sir Walter Ralegh reveals the remarkably broad spectrum of political angles involved in a paradigmatic contemporary reading of the epic: if it can be useful to think of the remarkably broad Ralegh as the reader after whom all subsequent readers may conveniently "fictionalize" themselves, we must recognize a profound need to entertain a very flexible attitude toward our functioning within the text. (And if even Ralegh asked for the plot outline Spenser provides in the "Letter," we may forgive ourselves for not being clear at all times about the sequence of events.)

The "Letter to Ralegh"

The first of the few general remarks Spenser makes in his letter about the nature of poetry (all of which follow Sidney's vocabulary in the *Apology* quite closely) is an assumption that provides the

27. For a discussion of the crucial differences between Spenser's and Sidney's poetics, see Michael Murrin, *The Veil of Allegory: Some Notes toward a Theory of Allegorical Rhetoric in the English Renaissance* (Chicago: University of Chicago Press, 1969), pp. 168–77, where the difference lies in the two poets' attitudes toward the divinity of poetic inspiration, Sidney adopting a less exalted view of the poet's truth than Spenser (but Spenser's being less exalted than Milton's).

very motive for writing the letter: because he knows, he tells Ralegh, "how doubtfully all Allegories may be construed," he is explaining his ultimate intentions:

> The generall end therefore of all the booke is to fashion a gentleman or noble person in vertuous and gentle discipline.[28]

Here the word "fashion" may be taken to apply first to Spenser's invention of the character of Prince Arthur; the word means not only to "represent" but to show the evolution in process throughout the narrative of the finished hero. However, "fashion" also applies to the reader, who is shaped in virtue and led into gentle discipline by his or her experience of the poem, much as Sidney's Cyrus begets other Cyruses. And that the reader may, in fact, be female, Spenser needs very crucially to allow. He intends in and by the poem to shape a "gentleman or noble person." Arthur therefore is sent out across the landscape of Faery Land in search of its queen—by whose "particular" significance Spenser directly tells us he means Queen Elizabeth, and by whose "general" significance he intends "glory." Usually in Renaissance poetics the "particular" indicates the "general": yet Gloriana is the "general" within the poem, while Queen Elizabeth is a historical "particular" outside of it. Spenser caps these odd distinctions between general and particular by making another very traditional distinction that nonetheless complicates our understanding of his sense of his readership. Spenser's perception of Elizabeth's dual nature gives his ideal reader a rather odd, if not unique, character.

> In that Faery Queene I meane glory in my generall intention, but in my particular I conceive the most excellent and glorious person of our soveraine the Queene, and her kingdome in Faery land. And yet in some place els, I doe otherwise shadow her. For considering she beareth two persons, the one of a most royall Queene or Empresse, the other of a most vertuous and beautiful Lady, this latter

28. *Spenser's Faerie Queene*, ed. J. C. Smith, 2 vols. (1909; rpt. Oxford: Clarendon Press, 1964), II, 485; hereafter cited in the text. Reprinted by permission of Oxford University Press.

part in some places I do expresse in Belphoebe fashioning her name
according to your owne excellent conceipt of Cynthia. (Phoebe and
Cynthia being both names of Diana.) [P. 486]

Like Ralegh's fragmentary "Cynthia," *The Faerie Queene* is not only
dedicated to Elizabeth, it is about her and, as an epic narrative, it is
therefore necessarily about the queen's two bodies—about her public atemporal princeliness and her private (temporal) female sexuality. Thus Spenser resolves the socially irresolvable issue of the two
bodies of the king into the convenient dispositions of poetic analysis
(Gloriana *and* Belphoebe; rule *and* chastity), analysis made more
complicated in the case of Queen Elizabeth, for whom at least one of
the two bodies was the wrong sex, and out of which (at least in the
earlier decades of the reign) was supposed to appear the next temporal embodiment of the atemporal kingship. The dispersal of the
poem's adumbrations of Elizabeth over a number of dramatis personae figures intractable political (and sexual) facts.[29]

Directly addressed in all the proems and often in the body of the
text itself, Elizabeth's "reading" is the most actively signaled reading of the poem within the text. If there is an ideal reader figured in
Ralegh in the letter, then there is a unique reader figured in Elizabeth, beside whom, and essentially for whom (in particular and
general significances) the ideal reader must function. That the
royal patroness of the poem is both a most royal governor and a
most beautiful lady, a deeply educated humanist and a brilliant political survivor, reveals how much Elizabeth's accidentally female
but politically powerful presence deflects and richly complicates the
usual relations between the writer and the reader of an epic. Spen-

---

29. For the basic discussion of the dual-body theory, see Ernst H. Kantorowicz,
The King's Two Bodies: A Study in Mediaeval Political Theology (Princeton: Princeton
University Press, 1957); for a discussion of the impact of the legal issues involved in
the problem of succession on the drama of Elizabeth's reign, see Marie Axton, *The
Queen's Two Bodies: Drama and the Elizabethan Succession* (London: Royal Historical
Society, 1977). Spenser elides the issue of the physical body, of course, by naming
the queen's two "persons"—a necessary abstraction in her case, and a locution that
connects her directly to his reader as "noble person."

ser's Elizabethan sense of some potential readers' female gender, here hinted at in the letter's distinction between "gentleman" and "noble person," can account for some of the stranger parts of his poem and the necessarily stranger responses to it, not the least important of which is, finally, Milton's response to the political implications of the sexual mythologies of Spenser's text.

The issue of Elizabeth's sex was not simple historically, and all the paradoxical tension it introduced into court culture not easily resolved by the sophisticated self-consciousness of Renaissance courtly compliment. We need to remember, therefore, that an essentially medieval mode of *amor cortois* formed part of the political style of Renaissance government administration, becoming a method by which men made or did not make brilliant careers for themselves.[30] Spenser appealed to an aristocratic set of courtiers-cum-public servants, who were, at the same time, no mean poets themselves, while holding such offices as governor of Flushing (Sidney) and "Wardein of the Stanneryes" (Ralegh). Conversely, Milton aimed at a small, he tells us, but select readership doubtless of private men, no longer perhaps in government service but able finally to rule not only themselves but also a type of family that, as historian Lawrence Stone has explained, had only recently turned

30. Defending Elizabeth's largely negative policies, Wallace T. MacCaffrey comments perceptively: "It may well be that the very task of asserting and maintaining by sheer force of will and personality her ascendancy over a violent, masculine political and social order exhausted all her energies and left nothing over for other enterprises" (*Queen Elizabeth and the Making of Policy, 1572–1588* [Princeton: Princeton University Press, 1981], p. 16). For a discussion of the impact of Castiglione's courtly ideals on the status of poetry in late Tudor England, see Daniel Javitch, *Poetry and Courtliness in Renaissance England* (Princeton: Princeton University Press, 1978). Oddly, Javitch does not stop to consider how much more complicated the whole courtly situation becomes when the prince is not in fact a man—as he was for Castiglione's court—but when the prince is herself a woman and the game she governs no mere literary pastime (as was the Duchess of Urbino's) but government and politics themselves. For a discussion of Elizabeth's impact on Spenser's literary career, see Louis Adrian Montrose, "'Eliza, Queene of shepheardes' and the Pastoral of Power," *English Literary Renaissance* 10 (1980), 153–82; also Jonathan Goldberg, *Endelesse Worke: Spenser and the Structures of Discourse* (Baltimore: Johns Hopkins University Press, 1981), pp. 127–74.

into the "nuclear" set of relations among a husband and wife and their children.[31] Spenser distinctly indicates that women belong in his readership; Milton, though less obviously, appears to rule them out. The specific terms of the two rhetorics—where each poet locates the female reader and the particular nature of the appeals made to her—will be very different because the two audiences were different.[32]

The one particular that both readerships would have agreed upon is the high moral effect of heroic poetry; and Milton's claims for the moral intentions of his verse go, if anything, far beyond Spenser's hopes to fashion the discipline of a court. If "church-outed by the prelates," Milton felt he had to give up poetry for the politics of prose, that prose is a record of his merely postponed ministry and his intentions to write something "doctrinal to the nation." Milton's sense of poetic mission was only more overtly didactic and oratorial than Spenser's. If Spenser aimed to make gentle readers more gentle in this world, Milton aimed, for fit and few, to save souls for the next. There is a crucial difference in the intensity of appeal made by the two poets—if Spenser seduces a reader into a response, then Milton demands one—but in the intricate maneuverings of the attitudes of the reader toward his or her own reading, Milton copies many of Spenser's methods.

In brief, the rhetorical strategy Milton learned from Spenser was how to make the reader interpret his or her own interpretations, to judge the moral quality of his or her own response to reading, to feel the work as a large rhetorical appeal to the will, and to make a choice. In other words, all that Sidney described in the *Apology*, Milton learned how to do from reading Spenser, and his manner of

31. For a discussion of the political isolation of Milton's imagined audience, see William Kerrigan, *The Prophetic Milton* (Charlottesville: University of Virginia Press, 1974): they were "a group of outcasts judged 'perverse' by their contemporaries" (p. 180n); for the strengthening of patriarchy within the newly developing nuclear family in seventeenth-century England, see Lawrence Stone, *The Family, Sex, and Marriage in England, 1500-1800* (1977; abridged ed., New York: Harper and Row, 1979), pp. 109-46.

32. See below, Chapter 4.

doing so is distinctly Spenserian rather than Sidneyan.[33] Yet there is one large difference between Milton and Spenser in the way they offer the reader a choice: Milton does not hold out Spenser's plurality of possibilities, his leisured sense of time to select among and possibly synthesize potential interpretations, to acknowledge the mediate nature of the truth-bearing fiction. Milton offers instead a binary either/or choice about a single truth;[34] all the self-consciousness his poem has about its own fictiveness—a poetic sense it uses the presence of *The Faerie Queene* in great part to · convey—does not detract from the pressure *Paradise Lost* puts on the reader to assent to the intimate significance of the poem's reality.

This difference in the rhetorical rhythm, so to speak, of the reader's self-consciousness, derives from the two epics' very different forms. In this regard, continental criticism with its essentially formalist concerns can help to suggest why relations between Milton and Spenser should have remained invisible to formal criticism. In choosing romance epic, Spenser chose an Italianate form generically hospitable to his native medieval interests (romance interlace had been a marked form in medieval narrative). A segmented, interwoven, carefully pieced structure, reinforced by Spenser's highly articulated book-canto-stanza organization with its tightly ordered rhyme scheme (only three rhymes in nine lines), the form is tailor-made for the kind of slow-motion analysis of moral and political responsiveness necessary to a courtier in the weblike organization of an aristocratic court. The poem's form then reflects the interweave of aristocratic and landed-gentry dependencies

33. Sidney's prose insists on a detached stance for the reader who is to analyze a given scene into its static, component parts. See in particular Forrest G. Robinson, *The Shape of Things Known: Sidney's Apology in Its Philosophical Tradition* (Cambridge, Mass.: Harvard University Press, 1972), pp. 146–50, for a description of this Sidneyan analysis. Conversely, Spenser involves the reader intimately within a narrative process of paratactic exfoliations of interpretation, which works against a Sidneyan labeling of parts. For Spenser's usual procedure, see Paul J. Alpers, *The Poetry of The Faerie Queene* (Princeton: Princeton University Press, 1967); also my *Language of Allegory*, pp. 282–89.

34. See in particular Leslie Brisman, *Milton's Poetry of Choice* (Ithaca, N.Y.: Cornell University Press, 1973).

among complexly interrelated family connections. Its form
matches its audience.

For all its silence on the nature of allegory, the "Letter to Ralegh" goes to great lengths to defend romance epic against the criticism that has, in fact, had a most telling effect on the poem's
reputation—that to eyes trained on neoclassical perspective, *The
Faerie Queene* had no single form:

> Thus much Sir, I have briefly ouerronne to direct your vnderstand-
> ing to the wel-head of the History, that from thence gathering the
> whole intention of the conceit, ye may as in a handfull gripe al the
> discourse, which otherwise may happily seeme tedious and con-
> fused. [P. 487]

The structure he in fact ascribes to the poem in the "Letter" is a
straightforward exposition of the multi-plotted, many-heroed romance epic, with its multiplicity of interwoven episodes. Not exactly what Milton would have understood Aristotle to mean by a
"single action." Yet Spenser still argues for the singleness of discourse in the poem. The problem is that the "historiographer's"
plot that Spenser provides (borrowing Sidney's term from the *Apology*) is not readily discernible in the details of the poet's version
actually presented by the poem. The poem's plot is even denser
than Spenser's description of it in the letter; embattled since his
friend Gabriel Harvey first objected to his "Elvish Queen," Spenser's defense of the poem's form does not do justice to its real power.
However un-Aristotelian in shape, the form functions as part of the
allegory, as symmetrical and silently artful self-commentary. If the
plot is tedious and confused, in the dimension of visual shape on
the page, the poem does allow itself the perfection of an arbitrary
artifice. The alexandrine-stopped stanzas with their intricately in-
terlocked rhythms suggest by analogy the self-anatomizing artistry
of the whole.[35] The static perfection of the page, however, insists on
the fundamental "readerliness" of the text, an essential nature that

35. For these larger self-anatomizing analogies, see James Nohrnberg, *The Analogy of The Faerie Queene* (Princeton: Princeton University Press, 1976), pp. xi–xii.

the rigid boundary markers of book, canto, and numbered stanza transform into an only slightly more analytical process during the diachronic experience of reading.[36] Growing like dense foliage over its own analyzing anatomy, the poem exists in a spatial dimension of forest and clearing; book and canto divisions of the linear sequence seem like mere signposts until there is leisure for a synchronic criticism.

Utterly opposite to the shape of *The Faerie Queene* are the formal proportions of *Paradise Lost*. Set next to Spenser's poem, Milton's epic does have the slender clarity of classical sculpture, which by contrast makes *The Faerie Queene* look authentically gothic. With a plot of Vergilian sinuosity, *Paradise Lost* has a "single" action that has the peculiar distinction of being the very first plot (in our Western tradition) to have a beginning. That its beginning is *the* beginning and its end *the* end is central to the difficulties the poem presents, as well as to its appeal.[37] Consciously defended by reference to classical precedent and with a significant nod to Shakespeare, the blank verse meter of the poem, Milton explains, takes its strength from "the sense variously drawn out from one verse to another, not in the jingling of like endings, a fault avoided by the learned ancients both in poetry and all good oratory." Oratorical, especially in its opening books, the poem has an auditory effect quite unlike the readerly silence of Spenser's narrative. It is an oral

36. By "readerly" I mean something akin to what Roland Barthes means when he says a text is "scriptible"—that is, one that is a "perpetual present," and that intends "structuration without structure," *S/Z*, trans. Richard Miller (New York: Hill and Wang, 1974), p. 5. *The Faerie Queene* is "writerly" in this sense because its goal is to make the reader into a "producer of the text" (p. 4), an aim it shares with all allegory. I do not follow Barthes's terms because they are inapt to Renaissance allegory, there being no texts of the time which correspond to his definition of "readerly." Because of the prevalent rhetorical training of all Renaissance readers, a training Sidney expected them to put to active use, none could be said to read in the way Barthes defines it (out of the tradition of the nineteenth-century expressive realist novel). For the opposite view of *The Faerie Queene* as a Barthesian "writerly" text, see Goldberg, *Endlesse Worke*.

37. Edward Said, *Beginnings: Intention and Method* (New York: Basic Books, 1975), pp. 279–81, discusses Milton's difficulties in writing about an origin that exists prior to language.

quality essentially connected to the first thoughts Milton had about casting the story of Adam in the form of a five-act (allegorical) tragedy.

When Milton divided his initially ten-book epic into the Vergilian twelve books of the second edition of the poem (1674), he put the finishing touches to what he must have finally chosen to see as the perfect epic form, as if the final form itself were an indication of a finer tuning, a more consciously willed choice. Why Milton did not publish the epic in the twelve-book form in the first place is itself something of a question—mere oversight? a simple doubling of the five-act structure (two books per act)? a Puritanical hesitancy to place the biblical story in a pagan form?[38] Whatever the reason, the readjustment of the poem's form reflects an evolutionary process within it, a process of selecting among alternatives to make the final, right, choice. Finally, the Vergilian model reinforces the paradigmatic moral experience of the patriarch who, in fathering a family, founds an empire. The interrelations within a single family experienced as a generational struggle against the father's politically overwhelming personal care for his children reflect a shift in the concerns of Milton's audience from the open lineage family-politics of Spenser's day.[39] This is not at all to suggest that Milton's great work of art is a simple response to changed cultural conditions. Rather the evolution of society toward the nuclear family revealed in its own underpinnings a nexus of political concerns that granted to Milton's genius a great and effective freedom to explore the historical origins of a social code so incredibly strong it is still, even if under siege, strongly with us today.

Spenser's aristocratic allegory offers a plurality of interpretive possibilities, and his originality lies in offering to the reader a seemingly infinite number of stories that hardly maintain their status as continuous fictions, so easily do they fade into their own interpretations. If Milton offers what seems a simpler either/or

38. For further discussion of the twelve-book revision in terms of dramatic form, see G. K. Hunter, *Paradise Lost* (London: Allen and Unwin, 1980), p. 38n.
39. Stone, *Family, Sex, and Marriage*, pp. 141–42.

choice, his originality lies in the very shouldering of the burden of
telling the first of stories, as well as the truest, and telling it so that
his reader must choose both to make it happen again within and to
enter upon a specifically paradigmatic set of internalized familial
relations.

Though the choices offered their readers are different in these
and other essentials, the process of making a choice is what Spenser
means to Milton. Spenser's kind of choosing, replicated in the complex articulations of his poem's formal structure, is a kind proper to
the painstaking needs of knowledge in a fallen world, a world that
looked to Milton in *Areopagitica* as densely interwoven as any landscape unraveled by Spenser's reader. It is almost as if Milton
learned to read the world by reading Spenser. In any event, his
remarks on Spenser in *Areopagitica* are justly famous, and they locate *The Faerie Queene,* moreover, at the moral and intellectual center
of Milton's imaginative world, a world whose outlines remain remarkably constant for the quarter-century between the publication
of the pamphlet and of *Paradise Lost.*

Areopagitica

A document central to Milton's moral vision in general and to
his attitude toward our "sage and serious poet Spenser," the *Areopagitica* is an early statement of Milton's rhetoric of reading—in it he
defends reading, just as Sidney had "apologized" for poetry. Had
Milton not learned from the sad experience of his divorce tracts to
give his pamphlets arcane Greek titles not readily recognizable by
unlearned readers, we might have had the work under the title
"The Doctrine and Discipline of Reading," for that is what
Milton's written "oration" is about. It is about reading books conceived, for rhetorical purposes, as living sentient beings, so that
Milton's argument against prior censorship takes on the dress of an
argument against something like state-ordered abortions.

> But that a Book in wors condition then a peccant soul, should be to
> stand before a Jury ere it be borne to the World, and undergo yet in

darknesse the judgement of *Rhadamanth* and his Collegues, ere it can passe the ferry backward into light, was never heard before, till that mysterious iniquity provokt and troubl'd at the first entrance of Reformation, sought out new limbo's and new hells wherein they might include our Books also within the number of their damned.[40]

All intellectual life has a right to swim up to the light—even monstrous, misshapen falsehood—for only in the light will truth be visible; otherwise one risks leaving truth as well as falsehood unborn in the womb of hell. If *The Christian Doctrine* enacts the Protestant assumption that each man is his own priest, then *Areopagitica* demonstrates that assumption's more fundamental axiom, that the "gift" of reason is for each man to be "his own chooser." *The Christian Doctrine* is also, of course, another defense of reading—of a particular reading of a particular Book. But when that reading itself became a book, Milton had so little trust in the press or his audience that, although it was written in the learned language, he did not publish it.[41]

Areopagitica failed to carry its immediate political point, and prior censorship was imposed by Cromwell's parliament. Its lack of success in its stated purpose does not, however, detract from its rhetorical defense of the specific kind of reading made necessary by a fallen universe. The central passage of *Areopagitica* is worth looking at again in some detail because of the peculiar way Milton makes the ways of fallen knowledge mimic Spenser's rhetoric of reading.

> Good and evill we know in the field of this World grow up together almost inseparably; and the knowledge of good is so involv'd and

40. *The Complete Prose Works of John Milton,* ed. Douglas Bush et al., 8 vols. (New Haven: Yale University Press, 1959), II, 505–6; hereafter cited in the text as *CPW.* Milton insists on the life of books in another passage: "who kills a Man kills a reasonable creature, Gods Image; but hee who destroyes a good Booke, kills reason it selfe, kills the Image of God, as it were in the eye. Many a man lives a burden to the Earth; but a good Booke is the pretious life-blood of a master spirit" (pp. 492–93).

41. For the story of its publication in the early nineteenth century, see *The Works of John Milton,* ed. F. A. Patterson et al., 18 vols. (New York: Columbia University Press, 1931–38), XVII, 425–28; hereafter cited as Columbia *Milton.* See also *CPW,* VII, 3–10.

interwoven with the knowledge of evill, and in so many cunning
resemblances hardly to be discern'd, that those confused seeds
which were impos'd on *Psyche* as an incessant labour to cull out, and
sort asunder, were not more intermixt. It was from out the rinde of
one apple tasted, that the knowledge of good and evill as two twins
cleaving together leapt forth into the World. And perhaps this is
that doom which *Adam* fell into of knowing good and evill, that is to
say of knowing good by evill. [*CPW*.II.514]

Sidney had also attempted to use the very licentiousness of poetry's
potential effect to defend its counter saving powers, resting his faith
in its ultimate usefulness on the reader's ability to "learn aright"
the author's artful morality. Milton, wishing to protect all manner
of discourse from the prior imposition of silence, argues that readers
will never learn aright how to distinguish good from evil unless they
are allowed a choice. A signal and very Spenserian-sounding pun in
Milton's well-known paragraph is his play with the idea of fallen
wisdom as a "sapience," which derives its means of knowing from
eating—*sapere,* to taste. Fallen knowledge is wisdom conceived as
evil food; to have such knowledge, to taste such sapience, is to be in
the difficult position of trying to distinguish between twins. Good
looks so much like evil, evil looks so much like good, one needs to go
through a process of learning to distinguish between them. In arguing for not choosing too soon about one's reading, but for letting the
process of choice by reason go on unimpeded, freely, Milton argues
for a very Spenserian sense of delay and postponement of necessary
choice: the process of reading which Milton defends in the *Areopagitica* is the very process of reading which Spenser had allegorized in
The Faerie Queene.

The reechoing landscape of language across which the Redcrosse
Knight journeys in Book I of *The Faerie Queene,* for instance, is a
paradigmatic presentation of the field of this world where evil is
good's twin and the heroic challenge of living in it is to learn to
discriminate that which in so many cunning resemblances is hardly
to be discerned. Thus Archimago, like Proteus, is himself a figure
of fallen polysemy and embodies in the text the potential of language to transform itself suddenly into something else. In the very

first canto the evil magus manages to trick the knight with a twinned copy of his lady, and then to disguise himself so that he looks exactly like the knight, becoming *his* twin; Spenser tells the reader

> Full iolly knight he seemde, and well addrest,
> And when he sate vpon his courser free,
> Saint George himself ye would haue deemed him to be.
> [I.ii.11]

Truth ought ideally to be whole, a unity. Archimago provides in Spenser's fiction a deeply divisive doubleness, a duplicitous, despairing, divorcing schizophrenia at work in the first half of the Book of Holiness and Wholeness, which reveals the need to read the field of fallen language very carefully. Because we are told the name of the Knight of Holiness only at the moment in the text when his evil twin has in fact appeared as Saint George (just as the narrator tells us Una's name when he describes the counterfeit of her which Archimago makes), Spenser subtly insists that distinguishing meaning in language, making choices between alternate interpretations—discerning and discriminating between good and evil's twinship—is finally possible. We first learn who Saint George is when we confront his evil twin, whom not even Una can immediately tell apart from the knight. The narrator's information provides the two names, and the distinctions; but we are to understand not merely that language can ultimately distinguish the false from the true, but that language can best express what is true when it confronts the false. In Spenser's practice in Book I the naming of good works quite designedly as a system of difference from evil.[42]

---

42. In a sense, allegorical narrative as Spenser practices it here would seem to anticipate a Saussurean understanding of language not as a nomenclature of things, but as a system of difference—that is, as a means of differentiating between perceived contraries (perception being based on the very act of discriminating the contrariety). I do not mean to argue that the analogy is exact, merely suggestive; but again it appears that this issue in language is something Spenser's narrative allegory takes up in the manifest activity of its literal surface. For a lucid discussion of this underlying premise of post-Saussurean literary practice, see Catherine Belsey, *Critical Practice*, pp. 37–55.

We can name and know the good only by seeing that it differs from evil. Reading in faeryland is crucially self-regarding, always aware of the potential duplicity inherent in the polysemy of allegory; falsity may parade as truth, but it is finally possible to tell them apart: such is the kind of reading Milton praises in *Areopagitica*.

Not surprisingly, the pamphlet's most famous paragraph also contains Milton's best-known reference to Spenser; its salient point celebrates Spenser's usual procedures:

> I cannot praise a fugitive and cloister'd virtue, unexercis'd & unbreath'd, that never sallies out and sees her adversary, but slinks out of the race, where that immortall garland is to be run for, not without dust and heat. Assuredly we bring not innocence into the world, we bring impurity much rather: that which purifies is triall, and triall is by what is contrary. That vertue therefore which is but a youngling in the contemplation of evill, and knows not the utmost that vice promises to her followers, and rejects it, is but a blank vertue, not a pure; her whitenesse is but an excrementall whitenesse; Which was why our sage and serious Poet *Spencer*, whom I dare be known to think a better teacher than *Scotus* or *Aquinas*, describing true temperance under the person of *Guion*, brings him in with his palmer through the cave of Mammon, and the bower of earthly blisse that he might see and know, and yet abstain. [*CPW*.II.515–16]

Setting aside for a moment Milton's notorious error about the particulars of narrative in canto vii of Book II (the Palmer does not accompany Guyon into the cave)—what is striking about his attitude toward Spenser is its polemic insistence ("I dare be known") on the Renaissance doctrine of a didactic, rhetorical poetics. Milton's terminology is distinctly Sidneyan: Spenser is a better teacher than are scholastic philosophers because he brings a character into knowledge—almost by the hand, as it were—with his Palmer, to experience the great allure of evil, to know it, and to reject it.

Much has been said about the error that Milton makes when he assumes that the Palmer accompanies Guyon into the Cave of Mammon, when, in fact, they have been separated for a whole canto prior to the hero's descent to hell. Harold Bloom has argued that this mistake is not idle, but a clear "misreading," caused by Milton's need to protect himself against Spenser's influence.

> Milton's is no ordinary error, no mere lapse in memory, but is itself a powerful misinterpretation of Spenser, and a strong defense against him. For Guyon is not so much Adam's precursor as he is Milton's own, the giant model imitated by the Abdiel of *Paradise Lost.* Milton re-writes Spenser so as to *increase the distance* between his poetic father and himself.[43]

Bloom goes on to cite Augustine's identification of memory with the father and to surmise that "a lapse in memory as preternatural as Milton's is a movement against the father." Abdiel does, of course, like Guyon, face his temptation alone. Yet I would suggest that Milton's mistake about the Palmer witnesses what was most crucial to Milton in Spenser's narrative procedures—that is, their ability to locate the reader as an active participant in the moral choices offered by the poem. In positing the presence of the Palmer in Mammon's cave, Milton testifies to the loaded complexity of the reading experience that all readers of *The Faerie Queene* share, and share most particularly at this juncture of the narrative, which is a notorious crux among critics of the epic. By positing the presence of the Palmer, Milton conveniently names the two interdependent elements of the reading experience as he describes it in *Areopagitica:* seeing-knowing/yet abstaining. We need to remind ourselves, too, that it is as paradigmatic readers that Milton calls up Guyon and his phantom companion: the landscape through which they move represents what the uncensored free-marketplace of ideas ought to be allowed to remain, a tangle of truth and falsity, good and evil, the negotiation through which improves, purifies, and thereby fashions the active reader into virtue. Guyon and the Palmer do paradigmatically what readers of books do.

   In a sense, the Palmer may schematize for us the reader's *interpretive* activities in allegory, that is, the process of labeling. Opposed to

---

43. Bloom, *Map of Misreading,* p. 128.

the interpreting Palmer, Guyon represents the reader's active affect, that which bends to the allure. Like the prosy Palmer, the reader usually has a better perspective on the facts than Guyon, because he or she reads the poem's stanzas provided by the omniscient narrator, while Guyon must "read" hell's unlabeled furniture. Yet crucially, in this episode in particular with the absence of the Palmer, the reader is made to resist temptation less ably than Guyon, while Guyon successfully abstains. The reader then participates in that element of the reading experience (feeling the appeal of the seductive evil) more strongly than does the character—Guyon in the Bower of Bliss episode, for instance—who concretizes it. I do not mean to reify the reading experience or simply to personify its "interpretive" element in the Palmer and its "affective" function in Guyon—though this scheme does make admirably clear the elements Milton specifically singles out. Rather, the two Spenserian characters together may figure forth the complicated dynamics involved in reading *The Faerie Queene*—a continuous process of interpretive refinement of ethical/political choices.

Milton's appropriation of Guyon and the Palmer in *Areopagitica* as paradigmatic readers is not merely Milton's invention. Like all of Spenser's heroes, Guyon in his quest inscribes a movement parallel to the reader's own reading of the text. Like the Redcrosse Knight, for instance, whose career in Book I unfolds as a process of learning to read correctly the theological and spiritual meanings embedded in the landscape through which he moves (a process that includes some very disastrous mistakes), Guyon in Book II experiences adventures that successively read out the difficulties of choosing to serve the spirit while living within (and with) the limits of the physical body.[44] The issues of knowledge and food so inextricably

44. Christopher Kendrick, "Milton: A Study in Ideology and Form" (Ph.D. diss., Yale University, 1981) in a suggestive Marxist reading of *Areopagitica* discusses the impact of Milton's monism (body and soul are one entity) on Milton's confrontation of the forces in emergent capitalism in seventeenth-century England. *Areopagitica*'s concern with re-membering the body of truth, profoundly recalls the emphasis on the body in Book II of *The Faerie Queene*.

intertwined in the passage in *Areopagitica* are already intricately confused by Spenser in Book II of *The Faerie Queene* as he anatomizes the necessary constraints put on human virtue by the need to stay physically alive in a fallen world. Guyon's experience in Mammon's cave includes a mistaken route that is a set of temptations that appeal to the whole body by addressing the reading "eye."

At the opening of the canto, Spenser shows us Guyon traveling alone, already bereft of the Palmer's company, in a stanza notable for its rhyming insistence on the connection between "reading" and "feeding."

> So *Guyon* having lost his trusty guide,
>   Late left beyond that *Ydle lake,* proceedes
>   Yet on his way, of none accompanide;
>   *And euermore himselfe with comfort feedes,*
>   *Of his owne vertues, and prayse-worthy deedes.*
>   So long he yode, yet no aduenture found,
>   Which fame of her shrill trompet worthy *reedes*:
>   For still he traueild through wide wastfull ground,
> That nought but desert wildernesse shew'd all around.
>   [II.vii.2; emphasis added]

The Redcrosse Knight, having found himself in a similar situation at the exact same point in his journey, also traveled alone to another gloomy glade from which he—though not by choice—made a descent to another hell, reaching the nadir of his career in Orgoglio's dungeon in the same canto in which Guyon makes his own deepest descent. At this midpoint marker, the analogizing anatomy of the poem indicates the two journeys' similarities and differences. Any reflection back to the episode in the first book will make the description of Guyon's "feeding" himself with the thought of one's own virtues seem an oral pleasure the self-sufficiency of which will become increasingly problematic. Yet, unlike his more earthly cousin, faery Guyon does not need to be extricated by Arthur from his predicament. Unlike the Redcrosse Knight, he exits from hell under his own power. But when he arrives back above ground, he faints dead away:

all so soone as his enfeebled spright
Gan *sucke* this vitall aire into his brest,
As ouercome with too exceeding might,
The life did flit away out of her nest,
And all his senses were with deadly fit opprest.
[II.vii.66]

"For want of food, and sleep, which two vpbeare, / Like mightie pillours, this fraile life of man, / That none without the same enduren can," Guyon faints. However virtuous one's desires and however much one's deeds are praiseworthy and legitimate food for self-comfort, they are no substitute for the physical stuff of mortal sustenance, and in contrast to his success in not eating hell's food, when Guyon returns to "sucke" the vital "aire" of this world, he finally succumbs to his own infirmity. Doubtless right to take up the challenge of the adventure, Guyon yet achieves his moral triumph only by stretching mortal possibilities to the farthest physical limits. It is not merely that Protestant morality places a higher value on the *vita activa* than the *vita contemplativa* (just as Milton rates Spenser a better teacher than two medieval "schoolmen"); it is also that the specific knowledge Guyon wins in his adventure is worth the risk. Guyon's error, if it can be called error, is one that Milton argues to be entirely praiseworthy, for readers of books.

> Since therefore the knowledge and survay of vice is in this world so necessary to the constituting of human vertue, and the scanning of error to the confirmation of truth, how can we more safely, and with lesse danger scout into the regions of sin and falsity then by reading all manner of tractats, and hearing all manner of reason? And this is the benefit which may be had of books promiscuously read. [*CPW*.II.516–17]

Still, there is danger in courting temptation. "I read thee rash, and heedlesse of thy selfe," Mammon first says to the knight on the brink of descent, and in a sense he is right. In view of the fact that the trip underground is a divagation, and that the Redcrosse Knight has been found morally culpable for a similar wandering by the wayside, the question remains, why does Guyon go to Mammon's cave?

He goes to see what is to be seen—in essence, to see, to know, and to abstain. At the outset of the temptation, he easily dismisses the allure of Mammon's "eye glutting gaine," by moralizing "All otherwise . . . I riches read, / And deeme them roote of all disquietnesse." But he is soon tempted, by curiosity if by nothing else, so when Mammon virtually crooks his finger and says, "Come thou . . . and see," Guyon goes. The immediate motive given, that Guyon needs to know the origins of the gains he is being offered before he would even consider accepting them (II.vii.19), appears in context to be patently senseless; Guyon has already refused all past and future offers Mammon could make, citing all the right moral reasons for refusing. Guyon's real, and very Elizabethan, reason for making the journey is not a desire to see the gold, but to see hell:

> What secret place (quoth he) can safely hold
> So huge a masse, and hide from heauens eye?
> [II.vii.20]

In the same vein, Guyon's very first question had challenged Mammon for perverting money by hiding it "apart / From the world's eye, and from her right vsaunce" (II.vii.7). Thus it is the very hiddenness of the place—hidden both from the eye of the world and from the eye of God—that Guyon finds so alluring. In a sense, what Spenser offers in the Mammon episode is the dark underside of money's world, the functions it performs that are usually hidden to the eye. Spenser's allegory takes as its province the usually hidden springs of human society, making manifest the latent contradictions of Elizabethan economic organization, which provide in part the fallen text that Guyon must be able to read. The economic text is not the only one Guyon learns to read, neither is it the only way the reader can understand Book II of *The Faerie Queene;* it is one of many commentaries intended by Spenser's text and, perhaps because newer to our current ways of reading, also now more interesting.

Guyon begins with a fully classical notion of the fall, in which avarice is both the conventional partner of gluttony and the sexual violator of Nature herself:

Then gan a cursed hand the quiet wombe
Of his great Grandmother with steele to wound,
And the hid treasures in her sacred tombe,
With Sacriledge to dig. Therein he found
Fountaines of gold and siluer to abound,
Of which the matter of his huge desire
And pompous pride eftsoones he did compound;
Then auarice gan through his veines inspire
His greedy flames, and kindled life-deuouring fire.
[II.vii.17]

Spenser makes clear the tricky predicament in which, as an acute
reader of the changing Elizabethan economic structure, Guyon
finds himself. Mammon answers Guyon's classical account of the
fall with modern economic theory:

Sonne (said he then) let be thy bitter scorne,
And leaue the rudenesse of that antique age
To them, that liu'd therein in state forlorne;
Thou that doest liue in later times, must wage
Thy workes for wealth, and life for gold engage.
If then thee list my offred grace to vse,
Take what thou please of all this surplusage;
[II.vii.18]

Mammon has neatly put his finger on the contradiction between
Guyon's wage-laboring knighthood and the ideals of feudal array
based on land tenure.[45] Guyon thus goes to hell in part to witness
the confusion caused in the natural basis of the feudal economy by
the monetary form. What he sees is hardly attractive, and seems, at
least to post-Dickensian eyes, a truly hellish process of the industrial
smelting of gold:

45. Perry Anderson, *Lineages of the Absolutist State* (London: NLB, 1974), p. 116,
points out that the last feudal array based on land tenure was called in 1385; all
subsequent soldiering was paid in cash. Anderson also explains that there was a
"progressive dissociation of the nobility from the basic military function which
defined it in the mediaevel social order, much earlier [in England] than anywhere
else on the continent" (p. 125). The main problem posed to Absolutism everywhere, according to Anderson, was the "contradiction between the monetary form
and the natural basis of the feudal economy" (p. 197n).

And hundred fornaces all burning bright;
By euery fornace many feends did bide,
Deformed creatures, horrible in sight,
And euery feend his busie paines applide,
To melt the golden metall, ready to be tride.
[II.vii.36]

Physically picturing the creation of money, of Mammon's surplus-age, Spenser insists on its basis in real labor: "And euery one did swincke, and euery one did sweat." Of course, this picture of devils laboring at furnaces is conventional, deriving no doubt from medieval pictures of the fires of hell. (But it is not to be found in Dante—where one would most expect to find it.) Its appropriateness to the development of late Elizabethan economy aptly reveals how Spenser's epic assiduously addresses the most basic problems of the imperial moment. In *The Crisis of the Aristocracy,* Lawrence Stone points out that the last half of the sixteenth century saw a "remarkable growth of mining activity. In this the nobility and great gentry took the lead, sometimes on a very large scale."[46] Stone estimates that 40 percent of the pre-1603 peerage were engaged in mining and industry on their estates, some of the leading proponents being Burleigh and Leicester. In a sense, Spenser here in elaborate analysis broaches the issue that Cervantes handles comically every time Don Quixote is surprised by a request that he pay his inn bills. Don Quixote is of course being asked to pay for bed and board—for sleep and food, those two necessities that, like mighty pillars, upbear "this fraile life of man," and for the want of which Guyon faints away at the end of the canto. Guyon goes to hell to see the fountain of the world's wealth because money is a necessary evil in the fallen world. By abstaining from its allure, Guyon succumbs to the physical consequences. Roughly put, in a money economy you need money to buy food. Thus we may perhaps see some of the politically necessary connections in what Harry Berger has noted to be a persistent pattern of confusions between the edible and the visible, in

46. Lawrence Stone, *The Crisis of the Aristocracy, 1558–1641* (Oxford: Clarendon Press, 1965), p. 339.

this canto.[47] Thus Guyon "gluts" his "mortal Eye" with all that which "liuing eye before did neuer see"; and so:

> 'th' Elfin knight with wonder all the way
> Did feed his eyes, and fild his inner thought.
> [II.vii.24]

As a culmination to the test, Mammon leads Guyon finally

> Into a gardin goodly garnished
> With hearbs and fruits, whose kinds mote not be red:
> Not such, as earth out of her fruitfull woomb
> Throwes forth to men, sweet and well sauoured,
> But direfull deadly blacke both leafe and bloom,
> Fit to adorne the dead, and decke the drery toombe.
> [II.vii.51]

In the midst of this garnished "Garden of Proserpina" is a tree "loaden all with fruit as thick as it might be"—not, however, as one might have anticipated, the pomegranates to which Proserpina herself succumbed, but the "golden apples glistring bright" of pagan myth—Hercules's, Atalanta's, as well as the one that started the Trojan war when Paris awarded it to Venus on Mount Ida. Yet the final temptation appears not to be this golden fruit—to which Guyon, with his desire for an adventure worthy of being read abroad by fame's trumpet, ought to have been at least potentially susceptible. Instead, Guyon encounters a character desperate for food:

> Lo *Tantalus*, I here tormented lye:
> Of whom high *Ioue* wont whylome feasted bee,
> Lo here I now for want of food doe dye:
> But if that thou be such, as I thee see,
> Of grace I pray thee, giue to eat and drinke to mee.
> [II.vii.59]

---

47. Harry Berger, Jr., *The Allegorical Temper: Vision and Reality in Book II of Spenser's Faerie Queene* (1957; rpt. Hamden, Conn.: Archon Books, 1967), pp. 23-24.

Having fallen himself from heavenly feasting to hellish famine, Tantalus tempts Guyon to the kind of pity that Vergil had to teach Dante, infernal pilgrim, to restrain. Yet Guyon is proof against the request:

> Nay, nay thou greedie *Tantalus* (quoth he)
> Abide the fortune of thy present fate,
> And unto all that liue in high degree
> Ensample be of mind intemperate,
> To teach them how to vse their present state.
>
> [II.vii.60]

In manner much like the Palmer, Guyon here "reads" out for us the meaning to be gleaned from the figure of Tantalus, as if misinterpretation—misreading—were also included in the possible perils of the place. The lesson that Tantalus is to give—"unto all that liue in high degree," to make temperate use of their present state—is in part a self-reflexive gesture at the fiction's own moral usefulness, as well as an ironic indication of the peril Guyon is presently in. Tantalus usefully figures Guyon's plight because his greed had been made by allegorizing mythographers to mean more than simple avarice; it meant intemperate desire for knowledge. Thus, in the various classical authors and the mythographers available to Spenser, Tantalus had incurred the gods' wrath by stealing their secrets—or their ambrosial food. As Frank Kermode reports, Tantalus had become a "type of blasphemous or intemperate knowledge."[48] The feasting of which he speaks to Guyon then refers not merely to the food he ate, but to the things he saw (that never mortal eye did view), and knew.

What is most striking from the hypothetical perspective of Milton's reading is that such knowledge involves the taking in of food; for just as Spenser assumed the Anglo-Irish, reared on the milk of Irish wet-nursing, learned their degenerate ways by learning a corrupt language,[49] so Milton most crucially associates the fall

---

48. Cited by Alpers, *Poetry of The Faerie Queene*, p. 245.
49. Edmund Spenser, *A View of the Present State of Ireland*, ed. W. L. Renwick (1934; rpt. St. Clare Shores, Mich.: Scholarly Press, 1971), p. 88.

of knowledge and of language with the eating of an apple. By forcing a relation between reading and feeding, Spenser anatomizes
gluttony and avarice as complexly interrelated issues in an increasingly complex society. Spenser's political stance may have formed
part of the attractiveness of the passage for Milton, for in so doing,
Spenser addresses issues of immediate moment to his contemporary aristocratic readers, and criticizes them. The conspicuous
gluttonizing of Elizabethan aristocrats late in the reign had apparently contributed to the economic decline of their class. Lawrence
Stone remarks on the various attempts to "maintain the open-
handed semi-public way of life of the medieval prince."[50] Thus
Burleigh is reported to have spent £ 629 for three days' celebration
of his daughter's marriage in 1584, providing for his guests' consumption 1,000 gallons of wine, 6 veals, 26 deer, 15 pigs, 14 sheep,
16 lambs, 4 kids, 6 hares, 36 swans, 2 storks, 41 turkeys, over 370
poultry, 49 curlews, 135 mallards, 354 teals, 1,049 plovers, 124
knotts, 280 stints, 109 pheasants, 277 partridges, 615 cocks, 485
snipe, 840 larks, 21 gulls, 71 rabbits, 23 pigeons, and 2 sturgeons.[51]
Such banqueting is a conspicuous attempt to maintain a style of
living associated with the increasingly impossible aristocratic ideal
of an earlier chivalric age (and economic organization). Such excess
we are taught in Book II to regard as suspect. According to Stone,
the yokels of Gloustershire spoke to the problem in elegant
aphorism: "a great houskeeper is sure of nothinge for his good
cheare save a great Turd at his gate." In the light of such realism,
Spenser's mention of the Port Esquiline, whereby the wastes of the
digestion in Alma's house are "avoided quite, and throwne out
priuily," does not seem an indecorum forced upon him by the need
to complete his "anatomy" metaphor, but simple recognition of the
physical and economic facts.

    When Guyon specifically burns the banqueting houses of Acra-
sia's bower, in which she had fed the lusts of various hoggish forms,
we see moral failure attacked by the virtue of temperance. But we

50. Stone, *Crisis,* p. 555.
51. Ibid., p. 560.

also see an attack aimed at the physical excess of one class of readers whom Spenser specifically addresses in this adventure of a curiously pedestrian knight. And that Guyon is pedestrian is, I think, of fundamental importance to the politics of the body that Spenser anatomizes in Book II. Unhorsed, Guyon may experience the lure of faeryland in ways that may more freely criticize the contradictions within its basic chivalric metaphor and ideals. Guyon's experiences thus provide in part a freelance laborer's critique of late Elizabethan economic realities, recognizing the hellish nature of the preindustrial mining of aristocratic land (in an effort to make it pay in nonfeudal ways)—but also taking a dim (shall we anachronistically say "middle-class"?) view of aristocratic indulgence in a conspicuous excess of food.

I do not mean to suggest that this economic reading is the final or only interpretation to make of the Mammon episode, but merely to suggest that this dimension of interpretation is one the text itself points out, as one of a number of possible directions commentary might take. The episode in the Cave of Mammon is a case study in the plural interpretive possibilities offered by Spenser's narrative. To take only a single figure: Tantalus can mean avarice simply, in which case he quite properly belongs in Mammon's hell; in addition to this, he can mean an intemperate desire for knowledge, in which case his greed may inculpate Guyon's greedy Faustian desire for experiential knowledge of immortal realms (a desire that Eve shares with him); third, because Tantalus grabs after the heroic apples of the Hesperides on Proserpina's tree and the fruit that ultimately "many noble Greekes and Troians made to bleed"—he therefore may image Guyon's lust for a heroic epic adventure, one to be "read" worthy by fame's shrill trumpet. Or, he may "mean" what Guyon says he means: a warning to all who live in high degree of the punishment given intemperance.

If, as Milton insists, out of the rind of one apple tasted the twins of good and evil knowledge leapt, then the way back toward goodness will be through experiencing the essence of that evil. If one falls by eating—like Tantalus—then one can repair ruin by the knowledge gained from not eating, but from seeing instead, from feeding eyes and inner thoughts, not taste, in order to gain that sapience by which one knows to abstain. Hell may be a dangerous place, but it is necessary to go there.

The specific knowledge we as readers experiencing the allegory gain is that we are fallen, are in fact not capable of comporting ourselves as well as Guyon does. Milton's mistake suggests that he understood this as well, understood the difference between reader's and protagonist's responses to evil, and that it is this crucial rhetorical gap that allows Spenser to work his moral magic. Milton's mistaken sentence about the Cave of Mammon, in making it parallel to the Bower of Bliss, overlooks the major difference between the two episodes—a difference underlined by the Palmer's absence from the first and by his presence in the second. In the Cave of Mammon, Guyon is not tempted whereas in the Bower of Bliss he is tempted—and would have been lured forward, moreover, by the sensual excess of the place had he not been restrained by the Palmer. On the way to the bower, Guyon and the Palmer pass a fountain in which naked nymphs splash at play:

> Withall she laughed, and she blusht withall
>   That blushing to her laughter gaue more grace,
>   And laughter to her blushing, as did fall:
>   Now when they spide the knight to slacke his pace,
>   Them to behold, and in his sparkling face
>   The secret signes of kindled lust appeare,
>   Their wanton meriments they did encreace,
>   And to him beckoned, to approach more neare,
> And shewd him many sights, that courage cold could reare.
>   [II.xii.68]

The difference between our sense of the beginnings of Guyon's sexual arousal here ("courage cold could reare") and of his former endurance of the stifling horrors of Mammon's cave has as much to do with Spenser's reading out of the threshold text ("The strong through pleasure soonest falles, the weake through smart") as it does to Spenser's habitual fidelity to physiological fact. Significantly, it is the Palmer who restrains the hero's ardors:

On which when gazing him the Palmer saw,
He much rebukt those wandring eyes of his,
And counseld well, him forward thence did draw.
[II.xii.69]

In the cave, Guyon restrains himself; in the bower, he must be restrained by the Palmer. Milton's rhetorical period in *Areopagitica,*
which renders the two episodes so parallel, then seems to overlook
this crucial difference—unless, that is, we take into account the
presence of the reader. If, in the Cave of Mammon, Guyon is self-
sufficient to resist temptation, then there *he* plays the part played
by the Palmer in the Bower of Bliss; the one who is tempted by
Mammon then is not Guyon, but the reader. And herein lies the
problem the canto has posed critics all along. As Harry Berger summarizes it:

> If it is true that Guyon is unaffected by the Cave's temptations and
> horrors, why have readers always responded differently to the epi-
> sode? . . . The problem, however, is not really difficult. . . . the
> reader is meant to react to the horror and the allurements of Mam-
> mon's cave. But he is then meant to see that Guyon does not react
> to them. This, I think, is the point of the episode. [P. 30]

The image of Philotime, in the "second temptation," is rightly attractive; but as this image is described for the reader she ought not
to be as attractive as she appears to Guyon. As narrator, Spenser
gives readers many more clues to the proper response to make to
Philotime than Mammon gives to Guyon; for the reader, the figure
is named "Ambition, rash desire to sty," while Mammon merely
calls her "Philotime" (love of honor). While Spenser points out the
artificiality of her beauty, Mammon calls her "fairest wight that
won'neth vnder skye" (II.vii.45,49). Moreover, we get the qualified, warning description first. Arguing that the bifurcation of
reader's and hero's responses is Spenser's main point in the whole
narrative account of Guyon's solitary adventures underground,
Berger claims that the narrative says to the reader: "Guyon is
clearly able to rely on his own powers, but you, Reader, had better

invoke some higher assistance, since it is apparent (experience has shown) that you and your kind are less able to resist" (p. 32).

Other critics tend to read back from Guyon's faint into his experiences in the cave. Seeing the faint as punishment, they assume Guyon must have made some mistake; the problem then is to find and label the error properly with the right allegorical name. But that is to label a mistake the reader, not Guyon, makes. For Milton, at least, to have risked the confrontation is itself virtuous and no mistake at all; and certainly implicit within his mistaken inclusion of the Palmer in his description of the two trials is the sense that reader and hero, both palmers in this pilgrimage through a fallen landscape, will need help in resisting temptation: our fallen wills will bend in the direction of the allure, if only by yearning to see to know, by desiring to feed our eyes, if not our mouths. Milton also seems to remember in his oversight that there was a bending toward the evil Mammon offered, if only—and I think this is what is really parallel about the two episodes—a readerly kind of "skeptogula"— a gluttony of the eyes, to see and know.[52] Feeding eyes is the only "mistake" Guyon appears to make, just as feeding himself with his own virtues is as close as he comes to the culpable arrogance for which the Redcrosse Knight is punished by Orgoglio. But Guyon already knows what the Redcrosse Knight learns, that he is "fraile flesh and earthly wight." Secret, forbidden knowledge is what we gorge ourselves upon.

As if to underscore the dangerous confusions between reading and feeding in canto vii, Spenser supplies a proper revision of the relations between two activities in the House of Alma episode of canto x, where Guyon and Arthur read the histories of their respective nations. There in the "house" of the body, the main activity of which is an allegorical anatomy of digestion, the heroes first read (for the whole of canto x) the texts of *Briton moniments* and the *Antiquite of Faerie;* and only after they have closed their books do they sit down to a ritual feast (II.x.77). In Alma's house reading (history)

52. For the "skeptophilia" in Book III of *The Faerie Queene,* see C. S. Lewis, *The Allegory of Love: A Study in Medieval Tradition* (1936; rpt. New York: Oxford University Press, 1958), pp. 331–33.

and feeding (feasting) are two complementary yet separate means of communion, the one with the past, the other with the present. For the tempted reader, right reading of the Mammon passage means a self-consciously open-ended interpretiveness. For Guyon it means abstention. In gaining knowledge by not eating but by seeing, by feeding eyes, not taste, in order to read well hell's images, Guyon's phantom companion becomes the prototype of Milton's reader. Milton's mistake in *Areopagitica* is finally a very significant one. It points to his recognition that there is an extra presence within the text—seeing, knowing, if not always abstaining. Allegory as a narrative genre always posits this kind of reader, interpreting his or her own interpretation, and Spenser no less than other allegorists incorporates such a reader into the experience of the text. Isabel MacCaffrey has written of Spenser's strategy this way:

> In most fictions, the author in one way or another manipulates the distance that separates character from reader; in the analytic mode of Spenser's allegory, he draws attention to the distance itself.[53]

This procedure is crucially at work in the experience of reading Book II, which is different from its doubling cousin, Book I, or its mirror-mate, Book V; for Guyon's experience, unlike those of the Redcrosse Knight or Artegall, is radically atemporal, while the reader's experience is always time-bound by the sequential action of reading. Spenser signals Guyon's transtemporal nature by making him a faery—Saint George and Artegall are not only human, they are Britons. Guyon, as a character more tied to the fictive realm of faeryland than his counterparts, need not really learn anything in his adventures; he is but a bit of the fiction after all. But for the reader to fail to become fashioned in virtuous and gentle discipline is for the poem to fail by leaving a mortal soul deformed in moral "shape"—a beastliness imaged last in Book II in the trans-

---

53. Isabel G. MacCaffrey, *Spenser's Allegory: The Anatomy of Imagination* (Princeton: Princeton University Press, 1976), p. 86.

formations of the Circean Bower of Bliss.

In aiming to fashion and transform its reader, *The Faerie Queene* always attends to the dangers of the process. If Guyon's adventures in Mammon's cave evade final interpretation as a way of escaping the ultimate fixity of hell, Guyon's experiences in the Bower of Bliss postpone the process of judgment as long as possible, but finally recognize the limits of poetry's transforming powers, and the irrefutable evil of the landscape. Guyon's experience in the garden is not different merely because he momentarily succumbs to temptation and must be restrained there; in the bower he must not merely abstain from, he must destroy the garden's pleasures.

> But all those pleasant bowres and Pallace braue,
>   *Guyon* broke downe, with rigour pittilesse;
>   Ne ought their goodly workmanship might saue
>   Them from the tempest of his wrathfulnesse,
>   But that their blisse he turn'd to balefulnesse:
>   Their groues he feld, their gardins did deface,
>   Their arbres spoyle, their Cabinets suppresse,
>   Their banket houses burne, their buildings race,
> And of the fairest late, now made the fowlest place.
>   [II.xii.83]

Guyon's power here seems hardly temperate, though perhaps violently potent in order that it may neutralize the huge opposing power of Acrasia. Only after the garden's destruction can the Palmer retransform the captive beasts back into their proper human shapes. And even here there are limits to the transforming powers of good.

> But one aboue the rest in speciall,
>   That had an hog beene late, hight *Grille* by name,
>   Repined greatly, and did him miscall,
> That had from hoggish forme him brought to naturall.
>   [II.xii.86]

The proper response to Grill's choice is not to force his conversion, however, but to let him be:

> The Donghill kind
> Delights in filth and foule incontinence:
> Let *Grill* be *Grill*, and haue his hoggish mind.
> [II.xii.87]

In such a way does Book II as a whole testify to the necessary keeping of limits, to keeping one's proper shape—a basic component of
temperance. As a *via media* counterposed to Grill's hoggishness, we
see it differentiated from a sloth both effeminately aristocratic (as in
Verdant's emasculated posture of repose) or piggishly primitive (as
in the Indian culture Europeans found in America).[54] At the close of
Book II we reach the limits to which temperance may travel, fiction
may conceive, and then, Spenser turns back:

> But let us hence depart, whilest wether serues and wind.
> [II.xii.87]

In witnessing the outermost limits of the Odyssean quest, Book II
reflects upon the triumph over self that is necessary for the foundation of any empire. Not accidentally, then, is the proem concerned
with locating faeryland (Guyon's nation) somewhere in the same
region as that previously undiscovered Virginia—the outermost
edge of the virgin queen's growing empire:

54. Stephen Greenblatt, *Renaissance Self-Fashioning: From More to Shakespeare* (Chicago: University of Chicago Press, 1980), sees Guyon's destruction of the bower as
"a painful sexual renunciation" (p. 175) limning the European response to the
native cultures of the New World (p. 179). While Greenblatt's suggestion that the
destruction of the bower images the repressions necessary to empire building is
attractive, it seems ideologically incomplete most crucially in positing the entire
Faerie Queene as uncritically mystified worship of Elizabeth's power. Spenser mounts
a critique of Elizabeth even in the first installment of the 1590 *Faerie Queene;* in the
later installment his criticism is even more drastic. Emphasizing the traditional
debate between art and nature in the Bower, Robin Hedlam Wells, *Spenser's Faerie
Queene and the Cult of Elizabeth* (London: Croom Helm, 1983), p. 69, observes that in
it Spenser warns Elizabeth about "the artifice with which her court was virtually
synonymous." Elizabeth's notorious reluctance to let Ralegh personally supervise
his voyages to the New World was frustrating, while Elizabeth's enforced refusals—
"No wars, my lords, no wars!"—would have been just as emasculating as Acrasia's
lust. Spenser's romance with Elizabeth's power is more complex than he would
have us at first suspect. See below, Chapter 4.

> Where is that happy land of Faery
> Which I so much do vaunt, yet no where show—
> ....
> Many great Regions are discouered
> Which to late age were neuer mentioned.
> Who euer heard of th' Indian *Peru?*
> Or who in ventrous vessell measured
> The *Amazons* huge riuer now found trew?
> Or fruitfullest *Virginia* who did euer vew?
>   [Proem.II.1–2]

Faeryland is located in the place of the questing human imagination, a peculiar Renaissance creature that does not, Spenser reminds us here, confine its quests to mental realms alone but sallies
out to seek new continents. The discovery of America, the founding
and colonizing of fruitfullest Virginia, had been, of course, the con-
suming interest of Spenser's intimate friend, Sir Walter Ralegh,
who shares the honors of the proem to Book II with the queen. Both
had been (along with Leicester) heavy investors in the joint stock
companies founded to fund the colonizing of America, at first seen
as "an abortive goldrush" according to Stone[55]—and therefore
sharing some of the excess that Spenser censures in the Mammon
episode. Drake's circumnavigation of the globe in 1580 had been
financed by the queen, Leicester (to whom Spenser had been secretary in 1579), and Hatton. Sir Walter Ralegh's desires to hatch
empires were centered on the same patroness whom Spenser addresses in his epic, and for whom "fruitfullest Virginia" was so
oxymoronically named. Spenser's focus in the first half of his epic
on this remarkable woman takes a number of perspectives—and in
part the text glances asquint at the elusive hopes held out by the
promise of the queen's favor. At least as seen from the hypothetical
perspective of Milton's parallel reading, we may see the allure of
the chain held by Philotime—"a rash desire to *sty*"—punningly
refigured in Grill's metamorphosis and Verdant's emasculation.
Acrasia may image an alluring primitive insouciance about sensu-

55. Stone, *Crisis,* p. 370.

ous delights—but her fair artful arbors and banquet houses may also shadow the court at whose center was the queen for whom Spenser's new land is named.[56] Acrasia's decolletage may image the queen's no less traditional dishabille—as virgin the queen could properly go about with bosom uncovered and did so even in old age[57] —and therefore Guyon's experience may inscribe the complicated set of attractions and repulsions inherent in a courtier's response to her erotic—because erotically presented—power. The maternal posture of Acrasia's dominance would only reassert another dimension of Elizabeth's remarkable posture of femaleness vis à vis her realm. Whatever the precise interconnections between narrative detail and political situation, we should see that here, in the center of the first installment of *The Faerie Queene,* Odysseus's journey becomes the dazzling pattern for men of the early Renaissance, but it is an odyssey that ends not with a homecoming to a loyal wife, but with the destruction of a queen's power. (No wonder Milton singled it out.)

Spenser not only acknowledges the perimeters of possibility for his own verse in appealing to the queen (and in this he was prophetic, for he did not finally win her favor), he realizes the limits of the transforming powers of his poem on the habits of his Grillish gentlemen. This self-limitation seems a peculiarly English form of self-protection in the expansive Renaissance; a similar self-limiting appears in Shakespeare's figure of Caliban, native of the vexed Bermudan isle, "a thing of darkness" whom Prospero in burying his book finally acknowledges as his own—and keeps controlled.

Thomas Greene describes the early Italian emphasis on the happier transforming powers of the new humanist knowledge:

56. Ralegh himself changed the name of the territory to Virginia (which included what is now Virginia, the Carolinas, and Georgia, as well as inland states), and Elizabeth rewarded him with a knighthood in 1585; for a discussion of Ralegh's Virginia colonizing, see Samuel Eliot Morison, *The European Discovery of America: The Northern Voyages* (New York: Oxford University Press, 1971), pp. 626-31.

57. "Extracts from Paul Hentzner's Travels in English, 1598," in *England as Seen by Foreigners in the Days of Elizabeth and James the First,* ed. William Brenchley Rye (1865; rpt. New York: Benjamin Blom, 1967), pp. 104-5.

Once one begins to dream of ever more noble forms to imprint on
the wax of consciousness, one begins to forget the limitations of that
wax. Or rather, taken in by the metaphor, one forgets the stubborn
consistency of the mind which renders the analogy inexact.[58]

Spenser did not neglect the inexactness of the analogy, neither did
he forget that a medieval poet had also used Ulysses as a particularly apt exemplum through whom to remember this recalcitrant
fact about human nature: Dante had made Ulysses the image of the
voyager who goes too far, the master of words who leads his men,
finally, too far astray, having reached, like Spenser's Tantalus, too
far for forbidden knowledge. Dante's portrait of Homer's (really
Vergil's) hero may be the real pretext for Spenser's own investiga-
tions into the personal costs of Empire—and of imperial art.
Dante's Ulysses carries a heavy freight of self-consciousness about
the potential demonic presumption inherent in the poet's shaping
powers, especially as the Christian poet overgoes the pagan.

The Ulysses passage of the *Inferno* was not lost on Milton either;
both Spenser and Milton use the context in which Dante places the
portrait of Ulysses to coordinate their own concerns about possibly
presumptuous artistry. We shall have to look more carefully at their
mutual source in Dante's text when in the next chapter we consider
their very similar grapplings with the problem posed by poetry's
demonic fictive powers, its ability to misshape as well as transform.
If finally what Guyon learns to abstain from in the Bower of Bliss is
the appeal of its dual allure, its man-made beauty and its fairest
civilizing nature, then what the poet Spenser also gives up at the
same time is the power such man-made art might hope to claim
ultimately over man's stubborn beastly nature. The reader needs to
choose to be transformed; and what Spenser's reader gives up at the
end of Book II is the fiction that his or her nature can be easily, or
permanently, changed by the poem. The ways through evil toward

58. Thomas M. Greene, "The Self in Renaissance Literature," in *The Disciplines of Criticism,* ed. Peter Demetz et al. (New Haven: Yale University Press,
1968), p. 251.

good are slow and given to many slidings backward. But poetry continues the lesson, repeatedly allowing man to see, to know, and to abstain: to choose not to bend toward the allure. To choose not to eat, as Spenser shows us in Book II, is arduous, slow—an entirely pedestrian process, hardly heroic at all (and so Guyon loses his horse long before he loses the Palmer). And Guyon may also, we have seen, himself choose wrongly.

Paradise Lost is the record of this offered wrong choice. All the poetry of *Paradise Lost* up to the point when Eve eats the apple is a preparation of the reader for the choice (inevitable, because known), so that the process Milton unravels is a very slow one. Yet when we come to Eve's decision, Milton manages to bring us to the moment in a way that makes the act occur in a flicker of an eyelid. Here is Milton's Eve making a notably significant choice:

> her rash hand in evil hour
> Forth reaching to the fruit, she plucked, she eat:
> [IX.781-82][59]

The iterative present participle "reaching" here promises the slowness of small narrative units where there will be time between "pluck'd" and the backreaching to stop, to reconsider, and so to abstain. But Eve "eat." The past tense here looks, if not sounds, like a present (possibly pronounced "et"); so even as Eve is in the process of making a choice still seemingly revocable, it is already made, irrevocably done in the instant the will freely wills, forever lost in the past moment, the first moment to pass away in loss. The world and its time are transformed in an instant. And it happens incredibly fast.

> Earth felt the wound, and nature from her seat
> Sighing through all her works gave signs of woe,
> That all was lost.
> [IX.782-83]

59. Alastair Fowler, ed., *Paradise Lost* (London: Longman, 1968), prints "ate" but notes that it was spelled "eat" in early editions; this edition hereafter cited in the text.

We know Milton had at least once before read this particular moment in history in terms of Spenser's epic, and it is from his reading of his predecessor's fallen landscape that Milton learned to describe his falling one:

> Greedily she engorged without restraint
> And knew not eating death.
> [IX.791–92]

In the same bifurcated way that we know Philotime is Ambition while Guyon only knows she is Philotime, and just as we see "allegories, while Guyon sees people"—just as there is often a measurable distance between what Spenser's protagonist knows and what we know—in the same way we feel weighted down by the fatal difference of knowing more than Eve what death is. What Milton offers is more than the inescapable dramatic irony that Eve's innocence is here mere pathetic ignorance, irony available to anyone who had chosen to tell this story. As readers of Spenser's Book II are aware, Milton wants us to be acutely alive to the hellish nature of ingesting wisdom at all.

> O Sovran virtuous, precious of all trees
> In Paradise, of operation blest
> To sapience, hitherto obscured, infamed,
> And thy fair fruit let hang, as to no end
> Created.
> [IX.795–99]

Our double understanding of what Eve does not know but will learn, what she does not yet perceive to have changed in her very ways of knowing, the change from unfallen to fallen wisdom, is signaled by the fatal doubleness of meaning in the word "Sapience." Out of the rind of one apple tasted leaps a new procedure for knowledge, of knowing one thing by its inheriting, doubling, twinned, and punning opposite. So, too, if in Mammon's world nothing is used well, all things having been perverted from their "right usance," then Eve, now verbally sophisticated, can hellishly claim that she finally has made right use of the apple. The apple could bear no "fruit," could have no end to which it was created, could have reached no result, until Eve used it. If we are free now to see separated, the two meanings of the word "fruit," we must realize that this excess of significance comes at great cost. Earlier, in an open, unburied, and innocent moment of wordplay, Eve had told the serpent that he had brought her to the interdicted tree to no purpose:

> Serpent, we might have spared our coming hither,
> Fruitless to me, though fruit be here to excess.
> [IX.647-48]

Here Eve is in control of a simple unfallen correspondence in what are now, to us, two separate literal and metaphorical meanings of the world. As long as the fruit bears no "fruit," as long as Eve abstains from putting it to any use, it is put to good use. Its right usance, like the black fruit in Mammon's garden, is simply not to bear "fruit" in anything other than itself, not to be turned into another action with grave consequences. Its proper fruitfulness is to be left hanging "fruitless." As long as the apple remains so, there is no mortal taste that brings death into the world and all our woe. The apple remains just an apple.

Anne Ferry has noted that it is by his using particularly this kind of language, with its balanced inclusion of both literal and figurative meanings (concrete and abstract meanings are true and indivisible), that Milton differs most from Spenser.[60] Ferry argues that "allegory, like extended simile . . . implies a separation between terms it is apparently comparing, between the familiar and the unknown, the portrait and its conception" (p. 92). She characterizes Spenser's language, then, as one that links an adjective suggesting abstract moral judgment with a noun representing a concrete thing, as in "mightie arms," or "cruel markes," while Milton's metaphorical language insists on unity of significance rather than sepa-

60. Anne D. Ferry, *Milton's Epic Voice: The Narrator in Paradise Lost* (Cambridge, Mass.: Harvard University Press, 1963), pp. 90–109.

ration between literal and metaphorical meaning (as in the first "fruit of that forbidden tree").

But Spenser's language, as we have learned, actually demands an intricate (allegorical) unity, when it relies on the polysemous density of individual words to incorporate twin meanings as part of their sacred nature.[61] Thus much of Guyon's experience underground can be seen in terms of a collapsing together of the ideas of feeding and reading. A simple rhyme is forced into the type of pun on which the first book pivots so deftly—in the sense that the Redcrosse Knight's story becomes the "whole" of holiness, where "despaire" is only one manifestation of a constantly repeated doubling-out of duplicitous divisiveness (dis-pair) as imaged by the hero's fragmented psyche, when he strays from his beloved Una.

When seen as dependent on this sort of wordplay, Spenser's allegorical polysemy becomes more relevant to Milton's linguistic program. Indeed, Spenser's wordplay may be said to be the basis for Milton's. Describing Milton's program, Ferry goes on to list the single words in the first lines of *Paradise Lost* which function simultaneously in terms of both their literal and their figurative meanings:

> "Fruit" means both "result" or consequence and "apple"; "mortal" signifies both "subject to death" and "human"; "taste" can be used to mean the general noun "experience" as well as the particular sensation associated with eating. [P. 93]

Yet coordinating all of these words and making them all merely versions (nearly puns) of one another is the actual meaning of "taste" that Ferry mistranslates as "experience." The most important meaning is "sapience," the etymological meaning that grounds knowledge in food. It is this meaning that Milton puns on

61. For discussion of Spenser's wordplay, see Martha Craig, "The Secret Wit of Spenser's Language," in *Elizabethan Poetry: Modern Essays in Criticism,* ed. Paul J. Alpers (New York: Oxford University Press, 1967), pp. 447–72; A. C. Hamilton, "Our New Poet: Spenser 'Well of English Undefyl'd,'" in *Essential Articles for the Study of Edmund Spenser* (Hamden, Conn.: Archon Books, 1972), pp. 488–506; Angus Fletcher, *The Prophetic Moment: An Essay on Spenser* (Chicago: University of Chicago Press, 1971), pp. 101–6; see also my *Language of Allegory,* pp. 33–42.

in *Areopagitica,* using the same pun that may be said silently to structure the reading of canto vii of Book II of *The Faerie Queene.* Insofar as Milton reveals to his reader the punning connection to "Sapience" in Eve's first postlapsarian speech, he replicates Spenser's methods of ensuring his reader's entanglement in the process of unfolding the wisdom hidden in fallen language. Milton's puns are in part a signature of the presence of *The Faerie Queene* within *Paradise Lost.*

Christopher Ricks has defended Milton's wordplay as being a part of the Grand Style of the poem.[62] Ricks is concerned—as were most of Milton's eighteenth-century editors—to defend the linguistic decorum of the puns that, once glimpsed, seemed to lie everywhere in *Paradise Lost,* silently impugning the correctness of the poet's taste. Ricks himself distinguished between successful and unsuccessful metaphor, wordplay, puns proper, and "silently speaking" non-puns, though he is naturally more interested in reading the poem than in classifying its words. He undertakes a defense of the following pun on "distaste" in the opening lines of Book IX.

> No more of talk where God or angel guest
> With man, as with his friend, familiar used
> To sit indulgent, and with him partake
> Rural repast, permitting him the while
> Venial discourse unblamed: I now must change
> Those notes to tragic; foul distrust, and breach
> Disloyal on the part of man, revolt
> And disobedience: on the part of heaven
> Now alienated, distance and distaste,
> Anger and just rebuke, and judgment given,
> That brought into this world a world of woe,
> Sin and her shadow Death, and Misery
> Death's harbinger.
> [IX.1-13]

It is odd that Ricks opens his astute comments on this passage by saying that "there does not at first seem to be much in the immedi-

62. Christopher Ricks, *Milton's Grand Style* (Oxford: Oxford University Press, 1963), pp. 66-75.

ate context which will invigorate the metaphor in 'distaste.'" "Distaste" should, however, be immediately appropriate, because Milton in these lines tells us that Book IX will chronicle the change from rural repasts, where man could sit down to share food with an angel, to Heaven's present alienated distaste for man, a loss that happened by way of the one apple tasted. Milton had already told us exactly what Raphael and Adam ate—raw fruits and vegetables (no fear lest dinner cool); how they could talk all they wanted, and how, while they were eating together the same food, Raphael also was feeding Adam the wonderful answers to his wonderful questions. Disobediently dieting on death, Adam and Eve fall away from this kind of simple and immediate feasting. The pressure on the word "distaste" is not, as Ricks points out, "exerted locally." "It is also exerted by the countless times that the Fall is described as the *tasting* of the apple. The real structure of the phrase is that of a brilliantly unspoken pun" (p. 70).

Not to taste the apple is all Adam and Eve had to do. They are asked for obedience by abstention, but that does not mean their state of innocence is negative. Out of an infinity of choice there was only one small thing they could do wrong: to eat or not eat not apples, but only the apples of a single tree. This easy binary either/or choice is quite simple compared with the potential for error in Guyon's complex trials. If Adam and Eve are blessed with the perfect absoluteness of a single choice, Guyon is faced with numerous possibilities for failure. He may not only not taste, he may not sleep, or covetously touch, or even lustfully eye anything:

> If euer couetous hand, or lustfull eye,
> Or lips he layd on thing, that likt him best
> Or euer sleepe his eyestrings did vntye,
> [II.vii.27]

the demon hovering over his shoulder with his cruel claws will rend the knight to pieces. We are not even sure if Guyon knows how endangered he is, while we do know that Eve has been told many times what she risks. Hemmed in by so many negative possibilities,

Guyon's experience testifies to an ease of freedom that we lost at the fall. By comparison it seems easy to keep the one injunction given to Adam and Eve. Eve's choice is the obverse of Guyon's, not merely because she makes the wrong decision (when it would have been easy not to err), but because her choice has made necessary the nature of his choosing:

> Here grows the cure of all, this fruit divine,
> Fair to the eye, inviting to the taste,
> Of virtue to make wise: what hinders then
> To reach, and feed at once both body and mind?
> [IX.776-79]

Eve, in feeding both body and mind, makes it forever necessary for temperate man not to attempt to make knowledge his only food. Guyon may either feed his mind and make his body suffer for it, or feed only his body—like Grill—and suffer for that. At their rural repast Raphael had told Adam when he asked to know more about God's universe:

> Enough is left besides to search and know.
> But knowledge is as food, and needs no less
> Her temperance over appetite, to know
> In measure what the mind may well contain.
> [VII.125-29]

The two kinds of choosing seem to pose the starkest of contrasts. Set against the mortal quickness and sheer simplicity of Adam and Eve's momentous choice at the dramatic center of *Paradise Lost* is the type of choice their decision makes necessary: Spenser's kind of choosing, a kind proper to the densely interwoven plurality of possibility in a fallen world where the fatal twins, good and evil, cohabit so closely that his characters must make a very slow paced, deliberative picking of their way through a landscape which may be good, or may be evil.

Milton's landscapes, unlike Spenser's, are more clearly labeled good and evil—heaven is heaven, hell hell, and paradise, while it lasts, a good place. But the process of negotiating the journey through them is filled with as many pitfalls, for both reader and narrator, as any thicket in faeryland. Because we bring not innocence into the world but impurity much rather, the reader of *Paradise Lost* needs to be just as wary of his or her responses as Spenser's reader does; Milton takes time out, as it were, from telling his story, to insist upon this most crucial fact about his reader's fallen perspective. Significantly, Milton does so at the densest moment of acknowledgment of his precursor's presence within his text—a moment structured by another brilliantly unspoken pun—on "sin." Its implications for the rhetoric of reading *Paradise Lost* are manifold.

CHAPTER 2

The Sin of Originality
and the Problem of Fiction

SIGNALING the presence of the Spenserian text within his own most obviously by the allegorical personification of Sin, the half-woman, half-snake who sits at hell's gate holding the keys, Milton witnesses his dependence on his "original" at a most crucial juncture for his poem. The gates of hell are shut fast against Satan until he can cajole Sin into opening them, and they therefore mark a threshold across which Satan must pass before he can begin his epic flight up through Chaos to the light, where he will work his own dark designs on God's creation. Sitting within the closed boundary of hell, and holding within herself the power to allow Satan to cross or not to cross, Sin is herself a threshold marker; she figures therefore a bizarre potential that the epic flight (and indeed the poem) will not be achieved, will not spring free of its constraints, or find its true epic expansiveness in Satan's journey across the vast spaces of Milton's created cosmos.

In light of Sin's potential blocking function, it is critical to realize how generically important Satan's flight is to Milton. Thomas Greene has argued that "perpetual expansiveness is the habit of the epic sensibility," and that Milton's poem "manifests as spacious ... an imagination as we are privileged to know."[1] Besides our

1. Thomas M. Greene, *The Descent from Heaven: A Study in Epic Continuity* (New Haven: Yale University Press, 1963), p. 378. For a discussion of the parallels between Satan's and the narrator's flights, see William Kerrigan, *The Prophetic Milton* (Charlottesville: University of Virginia Press, 1974), pp. 147–53.

precipitous drop into hell in the opening lines of the poem, our first experience of the physical vastness of Milton's imagined spaces is Satan's voyage. As the point of origin for this epic voyage, the particular place at which Sin sits is, therefore, crucial. It is most significant for his epic that at this place, and very specifically in terms of the dragon coiled at the center of *The Faerie Queene's* labyrinthine language, poised ready to spring—at this place, in this character, Milton considers the question of the language of *Paradise Lost* and its necessarily fallen, mediating fictiveness.

Sin and Errour: The Problem of Origin

The character upon whom Milton precisely models his Sin is, of course, Errour, the first of numerous and self-replicating antagonists whom the Redcrosse Knight must confront throughout the first book of *The Faerie Queene*. As such, Errour's presence at Book I's beginning has a pervasive influence over the conduct of the entire book. All of the knight's other enemies are in very important ways merely refigurations of the threat Errour poses, not the least of which is the temptation to assume that to vanquish her in martial combat is to become free of her power. Because the knight's initial ambiguous battle with the dragon is designed to undermine its own readability, the reader's experience with the incident's "allegory," counterpart to the knight's false sense of security, becomes a crucial part of the poem's allegorical rhetoric—that is, its active involvement of the reader in the exfoliations of the text. Milton appears to have understood this rhetorical aspect of Spenser's procedure quite well.

It is easy (because more comfortable) to forget the peculiarly slimy details of Errour's portrait. But because it is detail upon which Milton builds his own first female creator-figure, Sin, we should look again at Errour as the Redcrosse Knight first glimpses her:

Halfe like a serpent horribly displaide,
But th'other halfe did womans shape retaine,
Most lothsom, filthie, foule, and full of vile disdaine.
[I.i.14][2]

Throughout the Middle Ages and up through the Renaissance, the Edenic serpent had been imaged as a half-snake/half-woman.[3] As Spenser first presents her, Errour offers to knight and reader the fruit of the Tree of Knowledge. No longer merely twined about a single trunk, however, she lies now at the center of a whole seductive forest. In her, Spenser realizes the fantastic cancer of evil knowledge.

Una and the Redcrosse Knight become lost in the wood at the same time the reader loses the narrative thread in the extended tree catalogue of stanzas 8–9; the conjunction of narrative and reading experiences is typical of Spenser's rhetorical organization of the narrative. We may read, or interpret, both experiences to imply that the catalogue represents a "fallen" facility for naming—for controlling experience through a nomenclature that is shown to have, finally, little ability to control. What is being enacted is in part the proverb that Una and the Redcrosse Knight "cannot tell the forest for the trees"; but the epic catalogue, itself an emblem of the Orphic poet's controlling powers in epic, may also perform a subtle parody of the prelapsarian knowledge by which Adam named the animals.[4]

2. *Spenser's Faerie Queene,* ed. J. C. Smith (1909; rpt. Oxford: Clarendon Press, 1964), 2 vols.; hereafter cited in the text.
3. Michelangelo's serpent with full female torso in the Sistine Chapel temptation scene, and Raphael's female-headed snake in the loggia approaching that chapel are two Italian Renaissance versions. A similar (full-torso) serpent offers the apple on the northwest doorway of the Cathedral of Notre Dame in Paris. For other examples see Arnold Williams, *Common Expositor* (Chapel Hill: University of North Carolina Press, 1958), p. 116.
4. For a fuller discussion of the complicated notion of reading as narrative process in Book I of *The Faerie Queene,* see my *Language of Allegory: Defining the Genre* (Ithaca, N.Y.: Cornell University Press, 1979), pp. 255–60. For further problems with the catalogue, see below, pp. 101–3.

But because Spenser is interested in the reader's immediate visceral response and not merely in a recognition of the intricate verbal problems inherent in the scriptural basis of his fable, he continues the description of the dragoness with further detail:

> And as she lay upon the durtie ground,
>   Her huge long taile her den all ouerspred,
>   Yet was in knots and many boughtes vpwound,
>   Pointed with mortall sting. Of her there bred
>   A thousand yong ones, which she dayly fed,
>   Sucking vpon her poisonous dugs, eachone
>   Of sundry shapes, yet all ill fauored:
>   Soone as that vncouth light vpon them shone,
> Into her mouth they crept, and suddain all were gone.
>   [I.i.15]

To understate the effects of nauseated horror at the facts of monstrous female creation this stanza evokes is to miss part of Spenser's point; the thousand moiling, sucking creatures that disappear into her mouth, like so many snakes slithering from the light, image our subterranean terror at the very slime of origin. However hideous, they are appropriate for a book that chronicles the pains of spiritual rebirth. In his care to provide an immediate visceral response to the blatant ugliness of an evil that will appear much more appealingly disguised later, Spenser invests the scene with a cannibalistic progeny so self-destructively greedy as to pose no immediate threat to the hero. So when the knight finally manages to hack off her head, Errour's brood suck their mother's blood:

> Her scattred brood, soone as their Parent deare
>   They saw so rudely falling to the ground,
>   Groning full deadly, all with troublous feare,
>   Gathred themselues about her body round,
>   Weening their wonted entrance to haue found
>   At her wide mouth: but being there withstood
>   They flocked all about her bleeding wound,
>   And sucked vp their dying mothers blood,
> Making her death their life, and eke her hurt their good.

That detestable sight him much amazde,
  To see th'vnkindly Impes of heauen accurst,
Deuoure their dam; on whom while so he gazd,
  Hauing all satisfide their bloudy thurst,
  Their bellies swolne he saw with fulnesse burst,
And bowels gushing forth: well worthy end
  Of such as drunke her life, the which them nurst;
Now needeth him no lenger labour spend,
His foes haue slaine themselves, with whom he should contend.
                                                                    [I.i.25–26]

The spawn's matricidal suicide is only the final touch to the detestable and amazing picture of Errour's productions—which are all
like her, ambivalent in their sexual hermaphroditism. They are
"the same" Spenser tells us, as those bred by "old father Nile . . .
partly male and partly female" when his "fattie waues do fertile
slime outwell" (I.i.21). The sexual ambivalence of the figure is
matched by a verbal ambivalence that saturates the episode with an
interpretative potential for which the sexual confusion may itself be
a sign.

When Spenser explains of Errour that "Her vomit full of bookes
and papers was, / With loathly frogs and toades, which eyes did
lacke" (I.i.20), he signals by this bizarre fact that the reader is being
initiated into his or her own ignorance about reading, just as the
knight's unachieved valor is being tested. Una has explained that
"this is the wandring wood, this *Errours* den . . . Therefore I read
beware" (I.i.14), by which self-conscious wordplay Spenser insists
that the reader read self-conscious of his or her own running allegorical interpretation or a reading-out of the meaning of the episode. Those misshapen creatures that crawl back into Errour's
mouth are, Spenser tells us, "blacke as inke." Insofar as the reader
will tend to assume that the knight has vanquished Errour and that
the battle is therefore an object lesson in how to cope with the primal
fear it arouses, the reader will be wrong, will be misreading those
black inky creatures. The knight remains subject to Errour even
after he hacks off her head and after her brood (with whom he
should contend) destroy themselves. If the episode seduces the
knight into relying on his own unaided valor, the first thing the text

does is seduce the reader into thinking it is simple to interpret. The full meaning of the Errour episode is not, in fact, apparent until canto x, where the most authoritative text to be read about the incident finally appears, in the company of other female nurturing figures, Fidelia and Charissa. In the House of Holiness the Redcrosse Knight is taught by Fidelia to read scripture: "That her sacred Booke, with bloud ywrit / That none could read, except she did them teach, / She vnto him disclosed every whit" (I.x.19). In the same House, knight (and reader) find the refigured image of female nurturance in Charissa, "late in child-bed brought," who even though "a multitude of babes about her hong," teaches the knight the "ready path" to heaven—a path that is a narrow way up to the Mount of Contemplation, where he learns his origin, is reborn, and christened. There, his name and nation are finally "red aright" by Contemplation.

Yet, if the knight finally arrives in canto x at the point where his "errant" wandering can be put back on the straight and narrow path, still the major portion of the poem has dealt with his errancy and wandering—travel overseen by the forces named by the word for the first dragon-mother (*errare,* to wander). If Charissa's beneficence is the right reading of all those female attributes of nurturance, guidance, and fostering growth which we see perverted in Errour's malificence (evil it seems too neat to call the power of the "devouring mother," though this is doubtless the right archetype) then Errour images not merely the terrors of earthly origin but the punning duplicities inherent in fallen language. At the same time the double-sexedness of her monstrous femaleness figure the evil potential of a sexual ambiguity in itself not culpable in *The Faerie Queene* (witness Nature's ambiguous sex in the *Mutability Cantos*—a sign of her divine numinousness).

Satan's confrontation with Sin in Book II of *Paradise Lost* has many of the same rhetorical functions as the Redcrosse Knight's battle with Errour, and provides the same cueing of the reader's reading. It is equally important not to neglect the repulsive sexual detail of Milton's portrait or to dissolve it into the technique of mere trope. As Milton and Spenser conceive it, the process of reading carries real emotional freight. They discuss reading in terms laden with an emotional dread and desire that they expect us to bring to our own practice. Milton's epic voice tells us in great detail what Sin looks like at a moment of rebeginning for the poem, just before Satan sets out on his heroic journey across the wastes of Chaos:

> The one seemed woman to the waist, and fair,
> But ended foul in many a scaly fold
> Voluminous and vast, a serpent armed
> With mortal sting: about her middle round
> A cry of hell hounds never ceasing barked
> With wide Cerberian mouths full loud, and rung
> A hideous peal: yet, when they list would creep
> If aught disturbed their noise, into her womb,
> And kennel there, yet there still barked and howled
> Within unseen.
>   [II.650–59][5]

Incestuous progeny twice over, the barking, womb-burrowing hell-hounds are the spawn of Death's rape of his mother Sin, Death himself being the incestuous result of Sin's mating with her father Satan. Not merely a parody of the Trinity, that abstract balance of masculine powers about which we know Milton had real reservations (termed "subordinationism" or "Arian heresy"), Sin, her father Satan, her son Death, and the hellhounds present a hideous and more grotesquely literal parody of the act of origin than even Spenser's Errour does. The full narrative context stresses this relation of parent and progeny: the infernal meeting between Sin and Satan is framed by Death's threatened patricide. Just so, the hell-

---

5. John Milton, *Paradise Lost,* ed. Alastair Fowler (London: Longman, 1971); all subsequent references are to this edition, hereafter cited in the text. The seventeenth-century spelling printed in the Columbia Milton preserves a number of puns; thus "The one seem'd Woman to the waste, and fair, / But ended foul in many a scaly fould / Voluminous and vast" (II.650–53), pun not only on the obvious "foul" and "fould" but on the etymological connections between "waste" and "vast"; without pressing the contradictions of a folded emptiness, we can see that the language surrounding biform Sin has a fuller set of immediate ambivalences; she is associated with wordplay (Columbia *Milton,* II, 61).

hounds by creeping back into Sin's womb unbirth themselves. The peculiar sexual repulsiveness of these reburrowing creatures Milton appears to owe to Spenser, for he specifically distinguishes them from the dogs of classical myth: "Far less abhorred than these / Vexed Scylla bathing in the sea that parts / Calabria from the hoarse Trinacrian shore" (II.659–60). When transformed by Circe, Ovid's nymph Scylla merely found her legs changed into a girdle of barking dogs round her naked belly, as if, Ovid says, Cerberus had twined himself around her waist: in the *Metamorphoses* these mad dogs merely bark. As a monster in the *Odyssey*, Scylla had menaced Ulysses's voyage, gobbling six of his men, and in Vergil's poem, where she is further transformed into a rocky front facing Sicily's Carybdis, she threatens to destroy Aeneas's men. By then she retains no human form.

Although Milton owes the dogs' invasion of the mother to Spenser, he has overgone the specific sexuality of Spenser's portrait by one detail. While Errour's progeny cease sucking on her dugs and creep back into her mouth, Sin's hellhounds crawl back into her womb.[6] Spenser doubtless chose the orifice he does because of its typological associations with hell-mouth: when the Redcrosse Knight in canto xi finally slays the ultimate dragon through the mouth, at that moment he participates in the divinely imploded presence of Christ, and provides a typological refiguration of the harrowing of hell.

Of course, in *Paradise Lost* Sin sits at that very place— Hellmouth—and Satan's task is to talk her into opening the gates so that he may give birth to his grand design—which is to have the children of light come trooping back through the hellish maw, unmaking their creation in sin, tombing themselves in hell's womb.

Spenser's typological intention in having Errour's progeny crawl into her mouth is readily apparent only after one reads the whole book and watches the final battle, and so it is a detail the perfect propriety of which relies upon the reader's experienced interpretation. It is a function of the reader's right reading of Spenser's alle-

---

6. Fowler notes that Du Bartas's opossum in *Divine Weeks* (i,6) rewhelps her young, a legitimate error rather different from Milton's mythologizing of Sin.

gory. By placing Sin specifically at Hellmouth, Milton literalizes Spenser's allegorical detail, making physically present in his landscape the point of Spenser's interpretive tactic. Yet to say that Milton thus deallegorizes the figure would not be fair to allegory, to Milton, or to Spenser, for Spenser's allegory has a very real and literal impact of its own. That Sin is the original of which Errour and Scylla may be presumed mere copies is a function of Milton's poetic time scheme. The density of suggestion in this time scheme allows Sin to be like a type to Errour's antitype; Errour is what Sin will look like after she has arrived on earth and has infected man's language. Milton's portrait is more "original" because it portrays Sin closer to her temporal and therefore typological origin. By choosing the time scheme he does, Milton undermines all his precursors in epic, including Spenser. [7]

The idea of "originality" is a loaded one for Milton, especially in the context of his indebtedness to Spenser. If the Redcrosse Knight witnesses in the Errour episode a repulsive and ultimately suicidal matricide when the dragonets "devour their dam," Sin's first outcry in *Paradise Lost* is a startling shriek of disordered family relations that announces a threatened patricide:

> O Father what intends thy hand, she cried,
> Against thy only son? What fury, O son,
> Possesses thee to bend that mortal dart
> Against thy father's head?
>
> [II.727–730]

That a Spenserian personification should oversee this kind of Oedipal scene in Milton's narrative would doubtless provide much grist for a Freudian reading of Milton's relations to Spenser. But what is more immediately interesting is the trinitarian resonance of Sin's outcry, which subtly hints at Milton's transgression of another, far more privileged, set of received textual interpretations than those of *The Faerie Queene*. The parodic echo of the set terms for addressing

7. For a fuller discussion of Milton's typological legerdemain, see Harold Bloom, *A Map of Misreading* (New York: Oxford University Press, 1975), pp. 125–43.

the Trinity—Father, only begotten Son, Holy Spirit—belies the presence of one heresy that Milton appears to have allowed himself in his own very "original" reading of the text of Scripture. This is the only direct appearance of the otherwise invisible idea of the Trinity in the text of the poem, so few readers guessed until the publication of *The Christian Doctrine* how far from the beaten path of doctrine Milton had actually strayed. Milton obviously was not interested in distracting orthodox readers' attention by insisting on what would be taken as heresy. Yet here one sees a criticism of the idea of the Trinity implicit in an allegorical "reading" of the relations among Satan, Sin, and Death. Because this kind of reading is the very sort that Milton's (and Spenser's) allegory in fact works against, we can see how Milton makes such one-for-one translation (Satan = God; Sin = Holy Spirit; Death = Son) "discover" a Roman Catholic doctrine we know he rejected. Milton criticizes both the method of reading and its results.

The more important idea for Milton in Satan's confrontation with Sin is immediate and literally apparent in the details of incestuous, perverted relations between parent and progeny. Paradise was lost because of the lack of proper respect due a creator by his creatures. The same concern for origin and for proper relations between creature and creator is, of course, central to Spenser's Book I. Therefore, it is one of Milton's slyest jokes that Satan thinks the ugliest two creatures he has ever seen the only two he has ever created; he asks Sin:

> why
> In this infernal vale first met thou callst
> Me father, and that phantasm call'st my son?
> I know thee not, nor ever saw til now
> Sight more detestable than him and thee.
> [II.741–45]

The central irony of these filial relations is that Sin is a dutiful daughter and sexual partner, for she, unlike her disobedient father, remembers only too well her origin and to whom, therefore, she owes obedience.

Thou art my father, thou my author, thou
My being gavest me; whom should I obey
But thee, whom follow?

[II.864–66]

Sin has already argued how little she "owes" to God's commands above, which have forbidden her to unlock the gates, so the only other answer possible to give to her question of whom she should obey has already been given, in the negative.

It is important that Sin (like Satan) makes her decision with a rhetorical question, to which the respondent is not meant to respond, the speaker having answered in the very framing of the question, forestalling and therefore paralyzing further free choice. Such rendering passive the auditor's will is the core of Sin's rhetoric of irresponsibility. It has its own grammar as well, marked most of all by the passivity of its verbs. Sin knows that "fields were fought in Heaven," and that "Into my hand was given" the powerful key that unlocks hell's gate. "Fall" to Sin is a noun, not a verb; so, when she explains that she fell from heaven she says, "And in the general fall / I also." Events "befall" innocent victims who are powerless to choose otherwise. This special kind of diction bespeaks Sin's very special character. Hers is not a dramatic unity of personality, but the kind of allegorical characterization which animates the signal word hovering over her portrait. As she sits at hell's gate, her own nature yet unachieved but merely potential, a collection of signs (however repulsive), she is that kind of Sin which is itself a punishment for sin: she is quite specifically "original sin." A punishment for actual sin, for the fall of man, original sin, as Milton explains in *The Christian Doctrine,* consists in

> the deprivation of righteousness and liberty to do good, and in that
> slavish subjection to sin and the devil which constitutes as it were
> the death of the will.[8]

In her very slavish willessness, Sin is a snakily undulating parody

8. Columbia *Milton*, XV, 205.

of true obedience, a parody of the rights due proper and original authority.

The great saving humility that Milton achieves in this episode is that in predicating Sin's character on Errour's, he avoids making Satan's mistake: he pays due respect to *his* original, to Spenser. Equally important, Sin's echo of Errour engages the fiction in self-consciousness about its own fictiveness at the point when it most immediately and dramatically considers what the fiction as rhetoric must work with—the reader's own originally sinful will. If we fallen readers are often made to look with Satan's fallen eyes in the poem, what we can see in Sin is what he saw—as she puts it, "in me thy perfect image viewing." What one is supposed to experience in the peculiar hideousness of Sin's twice-deformed genitalia is, doubt-less, a revulsion from the stain of origin—for "we bring not inno-cence into the world," as Milton argues in *Areopagitica,* "but impur-ity much rather"—and original sin seasons for death the very flesh brought forth at birth. It is absolutely right then that the hideous-ness of Sin's physical appearance should call up that peculiar collec-tion of fears and desires.

If Errour is a parodic, perverted version of the good-mother fig-ure, to be revealed in canto x of the first book of *The Faerie Queene* in the nursing portrait of Charissa (and there are countless other posi-tive female nurturant figures throughout the rest of Spenser's epic), and is therefore "readable" only in terms of later figures in the text, then Sin's paradigmatic relations to Satan and death are a parody not of the nonappearing Trinity but of another real family, the rela-tions among whose members are the crucial concern of the poem. Satan's own creation of Sin and Death ape God's creation of Adam and Eve. It is the idea of creation itself, the giving birth to other creatures—or to blasphemous and perverted fables—that Sin's own story of origin images. In this hymn about creation, a celebra-tion of the birth of the world, born from the vast abyss made preg-nant by the spirit, all must tell stories of their own births—Sin's is only the first birth-story in the poem:

> All on a sudden miserable pain
> Surprised thee, dim thine eyes, and dizzy swum

In darkness, while thy head flames thick and fast
Threw forth, till on the left side opening wide,
Likest to thee in shape and countenance bright,
Then shining heavenly fair, a Goddess armed
Out of thy head I sprung: amazement seized
All the Host of Heaven; back they recoiled afraid
At first, and called me *Sin,* and for a sign
Portentous held me.

[II.752–60]

The story Sin here tells takes the plot to the furthermost chronological point of origin so far encountered in the narrative. Milton begins the story proper with "what time" Satan's pride had cast him from heaven; Sin was born before the War in heaven had even begun, at the time of Satan's first thinking its possibility. From then on, Milton's procedure is to unveil events gradually as the chronology makes further and further forays into "the beginning." Satan's idea of rebellion, his conception of Sin may, in fact, be the beginning point of the entire plot. We may be being asked to consider what *is* the beginning of the single action that encompasses all human actions?

The story of Sin's birth also parodies the cephalic birth of Athena. Sprung from Zeus's head, as Hesiod tells it in the *Theogony,* Athena, the goddess of wisdom, was born fully armed. Here Milton need not directly indicate that this tale was an errant fable the pagans told, "erring." He has already explained how to read the pagan gods in recounting Mulciber's fall (II.739–51). Here the context itself simply and silently comments. Sin is fallen wisdom; Satan has literally self-conceived the evil Sapience that will ultimately devour the innocent tasters of the apple. The Greeks had thought Athena was wisdom, a good knowledge.[9] But Sin reveals that they had only the fallen manner of knowing, a secondary knowledge based on signs or seeming. It is, Milton also knows, the only kind of knowledge from which his reader can begin to know good.

9. For a fuller discussion of this extremely fine point, see Philip J. Gallagher, "'Real or Allegoric': The Ontology of Sin and Death in *Paradise Lost,*" *Journal of English Literary Renaissance* 6 (1976), 332–34.

Sin's very name, as Milton assigns it here, functions much as the etymological wordplay on "error" had in alerting Spenser's reader to the potential threat posed by Errour's "wandring" wood. The angels call her "*Sin,* and for a sign / Portentuous" held her. "Sin" elides easily into the sound of "sign"—the like sounds as well as the appearance of the words on the page brings Sin's name near to a pun. As a near-pun, the word "sin" insists upon its own self-conscious significance as well, that is, its ability to make signs. The word plays as well on the further submerged pun in the Latin word for "left," for Sin, like Eve, is born from the *sinister* side of Satan's head. So Adam taunts Eve after they have fallen:

> but a rib
> Crooked by nature, bent as now appears
> More to the part sinister from me drawn.
> [X.864-86]

In being also a personification, specifically Spenserian, Sin is a piece of animated language. She is a character who is, in ways too numerous and closely layered to spell out, a sign.[10]

Very much like etymologically punning Errour, who sits at the center of her wandering wood, Sin's nature forces upon the reader an extreme form of word consciousness. And the fact that we become most aware of Milton's punning language in the context of his most overt reliance on his original, Spenser, vividly reveals the care with which Milton had read *The Faerie Queene* and noticed the significance of its polysemous punning. With the refiguration of serpentinely sapient Errour in the portrait of Sin, Milton insists that the reader take *The Faerie Queene* as a poem paradigmatic in the nature of its fallen wisdom. As we have seen, Guyon's adventures in Book II had closely accompanied Milton's thoughts on fallen wisdom in the *Areopagitica.* In Book II of *Paradise Lost* Errour's serpent wisdom,

---

10. For another discussion of the linguistic concerns broached by the allegory of Sin and Death, see Anne D. Ferry, *Milton's Epic Voice: The Narrator in Paradise Lost* (Cambridge, Mass.: Harvard University Press, 1963), pp. 116-46; by using a fairly mechanistic definition of allegory, Ferry misses much of Spenser's power in her otherwise acute and persuasive reading of the language of the two poets.

already a sign of Edenic evil for Spenser, is further glossed by the Hesiodic details Milton adds to Sin's story, tying it to the kind of knowledge contained in all those heroic poems of the past. More important, Milton witnesses by Sin's punlike name that fallen wisdom has its own kind of language, which necessarily participates in the immediate allusiveness of postlapsarian knowledge. If one can taste good and evil in tasting the same apple, the sapience thereby granted has inhering within it the kind of doubleness we associate with puns. Spenser's characters are all puns; Sin is as close to a pun as any of Milton's characters get. In this, at least, Milton has most assiduously studied and understood his "original's" allegorical procedure.

But if he understands that process well, he has an entirely different attitude toward the procedure's status. Spenser creates narrative out of language's ambivalent polysemy; Milton does not, but finds that polysemy a problem, evidence of the fall itself. Satan is not only the father of Sin, he is also the father of corrupting wordplay. The fallen angels' notorious punning about the artillery barrage verges on *bomphiologia,* or excessively inflated diction. Their puns are horrible and meant to be exactly that; as they ready the cannon shot Satan vaunts:

> Heaven witness thou anon, while we discharge
> Freely our part; ye who appointed stand
> Do as you have in charge, and briefly touch
> What we propound, and loud that all may hear.
> [X.564–67]

"Scoffing in ambiguous words" Satan exemplifies the "lore" of sin.

As herself the first instance of the fallen pun, Sin's double nature names the tricky business of fallen language so problematic to Milton in writing about the unfallen landscape of Eden. And here Milton's great originality appears. If Spenser's landscape is the quintessential fallen place of twinned knowledges, indistinguishable from each other, then Milton has attempted to describe an unfallen place, in fallen language. His problem seems an impossible one. But as Christopher Ricks long ago pointed out, Milton's procedure is fairly direct: he makes the punning possibilities of language work against themselves. Outlining Milton's method, Ricks notes how it relies on a remarkable amount of self-consciousness on the reader's part. For example, of Milton's use of the word "error" to characterize the river in paradise which flows "With mazie error under pendant shades," Ricks remarks:

> *Error* is here not exactly a pun, since it means only 'wandering'— but 'only' is a different thing from an absolutely simple use of the word, since the simple meaning is consciously and ominously excluded. Rather than the meaning being simply 'wandering', it is 'wandering (not error).' Certainly the word is a reminder of the Fall, in that it takes us back to a time when there were no infected words because there were no infected actions.[11]

The reader must work to unpun "error," "wandering," and "mazes," negativing the bad moral connotations of the ambivalent fallen words themselves. The proper "unfallen" meaning—mere wandering in a meandering path—is, of course, Spenser's huge fable-producing pun unfolded in the first ten cantos of *The Faerie Queene*. This is not to suggest that Milton got the idea and its uses directly from Spenser; Shakespeare, for example, does very similar things with the word *error* in *The Comedy of Errors*. However, Milton did, I think, rightly associate the polysemous potential of language underlying Spenser's epic with fallenness, with fables, and with the original sin out of which he was trying to jolt his reader. In effect, when Sin says after the fall in Book X that "I residing through the race, / His thoughts, his looks, words, actions all infect," she signals that her "infection" of language is to turn it into an ambiguous system of signs in which all the overlapping meanings of individual words display the "fall" that language has suffered from its original state of perfect clarity. Adam's first postlapsarian words are conscious of themselves as ambivalent signs; his pun is a central one for Milton:

11. Christopher Ricks, *Milton's Grand Style* (Oxford: Clarendon Press, 1963), p. 110.

> Eve, now I see thou art exact of taste,
> And elegant, of sapience no small part,
> Since both to each meaning savor we apply,
> And palate call judicious.
>
> [IX.1017–20]

Adam here, like Eve before him, has discovered the wonderful economy of a fallen language that can mean so much more than it seems to intend. To say that they have also dicovered language's own fictive powers is perhaps to approach in part what readers have found repulsive about God's ostentatiously plain speech in Book III.

Erected out of the very ambiguity that Milton's God's style eschews, the poetry of *The Faerie Queene* is quintessentially self-conscious about its own fallenness. Allegory is a genre of the fallen world, for in a prelapsarian world, at one with God, there is no "other" for language to work back to since there has been no fatal division. No distance, no divorce, no distaste between God and man, who has not yet known the coherence of good and evil in the rind of one apple tasted. "Hand in hand with wandering steps and slow," Adam and Eve finally arrive home in a world that looks like ours and is spelled like Spenser's language.

As the most self-consciously Spenserian of Milton's characters, Sin properly finds her origin in puns and a self-reflexively fictive use of language—the essence of fallen fable. That her presence breaks epic decorum is what eighteenth-century critics most censured about *Paradise Lost*. So Addison objected that Milton "has interwoven into the Texture of his Fable some Particulars which do not seem to have probability enough for an Epic Poem, particularly in the Action which he ascribes to Sin and Death."[12] Dr. Johnson concurred:

---

12. Joseph Addison, *Spectator*, No. 297; Addison added to the list the Limbo of Vanity, observing that "such Allegories favour the Spirit of Spencer and Ariosto" (*Selected Essays from the "Tatler," "The Spectator," and "The Guardian,"* ed. Daniel McDonald [New York: Bobbs-Merrill, 1973]).

Milton's allegory of Sin and Death is undoubtedly faulty. Sin is indeed the mother of Death, and may be allowed to be the portress of hell; but when they stop the journey of Satan, a journey described as real, and when Death offers him battle, the allegory is broken.[13]

Johnson objects further to the intermixture of real and figurative, of mythic and fictive, of truth with out-and-out lies; Sin and Death "cannot facilitate the passage by building a bridge, because the difficulty of Satan's passage is described as real and sensible, and the bridge ought to be only figurative." He concludes his analysis of the episode's failure by saying: "This unskillful allegory appears to me one of the greatest faults of the poem; and to this there was no temptation but the author's opinion of its beauty."

Strikingly unbeautiful, the original of all true ugliness in fact, Sin's allegory offers Milton a talisman to ward off the potential fall there is in bridging the far-flung realms of his poem. Sin and Death are there to do exactly what Johnson objects to their doing; they interrupt Satan's journey, interposing a moment in which Milton may self-reflexively consider the further progress of the poem. The two sit watch at the first interface we meet in Milton's cosmos—the boundary between hell and heaven. Later they span the space of our original and precipitous fall into the poem, when they finally build the bridge to earth in Book X, which Johnson thought already too real in Book II. Milton breaks epic decorum to reveal fiction's face. Sin's self-reflexive verbal fictiveness indicates the literary tour de force involved in Satan's voyage across the incredible spaces of Milton's cosmos. If Sin is uglier than Scylla and more repulsive than Errour it is because she is the original of all these exemplars of ugliness. In her portrait Milton undermines and ends up claiming priority over all precursors. Yet embodied within Sin's portrait is an ironic warning, as we have seen, against doing that very thing. If the center of *Paradise Lost* is a hymn of a creature to the creator, then for that creature to forget his original is the greatest sin. Satan handles the problem of his origins this way:

13. Samuel Johnson, *Lives of the English Poets*, ed. G. B. Hill, 3 vols. (Oxford: Clarendon Press, 1905), I, 185–86.

who saw
When this creation was? Remember'st thou
Thy making, while the maker gave thee being?
We know no time when we were not as now
Know none before us, self-begot, self-raised
By our own quickening power.

[V.856–63]

Self-separated from creator, a creature is damned to wander in endless mazes lost, a hell within and where he is, hell. Worse irony, of course, is Milton's joke against Satan's own creations. Not only does he not remember his own making, his own creation, he does not remember his having made, having created something else. It is as if Milton were saying that to forget one's dependence on a creator is to be utterly separate from, unallied to, one's own creations. Insofar as Sin is Satan's fiction, something he has made, Satan as poet cannot claim it, for he does not recognize the creation as his own.

The Redcrosse Knight thinks that "Vertue gives herself light through darkness for to wade." In the Errour episode, he learns that this is not true, and begins the process of perceiving that the manly virtues in which he puts so much faith are laughably impotent in the face of ultimate evil. He learns that if he is to survive he needs to align himself with the love that creator has for creature. If the first sin of originality, assuming the burden of one's own creation (as Satan does), seems like an admirable opposite to the willless passivity of original sin, then the clownish young knight's deluded self-confidence gives the lie to that fallen wisdom. He is free only when he learns of his origin, how fallen he is—mere Saint George, *georgos,* worker of earth. Milton's readers also learn how fallen their own origins are when they confront one mother-surrogate of their race in the figure of Sin. It is crucially important as well that at the very same moment in the text, Milton, no Satanic artist himself, most necessarily acknowledges his own fallen origins in Spenser's epic. In the most self-conscious fiction-making of his poem, he witnesses the original whose poetry has made his fiction possible. Milton makes rhetorical use of this moment, too, using the personification of Sin to warn his reader about the element of me-

diating fiction—something that needs to be *read*—that there necessarily is in his retelling of the awesome Truth. Dr. Johnson was
right; the allegory does not fit. But it is because of its very lack of fit
that the reader will notice the fiction—and be reminded that no
poem written in a fallen language can hope to adhere absolutely to
the truth. In face of the figure of Sin, both reader and poet are self-
conscious of origins—the reader of his or her own original sin,
Milton of his beginnings in Spenser's text. Both may thereby correct their responses for that unavoidable margin of error there is in
all fiction.

The Form of Fiction: Epic Convention

The landscapes of Sin's hell and Errour's den are in terms of
linguistic self-consciousness the same place: they are places for a
poet to acknowledge the very fallenness of all fiction, its essential
mediate errancy from truth. Errour's den and hell are even more
blatantly the same mental landscape: both are hell. And, as we saw
in Chapter 1, it is not surprising that Milton and Spenser should
begin their readers' educations into good with a visit to the home of
evil Sapience. Knowing good as we do only through evil, hell is the
logical place to begin a Christian epic.

It is, of course, where Dante had begun his. Enlarging the epic
descent to the underworld into the entire first cantica of the *Divine
Comedy,* Dante grapples with some of the aesthetic and spiritual
problems involved in following a pagan precursor along the path
that leads to Christian revelation. Yet to begin in the infernal re-
gions has a radically different impact on the reader of the two English Renaissance epics than it does on Dante's reader. It will be
useful to consider for a moment the differences between the medieval and the Renaissance poets' procedures. In the medieval Roman
Catholic fiction, hell is a real, historical place, contemporaneous
with the time Dante wrote the poem and with the time in which
Dante's reader reads. It is a place to which Dante, by divine inter-
vention, claims actually to have traveled led by Beatrice's interme-

diary, Vergil. Vergil's presence within the fiction as a poet is the main method by which Dante coordinates his complex relations to pagan art. Like most of Dante's personages, Vergil is a real, historical individual. His presence within the fiction underscores that the journey the poem records was historical, that it actually happened, and was, in fact, not a fiction at all.[14] The record may be fiction, an artful recreation of something real, and Dante—as we shall see—may have something to apologize for regarding the fictional ornament of the record. But he need not apologize or warn his reader about the poem's plot, for that belongs to God. Nonetheless Dante is powerfully aware of the power of poetry to mislead readers: hence the initiating episode of Paolo and Francesca, who fell to the first circle because they had allowed themselves to be corrupted by literature. Reading has great moral power. If it helps to damn the lovers, it may, conversely, aid in Dante's readers' salvation.

Like Dante, Spenser and Milton must also warn their readers about the power of poetry to mislead. But unlike Dante, they are both Renaissance poets who faced the problem of their classical precursors in epic with a fully articulated sense of Aristotle's demands about form. If Dante's entry into his fiction was not hemmed in by these same rules and was furthermore eased by the convenience of the dream-vision form, Spenser and Milton had to put into the generic shape of a classical, pagan, Greco-Roman epic—which had celebrated a mysterious human heroism—the truth of Judaeo-Christian revelation that celebrates a mysterious inhuman heroism. Dante could follow Vergil through the landscape of hell without implying any primacy of vision—priority is self-evident. Spenser and Milton had to grapple with the assumption of the primacy of classical form at the same time that they believed they had to better the ancients in art because they were better in the truth of their religion. Because their truth was greater, their poems must also be. Though he had the *Aeneid* by heart, Dante had no similar burden of classical form: the perfect replications of his

14. Charles S. Singleton, *Commedia: Elements of Structure,* Dante Studies 1 (Cambridge, Mass.: Harvard University Press, 1954), 84–98, grounds the historicity of the poem's journey in the incarnation.

poem's infinite triplicities were, doubtless, sufficient mimicry of God's art, and there was no need for another kind of mimesis. As Renaissance epic poets, Spenser and Milton needed to create fictions that, in Stanley Fish's term, would be "consumed" into the truth at the same time that the creative process both analyzed and annihilated an utterly alien poetic form.

Both Milton and Spenser arouse their reader's self-conscious reflections on the relation of fiction to truth by calling attention to the very virtuosity with which they fulfill the conventions of classical mimesis—the imitation here not of nature but of classical art. Their problem is turned into an asset, and both poets use the formal requirements of classical epic as foils for art's limits. Spenser no less than Milton defines Christian heroism for his reader by undermining pagan notions of proud valor, although, of course, Spenser's "paynims" are as different from Milton's demonized pantheon as Spenser's romance *copie* is from Milton's spare attic shape. Yet in each case the poet allows a formal property of epic to make a deep aesthetic appeal, which, by its rhetorical manipulation, is then made to function as a protection against an evil excess of artfulness in a treatment of revealed wisdom.

The formal rule was: the epic poet begins *in medias res,* thrusting into the midst of things. Thus Spenser catches the Redcrosse Knight and Una in the silhouetted middle distance, already on their way to restore the Garden of Eden. Historically, this event is one paradigmatically of the middle moment. If Christian history arches from the origins recorded in Genesis (and reenacted in *Paradise Lost*) to the ends of time promised in Revelation, then the Redcrosse Knight's refiguration of Christ's winning back paradise is the human playing-out of the drama of midpoint. Milton begins by thrusting his reader down to hell to observe the devils plotting how to make the garden fall; how *they* fell is narrated in the middle books, and is a ludicrous dress rehearsal for all the wars they shall cause later in man's history—wars that become the erroneous matter of "heroic" songs like the *Iliad.*

The tricky maneuvering by which Milton and Spenser translate their readers to these *medias* points exemplifies their shared rhetorical poetics. Each uses a series of verbal pyrotechnics to dazzle the reader's attention while he subtly moves the reader—Spenser through a mental space and Milton through time—irrevocably across a geographical and moral boundary impossible to recross. The details of each procedure are worth scrutinizing for their similarity of effect.

Spenser's legerdemain is accomplished by the famous tree catalogue nine stanzas into the first canto. Formally the catalogue derives directly from Chaucer's *Parlement of Foules*, where it serves the same function as a bridge (as in musical parlance) to another allegorical "space." Yet Spenser would have also known Chaucer's precursor Ovid just as well, and the nod at the *Metamorphoses* in Spenser's catalogue heralds the connection to Latin epic and to the issue crucially at stake in the writing and reading of this kind of poem. The catalogue proper begins innocently enough in stanza eight, a praise of God's creation:

> Much can they prayse the trees so straight and hy,
> The sayling Pine, the Cedar proud and tall,
> The vine-prop Elme, the Poplar never dry,
> The builder Oake, sole king of forrests all,
> The Aspine good for staves, the Cypresse funerall.
> [I.i.8]

Chaucer's catalogue in the *Parlement* comprises a whole rhyme royal stanza of seven lines, ending with "the victor palm, the laurel to devyne": Spenser's pyrotechnical display of continuing the catalogue past the initial four lines into an entire nine-line stanza begins precisely where Chaucer's leaves off, with the laurel. It adds a peculiarly Renaissance twist; while the victor gets a palm and the interpreter a laurel in Chaucer, Spenser conflates the two:

> The Laurel meed of mightie Conquerours
> And poets sage, the Firre, that weepeth still,
> The Willow worne of forlorne Paramours,
> The Eugh obedient to the benders will,
> The birch for shaftes, the Sallow for the mill,
> The Mirrhe sweete bleeding in the bitter wound,

> The warlike Beech, the Ash for nothing ill,
> The fruitfull Oliue, and the Platane round,
> The caruer Holme, the Maple seeldom inward sound.
>   [I.i.9]

For Renaissance Spenser, the laurel is crown both to the martial hero and to the poet whose song praises his victories, in the same way as the present hero and his lady are praising the trees so high. Yet in doing so the knight and Una become lost in the Wood of Errour. When the "Maple seeldom inward sound" ends a catalogue that has begun with such a dual-purposed laurel, we may suspect that Spenser is emblematizing the sort of license against which Sidney was defending poetry. By having both protagonists and reader get lost—the fictional characters in the fictive wood, and the flesh-and-blood reader in the virtuosity of the poet's art—Spenser witnesses the power of such poetry to mislead. The Ovidian context of the catalogue reinforces this warning. Orpheus had been a poet notable for his lack of success in leading a prisoner of hell out of its confines. Ovid's tree catalogue appears just after he narrates the pathetic tale of Orpheus's losing Euridice and of the poet's mad despair at her now second death. The catalogue reveals, then, Orpheus's leftover poetic powers. Walking on a treeless hillside, wanting shade, Orpheus sits down to rest. As the poet begins to sing, the trees come crowding around to shade him from the sun:

> For trees came crowding where the poet sang,
> The silver poplar and the bronze-leaved oak,
> The swaying lina, beechnut, maiden-laurel,
> Delicate hazel and spear-making ash,
> The shining silver fir, the ilex leaning.[15]

Spenser's landscape is made up of carefully layered texts that the reader must learn to read and read among, just as the Redcrosse Knight is taught to read rightly and take counsel properly from the landscape ("Therefore I read beware"). In reading Orpheus's cat-

15. Horace Gregory, trans., *Ovid, "The Metamorphoses"* (New York, Viking Press, 1958), p. 276.

alogue and judging its significance, we must surely notice that his wood is a curiously wandering wood itself—the mobility of which, of course, while imaging the poet's power, also reminds us of his lack of it. If he can make trees walk, he still cannot translate Euridice from hell.

Unlike Milton, Spenser does not directly claim the supremacy of revealed wisdom over the refined intelligence of the ancients; but he would doubtless have assumed that the truth of the story he tells would grant greater efficacy to him as Christian poet to lead his reader from out of hellish error into wisdom! At the very least, his Ovidian catalogue serves to get both reader and protagonists lost; it gets them to the first figuration of hell in the poem:

> At last resolving forward still to fare,
>   Till that some end they finde or in or out,
>   That path they take, that beaten seemed most bare,
>   And like to leade the labyrinth about;
>   Which when by tract they hunted had throughout,
>   At length it brought them to a hollow caue,
>   Amid the thickest woods.
>
> [I.i.11]

Spenser's subtle transportation of his reader across an invisible boundary into the "ways" of Errour, which comprise a landscape out of which the Redcrosse Knight does not travel until he reaches the House of Holiness, is silently accomplished by the tree catalogue. Here is rhetorical narrative at work. The reader's experiences as well as the protagonists' are meant to be "interpreted"— that is, to be judged for the acuity with which they deal with the means of knowledge in a fallen world. Countless signals pressure the reader to experience his or her own confusions at the level of reading the print on the page as replications of the protagonists' confusions in reading a landscape that mirrors their abilities either to mistake evil for, or to distinguish it from its twin, good. The reader's inability to read the impacted episode is mirrored by Una's inability to lead her knight out of the Wood of Errour, though she does at least have the wisdom to name the place. The catalogue gets us into a different kind of ontological space; it is a wood, not a plain (across which the gentle knight first rides in the opening line): this is to say no more than that the meanings knotted up within it, as Errour's tail is knotted up within itself, will be unraveled, will be made "plain" in the text that follows and comments upon this initiating episode.[16]

Milton's entry into hell—his initiating episode—makes the same kind of rhetorical maneuver as Spenser's, but rather than disorienting the reader's sense of spatial organization, he manipulates the reader's sense of time. The epic formula Milton plays upon in this threshold legerdemain is not the verbal virtuosity of an epic list— each item of which, with its accompanying epithet, displays the poet's ordering powers—but that formula whereby the poet addresses and appears to uncover for the reader the source of his power. If the tree catalogue displays the outward and visible sign of poetic power, the invocation of the Muse purports to allow an auditor to be present at that power's genesis. The Miltonic invocation is a masterly tour de force that undercuts itself and by undercutting protects against its own presumptuous artistry. Its rhetorical function is to dislocate the reader, to dazzle, and to begin the first extremely subtle steps in the process of exorcizing the reader's false notion of epic heroism.

Human thought requires process, a syntax at least of sequence. This is as true of unfallen as of fallen human experience, and so Raphael explains to Adam that he has ordered his narration of creation specifically for his pupil's "human ears" and "earthly notion." The precipitous drop into hell in the opening lines of the poem comprises one of Milton's striking and successful attempts to give at least a rhetorical, negative sense of God's eternal moment, by imploding sequence: he so compacts the ordinary order of sequence and causality as to dissolve momentarily the reader's sense of past, present, future.[17]

16. For a discussion of the Errour episode as a "threshold text," see my *Language of Allegory*, pp. 34–36.

17. For a discussion of this entangling procedure, see Stanley E. Fish, *Surprised by Sin: The Reader in Paradise Lost* (Berkeley: University of California Press, 1967), pp. 32–35.

The basis for this rhetorical effect is not merely Milton's attempt to register the Muse's voice, speaking omnipresently; the effect relies upon the extremely fine distinctions Milton makes in the sequence of events in the story he has chosen to tell. The impacted presentness of Satan's fall has typological resonances as Milton describes not the ultimate fall of Revelation, but its figural type, the first fall. What is of most immediate importance is the rhetorical effect, for he describes not the fall itself but the time just after:

> Him the Almighty Power
> Hurl'd headlong flaming from th'Ethereal Sky
> With hideous ruin and combustion down
> To bottomless perdition, there to dwell
> In adamantine chains and penal fire,
> Who durst defy the omnipotent to arms.
> Nine times the space that measures day and night
> To mortal men, he with his horrid crew
> Lay vanquished, rolling in the fiery gulf
> [I.44–52]

The suddenness of arrival in the verb "lay vanquisht"—when most readers expect to hear a further and deeper "fell"—is the syntactical equivalent of an express down-elevator coming to an abrupt stop. It is very similar to the syntactical suddenness of the reader's arrival, along with the Redcrosse Knight and Una, at that state of confused dislocation which Spenser has labeled for all concerned "the Wood of Errour." The grandly opulent sonorities of the reader's precipitous drop into hell are coda to an invocation in which the sequence-signals reinforce the abrupt appearance of Satan's prostrate posture. "Say first," the epic bard enjoins his Muse, "say first what cause / Moved our grand parents to fall off":

> Who first seduced them to that foul revolt?
> The infernal serpent, he it was, whose guile
> Stirred up with envy and revenge, deceived
> The mother of mankind, what time his pride . . .
> [I.33–36]

"Say first . . . say first . . . what cause . . . who first . . . what time . . . for now." The notion of "first"—itself a privileged, stressed notion in this poem about man's first disobedience and about what happened "in the beginning"—appears to function primarily as a temporal marker. But the first question—"Who first seduced them?"—insists on causality and blame. The first answer to this question—"The infernal serpent"—is only the first of many possible answers and has no primacy in its priority. If anything, the answer comes too quickly. The poet is, of course, thrusting into the midst of things. Built into epic convention of beginning *in medias res,* then, is the very idea that undercuts Milton's initial insistence on the "firstness" of the event. Because this is epic we know that something will later be shown to have happened prior to this "first" cause. The sheer opulency of the invocation, while entirely apt for the opening of a heroic poem, still comments, as Spenser's tree catalogue does, on the potential mistakenness, the Satanic power, of this kind of poetry. Such an invocation is appropriate to Satan's heroism—he who is the "first" cause of such desperate measures— but it is strangely inapt to, and entirely absent from, the anti-invocation of Book IX, for instance, which sings of the true heroism of "patient martyrdom unsung." The very "unsung" nature of true and patiently witnessing heroism renders suspect the whole tradition of the invocation, so deftly managed at the opening of the poem. Thus, at the same time that it overgoes all other fictions that begin *in medias res,* by attaching itself to the original sequence of events given by the only truly authoritative account of cosmo-graphy, *Paradise Lost* defends against hubris by insisting in its rheto-ric on its merely poetic conventionality; it here follows, after all, a fictional form.

Beginning in hell may be to begin where the reader's will already is, and thus starting there is rhetorically sound practice. But it is also to begin in a place pregnant with fable—with fictiveness itself—and therefore it is a very good place to begin to tell the special kind of truth which both Milton and Spenser were burdened with telling. The saving nature of this initial self-reflexive hellish humil-ity is clearer perhaps with Spenser than it is with Milton, for Milton's use of Satan as the cacographic archimage of the tradi-tional "epic" plot of *Paradise Lost* has been obscured by the romantic perspective from which it has been most influentially discussed. Archimago is clearly the organizer of Book I's plot. With his books and potently evil words, of which the narrator remarks directly to the reader, "Let none them read," Archimago is among other things the essential artificer. Conjured up from hell, "Legions of Sprights, the which like little flyes / Fluttering about his ever damned head" present hoary-haired Archimago as the Lord of Flies/Lord of Lies. The false dream with which he tempts the Redcrosse Knight in the form of a falsely fashioned Una merely enacts a dream we could in any case very comfortably assign to the Redcrosse Knight's own libidinous desires. Archimago's reign over the nether region's image-making powers gives a psychoanalytic legitimacy to his poetic power. Once set afoot, his plots work well and provide the springs of action in the first three-quarters of the book. So Spenser summarizes:

> But subtill *Archimago*, when his guests
> He saw diuided into double parts,
> And *Una* wandring in woods and forrests,
> Th'end of his drift, he praisd his diuelish artes,
> That had such might ouer true meaning hearts;
> Yet rests not so, but other meanes doth make,
> How he may worke unto her further smarts:
> For her he hated as the hissing snake,
> And in her many troubles did most pleasure take.
>
> [I.ii.9]

Archimago is able to further the power of the first avatar of evil hiding in the center of the first wood; his plots send Una wandering, as Satan's did Adam and Eve.[18]

Just as we appreciate first in *The Faerie Queene* the amazing intricacy of Archimago's image making, so we know *Paradise Lost* first and most immediately as Satan's poem, his saga, the epic about his grand heroic design. To borrow briefly some terms provided by

18. On Archimago as artist responsible for the allegory of Book I, see James Nohrnberg, *The Analogy of The Faerie Queene* (Princeton: Princeton University Press, 1976), pp. 758–59.

Tzvetan Todorov via the Russian formalists: "plot" is the actual chronological order of events, "fable" the order in which we are told them.[19] In these terms, Milton begins his fabling (his epic artistry) with the work of fabulist Satan. If God allows the events to happen as they do, and in what sequence they do, then it is all ultimately God's plot. But as we readers first perceive the events of the poem, we follow Satan's fable. In this reading, all events appear at first to originate with "The infernal serpent, he it was."

The spuriousness of the "choices" offered by the debate in hell over what the devils' "plot" should in fact be, while it gestures at a very complicated set of attitudes toward the rhetoric of oratory which the Renaissance inherited from the classical past, also parodies the real choice offered the reader in his or her experience of the poem. The devils have, finally, no choices. In effect, their story is over. Having already fallen, self-tempted, they have been hardened in their hearts; they are no longer free to choose the one thing that would give their story a plot—a developing climactic chronology. All they can do is repeat their mistakes. No longer free to choose, they can only change.

If Milton and Spenser begin their fictions in evil fabling, it is certainly not because they despair of fiction's ever attaining the truth. Rather by so doing they both exorcise the obsessive repetitiveness of fiction's ever-changing fixity; and do so in the context of classical art. Their exorcisms, however, take very different shapes. It will be useful to scrutinize Milton's handling of the Dantesque transformations of the devils in Book X and Spenser's focus on Malbecco's successive deformations in Book III so that we may sense their quite different entertainments of relations to that classical past and its fictions about transformations.

The Transformations of Fiction: Ovid and Dante

The metamorphosis of Satan and the fallen angels into serpents in Book X of *Paradise Lost* is a tour de force of poetic descrip-

19. Tzvetan Todorov, *The Poetics of Prose,* trans. Richard Howard (Ithaca, N.Y.: Cornell University Press, 1977), p. 26.

tion. Particularly when read in the context of the poetic tradition that begins in Ovid and continues through Dante and Spenser, the episode takes on something of the dimensions of an epic *topos*—but it is a *topos* that, since Dante, carries with it a self-consciousness about its potentially hubristic virtuosity. Milton's concerns for the legitimacy of the transformations themselves are further weighted with the complex motives he has in telling of such metamorphoses. In Book X, Milton is interpreting Scripture directly, specifically God's judgment on the serpent in Gen. 3.10:

> Because thou hast done this, thou art cursed above all cattle, and above every beast of the field; upon thy belly shalt thou go, and dust shalt thou eat all the days of thy life: and I will put enmity between thee and the woman, and between thy seed and her seed; it shall bruise thy head, and thou shalt bruise his heel.

As a record of Milton's care in interpreting Scripture for himself personally, *The Christian Doctrine* reveals its author's insistence on proper, Protestant practice: "no passage of Scripture is to be interpreted in more than one sense." The Old Testament, however, presents a special case, for "this one sense is sometimes a compound of the historical and typical." Yet even here, Milton's emphasis falls consistently on the necessary restraints that must be placed on interpretation; he denies the legitimacy of allegorical readings:

> Lastly, no inferences from the text are to be admitted, but such as follow necessarily and plainly from the words themselves; lest we should be constrained to receive what is not written for written, the shadow for the substance, the fallacies of human reasoning for the doctrines of God: for it is by the declarations of Scripture, and not by the conclusions of the schools, that our consciences are bound.
> [Columbia *Milton,* XVI, p. 265]

Reading, for Milton, is an act with eternal consequences. As a humanist, Milton was led to praise the superior authority of the Old Testament's textual history: "There can be no doubt that [the priests and prophets] handed down the sacred volumes in an uncorrupted state to be preserved in the temple by the priests their succes-

sors, who were in all ages most scrupulous in preventing altera-
tions, and who had themselves no grounds of suspicion to induce
them to make any change" (ibid., 277).

On the other hand, such a textual tradition did not hold true for
the New Testament: "on the contrary [it] has come down to us . . .
through the hands of a multitude of persons, subject to various
temptations; nor have we in any instance the original copy in the
author's handwriting" (ibid.). Milton was moved by this unhappy
fact to question the motives behind the corrupted textual tradition
of the Gospels: his conclusion hence reopens scriptural interpretation to a huge freedom.

> It is difficult to conjecture the purpose of Providence in committing
> the writings of the New Testament to such uncertain and variable
> guardianship, unless it were to teach us by this very circumstance
> that the Spirit which is given to us is a more certain guide than
> Scripture, whom therefore it is our duty to follow. [*ibid.*, 277-78]

Allied to this necessary freedom of interpretation is Milton's caveat
that the simplicity of Scripture ultimately pertains only to those
things crucial to salvation: "The Scriptures therefore . . . are plain
and perspicuous in all things necessary to salvation, and adapted to
the instruction of even the most unlearned, *through the medium of
diligent and constant reading*" (emphasis added). Whether or not the
exact interpretation of God's judgment on the serpent in Genesis is
necessary to the soul's salvation is a point open for debate. What is
certain from Milton's point of view is that the authority of the text
was not to be doubted, and that most centrally for the passage concerned, the judgment on the serpent might legitimately bear a typological reading.

Other than the description of creation, the judgments in Book X
are the closest the poem comes to the exact wording of the scriptural
text. Milton preserves the dialogue intact, merely rendering the
language into meter; he makes no comment about the judgment on
Adam and Eve, but the judgment given the serpent he interprets
freely. After Eve confesses quite simply that "the serpent me be-
guiled and I did eat," Milton explains:

> Which when the Lord God heard, without delay
> To judgment he proceeded on the accused
> Serpent though brute, unable to transfer
> The guilt on him who made him instrument
> Of mischief, and polluted from the end
> Of his creation; justly then accursed,
> As vitiated in nature; more to know
> Concerned not man (since he no further knew)
> Nor altered his offense: yet God at last
> To Satan first in sin his doom applied,
> Though in mysterious terms, judged as then best:
> And on the serpent thus his curse let fall.
>
> [X.163–74]

Milton has a problem with this curse, and appears here to be trying to have it both ways. On the one hand, Milton explains that God is "unable to transfer the guilt on" Satan, and "justly then" curses the snake itself, a creature who had merely been Satan's passive instrument, and could therefore be presumed innocent of the deed. Yet Milton then goes on to say explicitly that the curse applies "at last / To Satan first in sin"; the curse is given then in "mysterious terms"—we are not to read the serpent as literal snake, it appears, but as the "serpent" Satan. The figurative reading would appear to be rather close to the allegorical manner of reading which Milton rejects in *The Christian Doctrine,* were it not that Milton explicitly makes the mysterious interpretation strictly typological:

> So spake this oracle, then verified
> When Jesus son of Mary second Eve,
> Saw Satan fall like lightning down from heaven,
> Prince of the air;
>
> [X.182–85]

The sense of Scripture, then, is here single, sustaining the prophetic, typological meaning inherent in the literal. And, of course, the later moment interested Milton greatly—it is the climax of *Paradise Regained.* [20]

20. G. K. Hunter, *Paradise Lost* (London: Allen and Unwin, 1980), pp. 46–47.

This solution as to the mysterious meaning of the curse appears to be final. Yet we must still ask, if a typological interpretation solves the scriptural puzzle so neatly, why did Milton then deem it useful to give a Dantesque vision of Satan's transformation into the serpent form, and specifically to refer to the judgment in Genesis as he does?

> A monstrous serpent on his belly prone,
> Reluctant, but in vain, a greater power
> Now ruled him, punished in the shape he sinned,
> According to his doom:
>
> [X.514–17]

This contrapassolike punishment is God's justice rendered in a peculiarly poetic form, for Satan's punishment immediately follows his sarcastic vaunt about the apple—and not merely serpents but apples figure very largely in the hoary vision of this curse fulfilled:

> him by fraud I have seduced
> From his creator, and the more to increase
> Your wonder, with an apple; he thereat
> Offended, worth your laughter,
>
> [X.485–87]

Satan's description of the curse continues to worry the problem of its true interpretation.

> True is, me also he hath judged, or rather
> Me not, but the brute serpent in whose shape
> Man I deceived; that which to me belongs
> Is enmity, which he will put between
> Me and mankind; I am to bruise his heel;
> His seed, when is not set, shall bruise my head:
> A world who would not purchase with a bruise,
> Or much more grievous pain?
>
> [X.494–501]

Understanding the dual nature of the curse, Satan accepts the identity of, and yet the difference between, himself and the snake. What he does not know, of course, is the ultimate time scheme, or, finally, the nature of the hurt he shall receive. The biblical "bruise" is tailor-made for Satan's rhetoric, and its understatement, so unfitting to the enormity of the crime, needs interpretation. There is a sense that the long-delayed punishment is insufficient. If it need not be made clear to man, since "more to know concerned not him (since he no further knew) / Nor altered his offence," yet the doom must be made clear to Satan, who in his scoffing at the ridiculous instrument of his revenge (the apple), appears to be mired in an insufficiently literal understanding of his fate. The wittiness of the bruise must be shown to be God's irony, not Satan's.

The typological interpretation of the curse—that "seed" equals "Christ" and that "bruise" means the undoing of the fall for the happier paradise within—may give some hint as to the problem that concerns Milton in the identification of Satan with the serpent. The typological interpretation of the curse promises the incarnation. The curse then is the first time this crucial pivot point of redemptive history is mentioned in the biblical text. As the first and therefore most signal rendering of it in the Old Testament, the cursing of the serpent would have been important in any event. But what seems to be bothering Milton most about the connection between the cursing of the serpent and the incarnation is that Satan's entering the snake was in itself a kind of cacographic incarnation, a proleptic parody of the real thing which his own incarnation as serpent makes necessary.[21]

Milton makes Satan himself use the term "incarnate" to describe his entering the serpent; the precise lexical choice is not without its reverberations. Satan for his part laments the need to stoop so low:

> O foul descent! that I who erst contended
> With gods to sit the highest, am now constrained
> Into a beast, and mixed with bestial slime,
> This essence to incarnate and imbrute,
> That to the highth of deity aspired;
> But what will not ambition and revenge
> Descend to?
> [IX.163–69]

21. I am indebted to John Guillory for suggesting the point about Satan's incarnation to me.

As for Christ, so for Satan: incarnation is sacrifice.[22] Perhaps more
pivotally, the connection between language and these incarnations
is unavoidable. Christ is the Incarnate Word, while Satan incar-
nates language in the serpent, entering in at the mouth, and amazing Eve most of all by his ability to speak:

> "What may this mean? Language of man pronounced
> By tongue of brute, and human sense expressed?
> The first of these I thought denied
> To beasts, whom God on their creation-day
> Created mute to all articulate sound;
>   [IX.553–57]

Not insignificantly then, the first event of the transformation into
serpents is the nearly rhyming metamorphosis of speech into inarticulate sound; Satan ends his speech with a resounding cry:

> "But up and enter now into full *bliss.*"
>   So having said, a while he stood, expecting
> Their universal shout and high applause
> To fill his ear, when contrary he hears
> On all sides, from innumerable tongues
> A dismal universal *hiss,* the sound
> Of public scorn.
>   [X.503–9; emphasis added]

The transformation of the expected "bliss" into an inarticulate
"hiss"—as if an orator had failed to move his audience—begins the
punishment as an undoing of the first serpentine incarnation. If
Satan brings language to a brute snake, the first loss experienced in
the successive deformations is a loss of language. Surely Milton's
fictive and freely interpolated vision of Satan's punishment in the
form of the serpent comments nicely on the perversion of language
inherent in the first "incarnation" and the answering redemption
of the fall by the incarnate being of God's Logos.

22. Ricks remarks of the word, which Bentley called blasphemy, that the "silence of the context . . . makes the word effective—any nudge from the poet would
have been fatal" (*Milton's Grand Style,* p. 73); Milton saves his nudging for the
narrative of metamorphoses in Book X.

As nice as these distinctions are, there is still a hint that the presentation lies far beyond the necessities imposed upon Milton by the story he is telling. Or, as G. K. Hunter puts it, compared with Satan's earlier serpentine metamorphosis, "the imposition of snakiness on Satan and his peers in Book X seems arbitrary and unreal."[23] Its arbitrariness, according to Hunter, is only underscored by the fact that it is merely an "annual humbling"—"not a real change." Yet the story slides into even further inconsequentiality when Milton allows the idea of annual humbling to come from so uncertain a source: "some say" their pride is yearly dashed for certain numbered days (X.575). Added to this is yet another convention of hearsay: "However some tradition they dispersed among the heathen"—a poetic tradition open to further "fabling": "how the serpent, whom they called Ophion . . ." (X.580–81). While this neatly catches up another pagan myth and explains its origin in the demonic inspiration of all errant tales of pagan legend, it tends to evaporate into fiction the story Milton himself has told. The vision of the serpentine transformations is further bracketed by the appearance of Sin and Death both before (as they make their way to Eden) and after (as they finally arrive there): "Meanwhile in Paradise the hellish pair / Too soon arrived" (X.585–86). This allegorical envelope reveals, as does the fade into hearsay which concludes the piece, that the story occupies an ontological place different from the history that will be the ultimate and real answer to the parodic first "incarnation"—prophesied in the protoevangelum of the serpent's curse.[24] Noticing that the scene's difference from the rest of the poem has caused it to be judged "inappropriate," Irene Samuel has suggested that this moment in Milton finds its "evident analogue" in the ditch of the thieves in *Inferno*, 24–25. There, in a brilliant display of poetic powers, Dante describes a triple transfor-

---

23. Hunter, *Paradise Lost,* p. 127.

24. Isabel G. MacCaffrey, *Paradise Lost as "Myth"* (Cambridge, Mass.: Harvard University Press, 1959), p. 197, comments that Satan "is already beginning to live in a world of allegorical symbols instead of myth." Ferry remarks of the metamorphoses that "the fallen Archangel has shriveled to a serpent 'constrain'd' within an allegory" (*Milton's Epic Voice*, p. 138).

mation of men into serpents and serpents into men. [25] The propriety of Milton's use of the Dantean vision in his own poem may be more apparent if we look for a moment more closely at Dante's concerns with *his* pagan precursors. Milton, like Dante, places his truth within an inherited tradition of fiction. Dante's attitude toward Ovid and Lucan in describing the serpentine transformations is directly defiant.

> Taccia Lucano omai là dove tocca
>   del misero Sabello e di Nassidio,
>   e attenda a udir quel ch'or si scocca.
> Taccia di Cadmo e d'Aretusa Ovidio;
>   chè se quello in serpente e quella in fonte
>   converte poetando, io no lo 'nvidio;
>   [XXV.94–99]

Let Lucan now be silent with his tales of wretched Sabellus and Nasidius, and let him wait to hear what comes forth: Let Ovid be silent about Cadmus and Arethusa; for if in his lines he turns him into a serpent and her into a fountain, I do not grudge it to him. [26]

The minute particulars of the serpent and sinner exchanging limbs, as forms melt into each other, are a tour de force of grotesque description and Dante realizes that the poetic power exerted in the description is risky:

> Così vid'io la settima zavorra
>   mutare e trasmutare; e qui mi scusi
>   la novità se fior la penna abborra.
>   [XXV.142–45]

Thus I saw the seventh ballast change and interchange, and let the newness of it be my plea if in anything my pen be at fault. [P. 312–13]

Doubtless Dante's pride in overgoing his pagan predecessors is what makes him worry that his pen might be culpable and in need of excusing. His doubling of Ovid's exchanges insists not only on the

25. Irene Samuel, *Dante and Milton: The Commedia and Paradise Lost* (Ithaca, N.Y.: Cornell University Press, 1966), pp. 110–16, outlines the close parallels.

26. *Dante's Inferno,* trans. John D. Sinclair (New York: Oxford University Press, 1961), pp. 310–11.

tour de force, however, but also that there are finally no real evolutions in form, rather an infinitely reversible process, endlessly repeatable as part of God's eternal punishment. All of the miraculous particulars of the changes are then only one more image of the fixity of hell, imaged ultimately by Satan's stasis at its bottom point. Dante's reading of Ovid thus not only overgoes but also corrects the vision of pagan fiction by insisting on its infernal stasis, as metamorphoses that image no real movement.

That such movement is only illusory Dante demonstrates in the next canto, the ditch of the false counselors, where he listens to Ulysses's tragic story. At the opening of this canto Dante reflects upon the peril that such a pagan, heroic fiction poses for him as poet, indicating at the same time the peril involved in the poetic pyrotechnics of his earlier canto:

> più lo 'ngegno affreno ch' i' non soglio,
> perchè non corra che virtù nol guidi;
> sì che, se stella bona o miglior cosa
> m' ha dato 'l ben, ch' io stessi nol m'invidi.
> [XXVI.21–24]

and more than I am wont, I curb my powers lest they run where virtue does not guide them, so that, if favoring star or something better have granted me such a boon, I may not grudge it to myself. [Pp. 320–21]

Reining in his power more than before, he recognizes that poetry can lead him astray, where virtue does not guide him. Ulysses had led his men astray, past the pillars of Hercules, forward to a vision of Mount Purgatory on a journey that fell short of the goal and ended in a divinely willed shipwreck. This shipwreck before the shores of Mount Purgatory recalls Dante's first image of himself in the opening of the whole poem, as one who with "laboring breath has escaped from the deep to the shore" (I.23–24). Saved at the outset from the dangers that Ulysses courted, Dante recognizes the peril for him inherent in the fate of the tragic pagan. Restraining his poetic power, he goes beyond pagan fiction by witnessing such art's ultimate end in a static fixity, where all metamorphosis is eternally reversible, all forward movement an illusion.

Dante manages his self-restraint by a saving self-consciousness, referring directly to his activities as poet and juxtaposing them to Ulysses's headstrong progress. Irene Samuel has noticed that Milton follows Dante in insisting on the "ceaseless recurrence of the infection" of transformation, which Milton indicates by the prophesied annual recurrence.[27] But, as we have seen, this promised annual recurrence becomes the matter of fiction, of legendary hearsay, where nothing is a certainty, though open to further fiction-making of a demonic sort. More than Dante's insistence on the fixity of hell, Milton insists on the fictivity of hell's events. Hunter calls the episode "allegory"—a characteristic that adds to its arbitrary unreality. As we have noticed, the whole episode of the devils transformed into serpents in Book X is framed by the journey of Sin and Death to earth. Just as Sin and Death bring allegory within them to the real historical place of paradise, so Satan's journey back down to hell is part of the countering dissolve of his story into mere fiction, into endlessly repeatable transformations, which are choiceless and which therefore fade out of certain history.[28]

The episode, in commenting so closely on the curse in Genesis, makes an elaborate embellishment on the line of history which Milton narrates in the last two books of *Paradise Lost,* and as such its "fictivity"—its status as "mere" fiction—prepares by contrast for the true history that Michael will prophesy; that history, moreover, is emphatically different from the story of Satan's transformation because it offers choice and, therefore, the possibility for real and radical change. When the interpretation of the curse as it pertains to Satan, transformed into the snake in the "here and now" of hell's timelessness outside of human history, is bracketed by Milton's use of Spenserian technique we see once more the corrective that Spenser's presence offers Milton in controlling his readers' understanding of the relationship of his text to Scripture. Michael's true history culminates in the "bruise" promised the snake, but even here the

27. Samuel, *Dante and Milton,* p. 116.
28. A. J. Waldock comments that the Satans of Books II and X are "in different realms of discourse," in "Satan and the Technique of Degradation," in *Paradise Lost: A Collection of Critical Essays,* ed. Louis L. Martz (Englewood Cliffs, N.J.: Prentice-Hall, 1966), p. 96.

problem of correct interpretation, of right reading, is paramount. Adam first mistakenly assumes the "bruise" will have a literal meaning:

> O prophet of glad tidings, finisher
> Of utmost hope! Now clear I understand
> What oft my steadiest thoughts have searched in vain,
> Why our great expectation should be called
> The seed of woman: virgin Mother, hail,
> High in the love of heaven, yet from my loins
> Thou shalt proceed, and from thy womb the Son
> Of God most high; so God with man unites.
> Needs must the serpent now his capital bruise
> Expect with mortal pain: say where and when
> Their fight, what stroke shall bruise the Victor's heel.
> [XII.375–85]

Michael's correction follows immediately, and is needed most immediately to correct Adam's false sense of a local, historical battle. The incarnation, while a historical event, has its meaning in a psychological battleground, an arena that is generically the landscape of allegory. The meaning of the incarnation—Christ at work within each individual—is not, however, the kind of Ovidian allegory of transformation which Milton has labeled as merely fictive; it is real, and offers real change:

> To whom thus Michael. Dream not of their fight,
> As of a duel, or the local wounds
> Of head or heel: not therefore joins the Son
> Manhood to Godhead, with more strength to foil
> Thy enemy; nor so is overcome
> Satan, whose fall from heaven, a deadlier bruise,
> Disabled not to give thee thy death's wound:
> Not by destroying Satan, but his works
> In thee and in thy seed:
> [XII.386–95]

Milton needs to find terms more real than allegory for this "battle"—just as Satan continues to wonder about Christ's kingdom in *Paradise Regained*, whether it be "Real or Allegoric I discern not" [IV.390]. In part, Milton protects the future story of the effects of the incarnation from fading into allegory by having written allegory through to its fictive end in the Ovidian transformation scenes in hell. Typology is different from allegory because it works in real, historical time; the battle within, just as the paradise within, is more than a metaphorical fiction.[29]

To move now to the moment of most memorable Ovidian transformation in *The Faerie Queene*, where Spenser makes almost exactly the same point about fiction and history that Milton makes, is not to argue that one moment is a source for the other—as say, the ditch of the thieves is doubtless an analogue that Milton knew and used in Book X's serpentine metamorphoses. It is to see that in the successive deformations of Malbecco in canto x of Book III of *The Faerie Queene*, Spenser, like Milton, underscores the meaningful changes and opportunities offered his reader by the "history" underlying his epic, while at the same time emphasizing the static nature of mere fiction, associating it with a halted and futureless pagan myth.

Just as biblical history provides the spine of Milton's narrative, the Tudor myth of Arthur's connection to Trojan history is the spine of Spenser's poem. Milton had, of course, first thought of writing an Arthurian epic until he decided (following Polydore Vergil) that the myth had no basis in historical fact. Spenser would have known the arguments against the historicity of Arthur, but, writing for a Tudor sovereign, doubtless felt the appeal of the idea too strongly to neglect it on historical grounds.[30] A poet of mythic continuity, moreover, rather than historical disjunctions, Spenser tells us in

29. John Guillory, *Poetic Authority: Spenser, Milton, and Literary History* (New York: Columbia University Press, 1983), p. 170, credits the legitimacy of the metaphor of the paradise "within" to its "engagement with its Biblical model [Rev.—because of the presence of Michael, specifically], which engagement gives the metaphor a diachronic, historical meaning."

30. In some variant manuscript pages for *A View of the Present State of Ireland,* ed. W. L. Renwick (London: Eric Partridge, 1934), Spenser announces clearly that he does not believe in the Trojan myth: "But the Iryshe do hearin no otherwise than our vayne Englyshemen doe in the tale of Brutus, whome they devise to haue first conquered and inhabited this lande, it beeinge as impossible to prove that ther euer anie such Brutus of Albanye, as it is, that ther anie suche Gathelus of Spaine.... Lyke as wee and the French also woulde from the Troians" (p. 261).

each book that he is writing "legend." Within the limits of his acceptance of myth as fictionally usable fact, he is concerned to show the meaningful differences between the stasis of Ovidian art and the forward movement of human history.

Malbecco's position as Hellenore's jealous husband outwitted by Paridell places him directly within Spenser's parody of the Troy story in cantos ix and x of Book III. The "art" that Spenser must exorcise and place in distinction to his own is a paralyzed and paralyzing Petrarchism as much as it is the moral incompleteness of the mode of metamorphosis associated with Ovid.[31] Spenser is interested in a human love working through history; and only a love that can remember its history is true. Paridell opens his wooing program by recounting the sad history of Troy:

> *Troy,* that art now nought, but an idle name,
> And in thine ashes buried low dost lie,
> . . . .
> What boots it boast thy glorious descent,
> And fetch from heauen thy great Genealogie,
> Sith all thy worthy prayses being blent,
> Their of-spring hath embaste, and later glory shent.
>   [III.ix.33]

Britomart, of course, corrects this sense of history's loss; the line continues in her and shall grow on to future glory. She breaks into Paridell's narration:

> There there (said *Britomart*) a fresh appeard
> The glory of the later world to spring,
> And *Troy* againe out of her dust was reard,
> . . . .

---

31. For discussion of the Petrarchism, see Thomas P. Roche, *Kindly Flame* (Princeton: Princeton University Press, 1964), pp. 72–95, 129–31; Mark Rose, *Heroic Love: Studies in Sidney and Spenser* (Cambridge, Mass.: Harvard University Press, 1968), pp. 111–16; also my *Language of Allegory,* pp. 81–85. For the difference from Ovidian metamorphosis, see Paul J. Alpers, *The Poetry of The Faerie Queene* (Princeton: Princeton University Press, 1967), pp. 226–27, who argues that "whereas Malbecco's suicide leap and the description of his cave could pass for Ovidian narrative, the physiological stanza that follows could not."

> But a third kingdome yet is to arise,
> Out of the *Troians* scattered of-spring
> That in all glory and great enterprise,
> Both first and second *Troy* shall dare to equalise.
>
> [III.ix.44]

Daring to equalize Troy is, of course, the vaunt of the Renaissance as much as it is an example of Britomart's acceptance of her personal destiny and of, therefore, the validity of a love she first called disease. Troynovant will equalize the first Troy not only in the heroic enterprise of empire, but in epic celebration of it. The reprise of the first story within this third imperial retelling (the *Aeneid* being the second in this series) emphasizes its Petrarchan elements—primarily the adulterous love that is opposed to Britomart's fecund acceptance of her destiny in holy marriage. Malbecco would be Menelaus were the story an exact replica; that Menelaus is transformed in Spenser's retelling into the merely stock cuckolded husband suggests Spenser's care not merely to retell but to interpret the earlier fiction. Spenser does not directly denigrate his predecessors in the way Milton, protecting the sacred truth more directly, must do; but Spenser does imply that he shares something of Shakespeare's ironic attitude toward the story: it was all for a whore and a cuckold.

Paridell has forgotten the story of the second and third kingdoms:

> Ah fairest Lady knight, (said *Paridell*)
> Pardon I pray my heedlesse ouersight,
> Who had forgot, that whilome I heard tell
> From aged *Mnemon;*
>
> [III.ix.47]

Malbecco's metamorphosis also culminates in a strange forgetting. Spenser's changes are rung on Malbecco first in terms of similes— the epic, animal similes usual in Homer. From the midst of the goatherd where he has easily hidden because of his beard and horns, Malbecco rushes

> Like as a Beare
> That creeping close, amongst the hiues to reare
> An honey combe, the wakefull dogs espy,
> And him assayling, sore his carkasse teare,
> That creeping close, amongst the hiues to reare
> That hardly he with life away does fly,
>
> [III.x.53]

"Despite," "gealosie," and "scorne," then, "as a Snake," still lurked in his wounded mind. But the process is less external than Ovid's usual description. Spenser can say in a balancing of external description and internal commentary that Malbecco "ran away, ran with himselfe away"—the self itself disintegrating into its schizophrenic parts. When Malbecco attempts to throw himself over the precipice, he is foiled of suicide; the process is psychological, though it has a real physical effect:

> But through long anguish, and selfe-murdring thought
> He was so wasted and forpined quight,
> That all his substance was consum'd to nought,
> And nothing left, but like an aery Spright,
> That on the rockes he fell so flit and light.
> That he thereby receiu'd no hurt at all,
>
> [III.x.57]

We do not see the transformations themselves but the successive stages, after they have occurred; Malbecco's crooked claws appear syntactically before a process that might, in Ovid, have grown them:

> But chaunced on a craggy cliff to light;
> Whence he with crooked clawes so long did crall,
> That at the last he found a caue with entrance small.
>
> [III.x.57]

The cave signals the final transformation—for caves in the first installment of *The Faerie Queene* are the habitations of quiddities, abstract moral qualities personified. Like Despaire at his cave,

Malbecco is frustrated of successive suicides; he is fixed and fixed most immovably in a loss of memory:

> Yet can he neuer dye, but dying liues,
>   And doth himselfe with sorrow new sustaine,
>   That death and life attonce vnto him giues.
>   And painefull pleasure turns to pleasing paine.
>   There dwels he euer, miserable swaine,
>   Hatefull both to him selfe, and euery wight;
>   Where he through priuy griefe, and horrour vaine,
>   Is woxen so deform'd, that he has quight
> Forgot he was a man, and *Gealosie* is hight.
>   [III.x.60]

This transformation of a man into a word not only comments on the nature of jealousy itself, bane of lovers and so rightfully at issue in Book III, it also interprets the final effects of the loss of memory, of that consciousness of a developing history that ensures the only real change. It is that which distinguishes Paridell's parodic, from Britomart's true, love. Malbecco's story interprets Paridell's halted Trojan history; it is fixed, static, dead. More than a mere evaporation into fiction, as Milton manages with Satan, Spenser fades Malbecco into a word. The process is a reversal for Spenser. Usually we see him animate words—as for instance the word "Despaire"—but Malbecco fades into a word that cannot act, though of course it may still be spoken. In the transformations of Satan in Book X, Milton reverses his usual procedure as well. Historically and heroically real at the outset of the poem, Satan in Book X makes his last appearance as the matter for fable; his influence, after the fall, enters paradise in the guise of personifications.

The similar effect of the Ovidian transformations in *The Faerie Queene* and *Paradise Lost* suggests the function that pagan fiction has for both Christian poets. It marks a threshold of fictionality, an ontological boundary the crossing of which takes a character out of history, lodging him in a language that has less immediate contact with the world of evolving human destiny than before. Malbecco-turned-word and Satan-turned-matter-for-demonic-fable (even the inspiration for it) are strikingly similar in rhetorical effect. Both these transformations nicely demonstrate the thematic statements to be made by the different ontological possibilities open to characters in each poem. The negotiation of these different categories (a comic stock figure turned into a quiddity) is part of learning how to read *The Faerie Queene* in particular; categorizing its characters is a necessary part of the reader's grappling with the "allegory" of Spenser's epic.[32]

The task is even more crucial for the reader of *Paradise Lost* because the moment of transformation is unique. As MacCaffrey notices, with the bridge that Sin and Death complete while Satan is being transformed in hell, we see the literal turning into the figurative—we see the process "caught half way."[33] Insofar as Sin retains in Book X her Spenserian origin, what Milton is bringing into paradise is not merely a metaphorical way of talking about that internal battle that needs to be waged in other more real ways; he brings too a Spenserian self-consciousness about the very crossing of ontological boundaries, a real historical garden turning into (real, historical) psychology.

The bridge itself is placed securely at the main interface of Milton's physical cosmos; where it ends, the bridge connects infinite volumes:

> and now in little space
> The confines met of empyrean heaven
> And of this world, and on the left hand hell
> With long reach interposed; three several ways
> In sight, to each of these three places led.
> [X.320–24]

Hell's sinister reach is the signal mark of Sin. The "little space" here is to be sensed, however, as still physically real. Heaven is a

32. Rosemond Tuve, from whom I take the term "quiddity," establishes the categories in chap. 1 of *Allegorical Imagery: Some Mediaeval Books and Their Posterity* (Princeton: Princeton University Press, 1966); MacCaffrey discusses the "noun/adjective relation" as the "ontological foundation-stone of allegory" (*Spenser's Allegory,* pp. 82–84.), and her chap. 4, "Reader and Character," outlines the reader's process of negotiating these differences.

33. MacCaffrey, *Paradise Lost as "Myth,"* p. 200.

real place, hell is a real place (*pace* Satan's "Myself am hell"), "this world" is a real place, and so, for the moment, is the bridge. But we do not have to consider this landscape very long to remember how conventional it is in allegory (it is the opening scene of *Piers Plowman* with the ditch, the Tower of Truth, and the fair field full of folk) or to see therefore how Milton's "little space" hovers on the verge of becoming an allegorical "place," locating the realities of moral choice in a metaphorical landscape of crossroads.

   Milton shows the same hesitancy to allow his terms "the paradise within" to evaporate into metaphor, when he resists letting Sin and Death have physical powers over his world. Thus all that Sin and Death achieve in paradise is re-achieved in yet another description of the disordering of the universe by angelic agency. Thus, at Sin and Death's passing, the "blasted stars looked wan." It at first appears that their passage creates this stellar destruction. Later, however, we see angels twisting the cosmos at God's command; we see that the stars are blasted by God's, not Satan's, power:

> These changes in the heavens though slow, produced
> Like changes on sea and land, sideral blast,
> Vapours and mist.
>   [X.692–94]

In *Paradise Lost* Satan does not finally create even destruction, and in the creation of Sin and Death we see that he has authored something less than pure *res*. He can't do the real thing.

   Just as he cannot remember his origin, and so has forgotten his own history in creating Sin, Satan has no future beyond that which will be remembered in the texts of Ovidian metamorphoses, where mutation is mere repetitive change, unevolving. From the very moment of his conceiving his plan to revolt, Satan has hovered at the ontological abyss that he finally slips into in Book X, mirrored best in the face of fiction which Sin holds up to him even in heaven ("in me thy perfect image viewing"). Her serpentine transformation, like his in Book X, is matter for fable: their "histories" have no contact with the real, save, perhaps, for inspiring a literature whose only truth is its repetitive replication of the true pattern, a literature that yet can offer no choice out of the ceaseless flux, caught in the stasis of mere fiction.

This "fiction," offered as a commentary on the scriptural pro-toevangelum, is protected against its trespass on the real in the same way that Sin and Death have no real effect on paradise. Bracketing the story of Satan's metamorphosis with a frame of Spenserian self-consciousness about the fictivity of the narration, Milton is able to have it both ways: he tells the story, fulfilling the prophecy in hell, but then he takes it away and insists that its metaphorical truth is far different from the real "bruise" Satan will suffer later.

Of course it makes perfect sense that both Milton and Spenser should choose to represent the paralyzing effects of obsessive-compulsive sin in a fallen literary mode, one not benefiting from the truth of revelations. Generically, Ovid is perfect, and it makes per-fect sense too for fallen language to express so beautifully what the fall has done to language—thus the wittiness of the puns associated with Sin. For Spenser and Milton, the problem of fiction becomes thereby resolvable: all each poet need do in chronicling the effect of sin (its ways myriad, its ends the same end) is to warn the reader of the fallen nature of the tools used to give the reader the sense of sin. "And *Gealousie* is hight": language in *The Faerie Queene* can evapo-rate Malbecco as a character because that is what it feels like to be jealous—the obsession blanking out all other marks of human indi-viduality. Satan's ironic remark "with an apple" becomes the basis for a fantasia on the three curses—not merely Satan's "bruise," but the hellish vision of Adam and Eve's (and reader's) death in the ashes chewed by the serpents; Eve "knew not eating death," nei-ther do they, nor do we until we are forced to imagine what it might taste like.

This is to say no more than Sidney said when he argued that "for the poet, he nothing affirms, and therefore never lieth. For, as I take it, to lie is to affirm that to be true which is false; so as the other artists, and especially the historian, affirming many things, can, in the cloudy knowledge of mankind, hardly escape from many lies."[34] In a fallen world the only safe claim for a truth is a poetic one. Only the poet "never maketh any circles about your imagination to conjure you to believe for true what he writes." The pivotal point of this process is, again, the reader's self-consciousness, which Sidney assumes is basic: "What child is there that, coming to a play, and seeing Thebes written in great letters upon an old door, doth believe that it is Thebes? If then a man can arrive at that child's age, to know that the poets' persons and doings are but pictures what should be, and not stories what have been, they will never give the lie to things not affirmatively but allegorically and figuratively written." In this readerly self-consciousness lies not only poetry's claim to "truth" but also the site of the text's political activity, persuading the reader to choose what should be.

Sidney's discussion of the poet's signals to the reader of the basic fictivity of the idealized world he creates bears on the problems posed Spenser and Milton by their need to say the sacred truth, for the problem of truth is more difficult for both poets than the problem of fiction. Sidney assumes that one of the ways by which the poet signals his fiction making is specifically his invocation of the Muses: "He citeth not authorities of other histories, but even for his entry calleth the sweet Muses to inspire into him a good invention." For Sidney an appeal to the (pagan) Muses is a self-conscious device for signaling the making of fiction. For Spenser and especially for Milton, such an invocation makes rather different claims, as we shall see. For Spenser, the prophetic possibilities of his narrative are pinned down by Sidneyan reality principles, and so Spenser's presence within *Paradise Lost* helps to protect Milton against a potential trespass even greater than the violation of prophetic (scriptural) history by the necessary mediations of Ovidian fictions. Spenser's presence helps to protect against a trespass on the ineffable language of God himself. And to the problems posed Milton by his calling down of that sacred language we should now turn.

34. Sir Philip Sidney, *An Apology for Poetry,* ed. Forrest G. Robinson (Indianapolis: Bobbs-Merrill, 1970), p. 57.

CHAPTER *3*

Ineffability, Prophecy, and the Problem of Truth

W HEN Milton first thought of writing a drama of the fall, he posed himself a difficult—some might say insuperable—problem: how to present events that happened before the fall, which the audience would not be able to understand by virtue of their "sinful state." Adam and Eve's initial nakedness (posing an immediate impasse to seventeenth-century stagecraft) can stand witness to the more subtle ineffabilities that confronted Milton. Successive drafts of the projected play contained in the Trinity manuscript all answer the question by dodging it; the third draft, the first to be titled "Paradise Lost," sketches a play in which Moses, acting as prologue, not only describes his own miraculous state of "corporeal incorruption," but also explains to the audience that "they cannot see Adam in this state of innocence by reason of their sin."[1] Instead of the unpresentable Edenic interlude, then, Milton envisioned his first two acts as, first, a traditional debate among three of the four allegorical "daughters of God"—Justice, Mercy, and Wisdom— on what "should become of man if he fall," and, second, a celebration of Adam and Eve's nuptials by such creatures as "Heavenly Love" and "Evening Star." We are not scheduled to meet any of the principals familiar to us from the epic until Act III, a planned

1. Alastair Fowler, ed., *Paradise Lost* (1968; rpt. London: Longman, 1971), p. 4; all subsequent citations of *Paradise Lost* are to this edition.

presentation of "Lucifer contriving Adam's ruin," neither would we glimpse Adam and Eve directly until Act IV when we could see them already "fallen." Milton's reluctance to risk confronting his postlapsarian audience with a prelapsarian experience is maintained through the fourth and last manuscript draft of "Adam Unparadized," which also delays introducing the original couple until after they have fallen (and can be presented clothed in their shared sinfulness).[2]

Milton in these early drafts appears to have taken into account at least some of the more particular difficulties posed by the story he chose to tell, problems that Dr. Johnson named as central to the imperfections of the epic Milton eventually wrote:

> The plan of *Paradise Lost* has this inconvenience, that it comprises neither human actions nor human manners. The man and woman who act and suffer are in a state which no other man or woman can ever know. The reader finds no transaction in which he can by any effort of the imagination place himself; he has therefore little natural curiosity or sympathy.[3]

For Dr. Johnson—as for Milton at least initially—prelapsarian innocence is utterly inconceivable for fallen mankind, virtually unimaginable and unknowable. Milton's solution in the Trinity manuscript—to substitute allegorical characters for a direct presentation of the happy couple—only emphasizes the problem. Fallen mankind can appreciate the situation only mediately, not directly; only through animated language, through the darkened glass of

2. Ibid., p. 5: "Man next and Eve having by this time been seduced by the serpent appears confusedly covered with leaves."

3. Samuel Johnson, *The Lives of the Poets: Selections*, ed. Warren Fleischauer (Chicago: Henry Regnery, 1964), p. 26. Virginia Woolf echoes this objection in *A Writer's Diary* for very different reasons: "Has any great poem ever let in so little light upon one's own joys and sorrows? I get no help in judging life; I scarcely feel that Milton lived or knew men and women; except for the peevish personalities about marriage and the woman's duties" (New York: Harcourt Brace, 1954), pp. 5–6; cited by Sandra M. Gilbert and Susan Gubar, *The Madwoman in the Attic: The Woman Writer and the Nineteenth-Century Literary Imagination* (New Haven: Yale University Press, 1979), p. 190. Woolf's objections respond to a very interesting location of the female imagination in *Paradise Lost*. See discussion below, Chapter 4.

figuration (personification), not "face to face." It is perhaps all the more startling, then, that *Paradise Lost* in its ultimate manifestation presents not only prelapsarian Adam and Eve at great length (provoking Johnson's complaint) but other celestial characters as well, not to mention God the Father himself. In light of Milton's first reservations, the audacity of the ultimate attempt is brilliantly bold.

We must wonder what allowed Milton to shed his hesitancy about presenting the unpresentable, about saying the ineffable. Fundamental to the transformations involved in the leap Milton took is, of course, the switch in genres. What then becomes immediately interesting in the change from drama to epic is the potential in the tradition of epic to provide a bridge between the sinful limits of the audience's understanding and the unspeakable bliss of prelapsarian union. The reflexive techniques of the Shakespearean theater would not have served Milton's purpose; any stagecraft that calls attention to the fictional frame of the action and that alerts the audience to their own "willing suspension of disbelief" would work in the opposite direction from that which Milton needed. If Shakespearean stagecraft calls attention to its own immediate artifice, Milton must insist that his story is true.

The most striking difference between manuscript play and final epic is the loss of allegorical characters, a loss especially intriguing because those numerous characters had in part answered the problem of the story's ineffability. It is as if the choice of epic, a more mediate narrative form than drama, allowed the poet to discard the allegory. Yet this loss is something of a paradox when we consider that Milton's immediate predecessor in the tradition of epic was Spenser. In the Trinity manuscript Milton had also jotted down ideas for a heroic poem—which he elsewhere discusses—along the lines of Tasso and Spenser, built upon Arthurian material or the story of some renowned knight or biblical character.[4] To drop both the idea of a British, national epic and the use of allegorical characters from his treatment of the fall was to make two moves away from

---

4. For the list of topics from the Trinity MS, see *The Poetical Works of John Milton: Facsimile Edition*, ed. Harris Francis Fletcher, 4 vols. (Urbana: University of Illinois Press, 1945), II, 20–22.

Spenser. Both are also moves toward a historical, literal basis for fiction. Similarly, both rejections are tied to Milton's having taken upon himself the stature of the Mosaic bard, effected when he substitutes his own voice for the dismissed dramatic prologue of the manuscript drafts. Thus all three choices are intricately connected to his new understanding that it would be possible, after all, to celebrate for a postlapsarian audience the ineffable beauty of prelapsarian unions, both between God and man and between man and woman.

Much of Milton's originality lies in the audacious unallegorical literalness of his account; his account is, however, organized by an all-pervasive self-consciousness about the mediated "literariness" of his undertaking. As we have seen, *The Faerie Queene* and its self-reflexive language become a convenient context in which Milton shapes his own self-reflexive concerns about his poem's potentially presumptuous artistry. Spenser's indications of the problematic status of his text's language, and the means by which he distinguishes his fabled "true history" from false pagan fiction, offer Milton techniques for doing the same. Yet paradoxically, the more Milton incorporates into *Paradise Lost* references to the self-conscious mediateness of Spenser's sort of allegory, the more he is able to suggest an opposite potential in his own epic. In his insistence on the paradigmatic nature of the fallen language of *The Faerie Queene,* Milton marks the interfaces of his own fiction's limits. The ways the seams of the text fold in upon themselves reveal that if the stitchery is Milton's, the fabric is God's.

The Limits of Vision

The Spenserian text most obviously analogous to the moment of greatest ineffability in *Paradise Lost*—the blind poet's invocation to Light in Book III—is the vision offered the Redcrosse Knight by Contemplation in canto x of Book I of *The Faerie Queene*. By scrutinizing the similarities and differences between the two moments of poetic and prophetic inspiration we can appreciate the difficulties confronting any singer of eternal stillness; such a comparison should indicate how Milton's song inherited some of its potentialities from Spenser's.

Spenser's vision looks out from the pinnacle of the "highest Mount," which has a number of complexly interconnected analogues; it is "Such one" as that from which Moses received, "writ in stone / With bloudy letters by the hand of God," the prophecy of his own death; "Or," Spenser tells us, it is "like that sacred hill," which was this first mount's antitype, the fulfillment of its *figura*— that is, the Mount of Olives, where Christ often walked, he who redeemed the kind of death left so incomplete on Sinai. The third analogue is more surprising: "Or like that pleasaunt Mount, that is for ay / Through famous poets verse each where renownd."[5] Parnassus has no inevitable, sacred link to the other two mounts, which are—at least to typological ways of thinking—essentially the same mountain. There are a number of ways to accommodate what seems to be Spenser's astoundingly blithe suggestion of equality among the three places, implied by the three connecting "Or's." Isabel MacCaffrey speaks of this moment as a "reconciliation of mythologies," and an "assimilation of pagan myth."

> ... in choosing Parnassus, Spenser "says" more; he does not merely affirm the seriousness of pagan imaginings, but speaks directly of poets and poetry. We are to ponder the content, not merely the form, of this allusion; to consider the relation between the "thrise learned Ladies" and their lays, and the awful events of Sinai and the Mount of Olives.[6]

MacCaffrey's point is that "allegory admits vision," and this is surely Spenser's point with the nine learned Ladies' play on the mountaintop.

But surely one effect of Spenser's making the surprising comparison is to insist on the very mediateness of his own myth, that is, of

---

5. *Spenser's Faerie Queene*, ed. J. C. Smith, 2 vols. (1909; rpt. Oxford: Clarendon Press, 1964), I.x.53–54; hereafter cited in the text.
6. Isabel G. MacCaffrey, *Spenser's Allegory: The Anatomy of Imagination* (Princeton: Princeton University Press, 1976), p. 77.

Mount Contemplation's association with the first two mountains. To find Parnassus at the end of the list is both to celebrate it and to recognize the limits of the power it evokes by metonymy. The Muses, with their "heavenly" notes and lovely "lays," allow poets to envision mounts that are analogous to the mountains of Scripture; but analogy is not identity. Spenser does not equate Parnassus with Sinai or secular poetry with sacred prophecy. If Moses received his vision as a type of Christ, fulfilled finally on the Mount of Olives, Spenser assuredly does not offer himself as a further type, or *The Faerie Queene* as scripture. *The Faerie Queene* is not writ in stone by the hand of God, and it is important for Spenser's purposes of vision that the reader realize this difference.

With the mention of Parnassus Spenser indicates his own saving awareness that Mount Contemplation is merely like the other three mountains. He reminds the reader that his stanza had begun "Such . . . as." Poetry, by offering analogous vision and language parallel to God's, is heaven*ly*—*like* to God's Word, but not that ineffable language itself. While Spenser grants the language of his poem great power, he denies it the ultimate potency of divine origin.

Still, from this carefully defined vantage, Spenser can glimpse, if he cannot sing about, the beauty of the eternal city:

> Whose wals and towres were builded high and strong
> Of perle and precious stone, that earthly tong
> Cannot describe, nor wit of man can tell;
> *Too high a ditty for my simple song;*
> The Citie of the great king hight it well,
> Wherein eternall peace and happinesse doth dwell.
> [I.x.55; emphasis added]

The song Spenser does sing, in being lower, may yet suggest by analogy the song that is too high for him. Thus, when shown the vision of the heavenly city, the Redcrosse Knight compares it to Cleopolis, capital city of Gloriana's faeryland, a city of earthly glory, which while lesser is still for Spenser a fictive analogue of the New Jerusalem:

Till now, said then the knight, I weened well,
That great *Cleopolis,* where I haue beene,
In which that fairest *Faerie Queene* doth dwell,
The Fairest Citie was, that might be seene;
And that bright towre all built of christall cleene,
Panthea, seemd the brightest thing, that was;
But now by proofe all otherwise I weene;
For this great Citie that does far surpas,
And this bright Angels towre quite dims that towre of glas.
[I.x.58]

It is Contemplation, rather than the knight, who gives the earthly
city its proper credit:

well beseemes all knights of noble name,
That couet in th'immortall booke of fame
To be eternized, that same to haunt,
And doen their seruice to that soueraigne Dame,
That glorie does to them for guerdon graunt,
For she is heauenly borne, and heauen may iustly vaunt.
[I.x.59]

For Milton, fame is the last infirmity of noble mind; for Spenser, it
is still a worthy goal in Book I, which, however, once met requires a
turning away from earthly conquest to the peaceable pain of travel
to the New Jerusalem. In the same way poetic inspiration itself is
sacred and no less praiseworthy than religious prophecy, of which
poetic prophecy is a legitimate analogue.

Thus Contemplation, foreseeing, foretells the knight's victory:
"thou Saint *George* shalt called bee, / Saint *George* of mery England,
the signe of victoree" (I.x.61). Yet this "George" must be further
read back into his origins: if the New Jerusalem glimpsed from the
mountaintop is to be his future home in the time after the apocalyptic end of time, he must meanwhile learn of his first home—a
"heaped furrow," smallest of lowly declivities, "Where thee a
Ploughman all vnweeting fond, / As he his toylesome teme that way
did guyde, / And brought thee vp in ploughmans state to byde"
(I.x.66). Saint George is, as we saw, *georgos,* "worker of earth,"

who must learn to return from the height of vision to the level plain
on which his journey begins, and ends.

> O holy Sire (quoth he) how shall I quight
>   The many fauours I with thee haue found,
>   That hast my name and nation red aright,
>   And taught the way that does to heauen bound?
>   This said, adowne he looked to the ground,
>   To haue returnd, but dazed were his eyne,
>   Through passing brightnesse, which did quite confound
>   His feeble sence, and too exceeding shyne.
> So darke are earthly things compard to things diuine.
>   [I.x.67]

At the moment of vision the usual relations between sign and signified, between literal thing and its significance, seem reversed, for in
this episode allegorical procedures are made a part of the literal
action of the poem. Spenser has called *The Faerie Queene* a "dark
conceit," by which we may understand that if significance is hard to
see, phenomena are clear enough. At the moment of vision, when
the Redcrosse Knight is allowed to read, and be read into, pure
significance, he turns back to the phenomena of this world and they
seem dark. Cleopolis is not a bright but a dim city when compared
with heaven's Jerusalem. On the moutaintop he, like Contemplation, is blind to signs. "So darke are earthly things compard to
things diuine." It is out of this kind of moment, merely glimpsed,
that he must learn to read the world; yet Spenser makes Contemplation read his very name, George, to insist upon the usual disjunction there is between our normal experience, lost in the earthly
darkness of signs, and the meaning of this episode, which, by its
self-reflexive reference to the experience of reading, seems to negate
its own mediateness and to offer instead the purity of blinding light.

It is the merest glimpse, however, and although the vision is rap-
turous, the place—even though it is itself only an analogue to other
sacred places—is not a place where earthly man may stay. The Redcrosse Knight must go back down the mountainside and work the
significance of this vision in the world through his labor—the slaying of the dragon. We as readers may see in that act an achievement

of the terms of the vision: by slaying the dragon, Eden—as New Jerusalem—is restored. The apparent medieval distinction between the contemplative vision and the active quest is resolved by reading the allegory:ᶦthe metaphor of chivalry (fulfilling Gloriana's charge to slay the dragon) is also to prepare the way to the heavenly city; at the same time that the metaphor of chivalry reveals distinctions between, it also conflates, heavenly and earthly desire.ᶦ

If the Contemplation episode offers an anatomy of the reading experience itself—in terms of our interpretation of Saint George's newly revealed identity—Spenser offers a parallel experience in terms of the figure of Contemplation. The blind seer, rather than Mercy, "reads" the way to heaven for us because Spenser may, by Contemplation's blindness, by his fasting, by his spare thinness, indicate with a more transparent clarity the skeletal structure of significance which his story attempts to incarnate: "Each bone might through his body well be red." Even pure significance is something that may only be appreciated by the mediated act of reading. Spenser's epic begins, after all, with the Legend of Holiness, which is essentially and only a text to be read.[7]

While the splendid joys of the citizenry of heaven prove "too high a ditty" for Spenser's song, Milton's song spans the leap of fiction to partake of that citizenship's choiring: here is his greatest difference from Spenser.

> Hail, Son of God, saviour of men, thy name
> Shall be the copious matter of my song
> Henceforth, and never shall my harp thy praise
> Forget, nor from thy Father's praise disjoin.
>   Thus they in heaven, above the starry sphere,
> Their happy hours in joy and hymning spent.
>   [III.412-17]

Behind Milton's implicit claim that his song joins the heavenly choirs' is a larger presumption—that his poem reports what is, or could have been, heard there. Because the angels' song is given in

---

7. For further discussion of the pun on "read," see my *Language of Allegory: Defining the Genre* (Ithaca, N.Y., Cornell University Press, 1979), pp. 227-38, 254-60.

direct discourse, it is not until the epic voice steps back to describe
their hymning that we realize the possessive pronoun belongs to
each singular angel, not to him. (The pronoun's singularity—
"my" when metrically a plural "our" would have done as well—
invites the momentary confusion.) In this directness of discourse,
Milton's muse functions differently (if also still mediately) from
Spenser's, for Spenser's language is never heard, or even over-
heard; words are always *read*. Spenser implies the potent danger of
Archimago's evil words by the images they silently create, visions
able to lure the Redcrosse Knight astray, and by the injunction to
the reader, "let none them read." Conversely, Milton lets the
reader hear first the full power of Satan's seductive speech. Contemplation, in physical appearance and in the service he performs
for the Redcrosse Knight, exists in the realm of reading: his is a
nearly silent, unvoiced action of the internal eye, while the blind
bard of *Paradise Lost* is rightly called by convention "the epic voice."
Doubtless this difference is due in part to the genesis of *Paradise Lost*
as a stage play.[8] If Edward Philips was correct in assuming that
Satan's address to the sun had been written before the poem itself
was begun, we need to keep in mind the trace such an origin would
leave in the final epic.

This aural origin contrasts directly with the readerly nature of
Spenser's text, unfolding out of "antique rolles." All the titular
heroes of the various legends of *The Faerie Queene* are, in one way or
another, readers; faeryland is a bookish place. There are, by contrast, no readers in *Paradise Lost,* and if anyone can be said to do
anything so mediate as to read, what they read is not sign but phe-
nomenal signified—as in Adam's naming of the animals (or Eve's
naming of the plants). In the context of these two distinctly different
presentations of the text, Spenser's in an unvoiced (if not exactly

8. See G. K. Hunter, *Paradise Lost* (London: Allen and Unwin, 1980), pp. 77–
83, for a discussion of the dramatic structure of the drafts; see also J. M. Evans,
Paradise Lost and the Genesis Tradition (Oxford: Clarendon Press, 1968), pp. 207–16,
for a discussion of the parallels between Hugo Grotius's five-act Latin drama *Ada-
mus Exul* (1601) and the manuscript drafts.

silent) realm of reading, and Milton's in the auditory, dramatic conflict of heard "voices," Harold Bloom's remarks about relations between them become provocative:

> Influence-anxieties of all kinds, with all their afflictions or secondariness . . . inhibit *writing,* but not nearly so much the oral, logocentric tradition of prophetic speech. Insofar as Spenser . . . truly was Milton's Great Original, then even Milton was inhibited, for Spenserian vision became an attribute of Milton's id-component. But Milton's prophetic, oral original was Moses, who became an attribute of the Miltonic superego, and thus stimulated the largest power of *Paradise Lost,* which is its marvelous freedom in expanding Scripture to its own purposes.[9]

As we have seen, Milton appropriates Mosaic stature for himself by becoming the epic voice inspired by Moses' muse; at the same time he dismisses mediating Spenserian allegory by electing to write in epic form the story he had first conceived as drama, and, ironically, by rejecting the literally "voiced" discourse of a stage play. The epic voice of the narrative poem substitutes for Moses as prologue to the play. With this second choice, Milton makes a decision to elect what Bloom would call the prior mode of prophetic speech. Yet while Bloom's distinction points to the difference between Milton's dramatic, prophetic immediacy in Book III and Spenser's mediated reading of the distance between human song and divine agency in Book I, we must remember that Milton first conceived Moses' story as stage speech. Moreover, as we have seen in the episode of serpentine transformations, in great part Spenser's presence within his text provides Milton the protection of framing some of his more audacious interpolations into the scriptural text.

While Milton's dialogue in heaven prophesies all human history, Contemplation's prophecy to the Redcrosse Knight gives a lesson in interpretation—that is, in how to read the text of the poem within its apocalyptic context. Milton's text of the voice, so to speak, is also

9. Harold Bloom, *A Map of Misreading* (New York: Oxford University Press, 1975), p. 50.

apocalyptic, typologically acknowledging ends in beginnings, but unlike Spenser's visionary moment, Milton insists on the permeability of the boundary between the human and the divine. The vision we get in Book III of *Paradise Lost* takes us in the direction that Spenser's Redcrosse Knight looks, only to discover that he is blinded: we look down from Milton's heaven, not upward at it.

Similarly, while Milton's invocation in Book III is to light, what he "sees" when that light is granted is not anything in heaven, though it is something to be heard there, something that is bound up with our new perspective on the events of the poem. One new aspect is surely the extremely personal anguish of the invocation, which pivots on Milton's own historical, physical blindness, a fact that is in itself no mere poetic figure, though poetry can transform its mere literalness. It is also crucial to realize that, from the point of view of Milton's contemporary readers, Milton's blindness was not merely a personal literal fact, it was a public and highly charged political one as well. Salmasius had slandered Milton's blindness in *Defensio Regia pro Carolo Primo* (1649), and later, in *Regii Sanguinis Clamor ad Coelum adversus Parricidas Anglicanos* (1652), Milton's blindness had been attacked again. Milton's first *Defense of the English People* had made him famous both on the continent and in England, and so when he defended himself in the *Second Defense* (1654) against the attacks on his loss of sight, he was speaking not as a private person but for the (very) public record.[10] Milton defended his blindness as a holy sacrifice for a political cause:

> Hence when that office against the royal defence was publicly assigned to me, and at a time when not only my health was unfavorable, but when I had nearly lost the sight of my other eye; and my physicians expressly foretold, that if I undertook the task I should in a short time lose both—in no wise dismayed at this warning, methought it was no physician's voice I heard—not the voice even of Aesculapius from the shrine of Epidaurus—but some diviner monitor within; methought, that, by a certain fatality in my birth,

10. Christopher Hill, *Milton and the English Revolution* (New York: Viking Press, 1977), outlines the "fantastic success" of Milton's defenses: "His English tracts probably reached a wider audience than did his poems" (p. 183).

two destinies were set before me, on the one hand, blindness, on
the other duty—that I must necessarily incur the loss of my eyes, or
desert a sovereign duty.[11]

If Contemplation's blindness was a conventional sign of his "higher
thoughts," his blindness to the things of this world, and the Redcrosse Knight's dazed eyes evidence of the height of his unwonted
vision, Milton's blindness was from the first, and ought still to remain in the poem, a literal, historical, and political fact—however
much Milton places that fact within its proper literary context of
prophecy:

> Those other two equalled with me in fate,
> So were I equalled with them in renown,
> Blind Thamyris, and blind Maeonides,
> And Tiresias and Phineus prophets old.
> [III.33–36]

Though very different from these pagan precursors, not merely in
his lesser fame but in the greater truth of his vision, Milton in this
brief list outlines the forbidden sacred and sexual knowledge that
will be the matter of his song. Although framed in a specifically
pagan literary context, the historical actuality of his blindness reinforces its literalness, insisting on (as his dismissal of the allegory had
also implied) the potential there is in the poem for literally telling
the truth.

If the invocation to Book III radically differs from the invocation
to Book I by reason of its particular, personal note, it also differs in
its ascription of his poetic power to call down the Muse. In Book III,

11. Columbia *Milton*, VIII, 67–69. Sonnet XVI ("When I consider how my
light is spent") also bears on the connection of Milton's blindness to his political/
poetic vocation where the question is "Doth God exact day-labour, light denied"?
The sonnet associates gardening-labor/money-payments (investments) from the
parables with Milton's blindness as being a block to his poetic vocation; the issue of
labor and vocation, the doing of God's "work," is bound up with inspiration and
with the troublesome divisions of labor in the garden. See below, pp. 229–31.

Milton himself chooses which of the mounts he prefers to haunt. In the opening to Book I he offers three mounts and invites the Muse to choose among them (Oreb, Sinai, Sion). In the invocation to Book III the poet chooses Sion:

> Yet not the more
> Cease I to wander where the Muses haunt
> Clear spring, or shady grove, or sunny hill,
> Smit with the love of sacred song; but chief
> Thee Sion and the flowery brooks beneath
> That wash thy hallowed feet, and warbling flow,
> Nightly I visit.
>
> [III.26–32]

Immediately hereafter, Milton lists the blind pagan poets and prophets who share "sometimes" in his nocturnal musings, and so grants the pagan tradition the power to help shape his love of Sion's song. In such a way Milton turns his affliction into poetic (if not prophetic) election; and if he nowhere hints that the fact of his blindness is God's visible sign of his vocation in prophecy, it is perhaps because he intends that not the poet but the poem should be that final sign.

Only the poem in its audaciously ineffable subject can acquit Milton of the presumption there is in the claim that his blindness is recompensed in true vision. Moreover he asks for vision not only for his own "seeing," but for the audience's understanding; the request is not only for the power to see but also to tell:

> So much the rather thou celestial Light
> Shine inward, and the mind through all her powers
> Irradiate, there plant eyes, all mist from thence
> Purge and disperse, that I may see and tell
> Of things invisible to mortal sight.
>
> [III.51–55]

The sight we get, again paradoxically, is not of the things invisible, how they might look were we able to see them, but of how those invisible entities see—how, in fact, they can be said to see us. It is not a question of seeing God face to face, but of seeing ourselves as God sees us. We share God's perspective, which may seem finally a more audacious thing for Milton to offer the reader, though in fact it is not: we simply see what we always see, God's created universe, his creatures, only this time we see them in a new light.

> Now had the almighty Father from above,
> From the pure empyrean where he sits
> High throned above all highth, bent down his eye,
> His own works and their works at once to view;
> [III.56–59]

We also "see" the sanctities of heaven receiving from "his sight" (their seeing God? or their being seen by him?—or both?) "Beatitude past utterance." Here Milton assigns to angels the incapacity to utter their beatitude, but it is an incapacity that merely witnesses their bliss.

Not seeing God but following his glance, we focus on a creature we have already watched in grotesque, Brobdignagian close-up throughout the first two books. Now, in God's perspective, we see him as a mere creature crossing a boundary.

>   Satan there
> Coasting the wall of heaven on this side night
> In the dun air sublime . . .
> . . . .
> Him God beholding from his prospect high,
> Wherein past, present, future he beholds,
> Thus to his only Son forseeing spake.
> [III.70–79]

No doubt the dialogue we overhear in Book III had its origins in the debate among Justice, Mercy, and Wisdom which Milton canceled when he turned from drama to epic. God takes the part of Justice and the Son that of Mercy as they discuss what "will happen should man fall." With its laying bare the theological, dogmatic bones of the narrative as God looks backward, forward, omnipresent in time as well as space, the opening speech has been notable for the effi-

ciency with which it demonstrates what has happened to the understanding of human beings "by reason of their sin." As much critical
testimony witnesses, the position of the reader with respect to the
fiction becomes distinctly uncomfortable.[12] More than at other moments, the dialogue here immediately approaches the pinnacle of
inspiration figured in the character of the prophet Moses; the blind
bard, blessed with prophetic insight, can repeat the voices heard,
and if he cannot overcome the audience's incapacity, he can at least
confront them with the fact of their discomfort.

The bard's blindness not only avails Milton of Contemplation's
perspective (and more), it complicates the interaction between seeing and hearing which so marks the dialogue. In this conversation,
silence is for ten lines quite "deadly" (when no one answers God's
question and offers to sacrifice), and for a moment the Son, as
Word, is "silent yet spake." The complications of the bard's blindness and insight may also be involved in the irony that occurs when
Milton makes the last words of the book take place on another
mountaintop, with another kind of inspiration, and in a graver kind
of light. Thus, at the very end of Book III, Satan,

> Down from the ecliptic, sped with hoped success,
> Throws his steep flight in many an airy wheel,
> Nor stayed, till on Niphates' top he lights.
> [III.740-42]

As this last example illustrates, Milton's vision of the ineffable being of God is organized, not as Spenser's was, in terms of a slow and
arduous ascent, but from the top down. Nowhere is the difference
between the two visions more apparent than in the way the downward spiraling exit from the height of Milton's vision in Book III
retraces the steps of the Redcrosse Knight's laborious ascent in
Book I of *The Faerie Queene*. I do not mean to suggest that Milton, in
overgoing Spenser, rewrote Contemplation's vision to specifica-

---

12. For Milton's general program of confronting his readers in this way, see
Stanley E. Fish, *Surprised by Sin: The Reader in Paradise Lost* (Berkeley: University of
California Press, 1967).

tion, reversing it, but that both poets, working in a cohesive tradition, necessarily used the same tools (Dante had also used them). Milton used these instruments for his own effects.[13]
    Immediately after Milton ambiguously takes up his harp in the choiring of angels' praise, the epic voice moves to Satan's progress:

> Thus they in heaven, above the starry sphere,
> Their happy hours in joy and hymning spent.
> Mean while upon the firm opacous globe
> Of this round world, whose first convex divides
> The luminous inferior orbs, enclosed
> From Chaos and the inroad of darkness old,
> Satan alighted walks:
>
> [III.416–22]

The troublesome verb "alighted" again twists the radical opposition between lightness and darkness, blindness and insight, into the downward torque of gravity (here, for the moment, under Satan's control). This *entrelacement* of Satan's journey and the heavenly conversation allows the dialogue to be bracketed by a saving self-consciousness that appears to owe much to Spenser. The foregoing part of the "bracket" (the left side, so to speak), is provided by Satan's flight (itself within the realm of deceptive fiction); it is moreover a flight through Chaos which takes off from that most Spenserian threshold in the poem—hell's gate, at which Sin had sat. At the end of Book II, Chaos was a space in the process of being "allegorized." Sin and Death can labor there and create. The closing or "right" side of the bracket is Satan's making his way through another "allegorical" landscape, the Paradise of Fools, with its monastic trash flying in the wind, literalizing (with Spenser's technique) life's *vanitas*. The brackets can be seen to act as a neat (allegorical) envelope for the most literally rendered scene in the poem, the dialogue in heaven between God and Christ (dialogue, oddly

---

13. For a discussion of Milton's indebtedness to Spenser for the "iconographies of mental shift," see Angus Fletcher, "Positive Negation: Threshold, Sequence, and Personification in Coleridge," in *New Perspectives on Coleridge and Wordsworth*, ed. Geoffrey Hartman (New York: Columbia University Press, 1972), p. 137.

enough, that was originally scheduled to take place between personified abstractions). Such bracketing, insofar as it works to or-
ganize the reading experience, does so by making the reader aware
of the text's own gestures at its fictive instruments. What takes
place within the "protected" framing limits of these self-conscious
brackets is "true"—at least as true as that which warns about possible mediating fictiveness can aspire toward absolute truth. There is
much to be said for the point of view that insists that the "real"
poem lies outside the brackets—the fallen beautiful envelope that
has refused for generations of readers to consume itself away. But
there is also in the intricate balances of the poem's self-
consciousness a way to read *Paradise Lost* so that the truth within the
brackets insists on the physical verity of what the reader might at
first assume to be merely the acceptable artifice of analogy. Take as
an example the closing side of the bracket of Book III. There, the
allegory is as usual associated with Satan, and his perspective—
always mediate—signals the need for the reader's ever greater self-
consciousness; in the Paradise of Fools those who have sought their
"reward on earth, the fruits / Of painful superstition and blind zeal,
/ Nought seeking but the praise of men," find their fit retribution
alongside all the "unaccomplished works of nature's hand." This
landscape of punished presumption is vaguely located in the general scheme, except for one detail: after his arrival, from there "far
distant," Satan sees the magnificent sparkling structure of Jacob's
ladder:

> The work as of a kingly palace gate
> With frontispiece of diamond and gold
> Embellished, thick with sparkling orient gems
> The portal shone, inimitable on earth
> By model, or by shading pencil drawn.
> The stairs were such as whereon Jacob saw
> Angels ascending and descending, bands
> Of guardians bright,
>
> [III.505–12]

The beauty of the stairs, though distinctly inimitable by other than
verbal human arts, is, strikingly enough, not ineffable: Milton's

song describes it, assigning limits to the plastic arts. While they have to be described by analogy, "as of a kingly palace," stairs "such as" Jacob saw, they are approachable by Milton's muse:

> Each stair mysteriously was meant, nor stood
> There always, but drawn up to heaven sometimes
> Viewless, and underneath a bright sea flowed
> Of jasper, or of liquid pearl, whereon
> Who after came, sailing arrived,
> Wafted by angels, or flew o'er the lake
> Rapt in a chariot drawn by fiery steeds.
>   [III.515-22]

The vision here is of the stairs prior to any biblical (Elijah, or Lazarus in the parable in Luke 16) or postbiblical vision, including Dante's—from whose *Purgatorio* II, with its souls wafted by angels' wings, Milton doubtless got the image of sailing. Dante had, of course, also used the image of the Ladder of Golden Light to reveal the realm of Saturn in paradise (*Paradiso*.XXII). A traditional emblem of contemplation before Dante, the stairs had figured notably in the *Consolation of Philosophy* as embroidery on Lady Philosophy's gown.[14]

Isabel MacCaffrey has interestingly argued that the ladder that Satan sees here images the mystery of the incarnation. Rightly hesitant about invoking the biblical exegetes whom Milton mistrusted, MacCaffrey yet outlines the tradition of seeing the ladder, in Calvin's terms, as a "symbol of Christ" in his role as mediator between God and man.[15] In this reading, Satan's response to the stairs is of a piece with his response to the Son; thus, as James Sims puts it, "Satan's leap from the stair is a disdainful act. . . . He has rejected the Son as Messiah in Heaven, spurned him as Jacob's ladder on the rim of the world, and is soon to express his hatred for

14. Boethius, *The Consolation of Philosophy,* trans. Richard Green, The Library of the Liberal Arts (Indianapolis and New York: Bobbs-Merrill, 1962), Prose 1, p. 3; for further discussion of such embroidery, see below, pp. 164–65.

15. Isabel G. MacCaffrey, "The Theme of *Paradise Lost,* Book III," in *New Essays on Paradise Lost,* ed. Thomas Kranidas (Berkeley: University of California Press, 1971), pp. 78–79.

the Son as the Sun of Righteousness."[16] Because Satan gets to the
ladder from the Paradise of Fools, we may the more easily invoke
allegorical interpretations of it—especially because the explicitly
"mysterious" meaning of the stairs invites commentary so directly.
Yet to argue, as MacCaffrey and others do, that the stairs "shadow
... distantly ... the mediatory function of Christ" is to hold that
Milton presents Christ in allegory. The redundancy of the technique makes it questionable; we have already, as MacCaffrey notices, seen Christ take on a mediating role in the dialogue in heaven.
It seems useful to doubt that Milton would then turn to an allegorical presentation of Christ when he had already presented him in
propria persona. While MacCaffrey's argument makes all the details
of the book cohere into a single theme—concerning man's various
legitimate ways of knowing God and the limits placed upon those
ways—it unnecessarily erases an image that Milton places directly
before the reader.

The stairs lead, by direct scriptural quotation, to "the gate of
Heaven." Jacob sees them in a dream, and Milton seems to appropriate for himself with their presentation something of the power of
Adam's dream—a dreaming the real. In Milton's cosmos, heaven
and hell have real gates—the space between, the intermediate dis-
tances, may be bridged by fiction self-conscious of its own
fictiveness—but the coordinates are to be sensed as literally, geo-
graphically, there. The physical objects within the cosmos that
Milton presents to our mortal sight are to be contemplated by our
imaginations for their possible, mysterious meanings; but Milton's
truth is that they are not created by this process (as Spenser suggests
his are). The gates of heaven and hell exist independently of our
abilities to interpret them. It is of course right that Sin be able to
open, but not to close, hell's gate. And in the same way, Satan
spurns the stairs as one other avenue of renewed relationship with
God. To allegorize the stairs denies their remarkable presentness
within the poem and blurs a large distinction between Milton and
his precursor.

Spenser's Contemplation offers no specific vision of stairs or lad-

16. Cited by MacCaffrey, in *New Essays,* p. 81.

ders, but his vision insists most naturally upon ascent and descent:

> As he thereon stood gazing, he might see
> The blessed Angels to and fro descend
> From highest heauen, in gladsome companee,
> And with great ioy into that Citie wend,
> As commonly as friend does with his frend.
>
> [I.x.56]

If Spenser turns our vision upward to outstrip our sense of wonder, seeing for the moment beyond his poem's usual ken, then Milton works his way downward to the physically and historically real. The Redcrosse Knight sees in a moment's vision the whole city of Jerusalem: Satan from the bottom step

> Looks down with wonder at the sudden view
> Of all this world at once.
>
> [III.542–43]

The Redcrosse Knight had seen nothing when he looked downward, being momentarily blinded. If there is but "A little path, that was both steepe and long / Which to a goodly Citie led his view" in Book I of *The Faerie Queene,* this passageway is seen in *Paradise Lost* to be:

> A passage down to earth, a passage wide,
> Wider by far than that of after-times
> Over Mount Sion, and though that were large,
> Over the Promised Land to God so dear,
> By which, to visit oft those happy tribes,
> On high behests his angels to and fro
> Passed frequent, and his eye with choice regard
> From Paneas the fount of Jordan's flood
> To Beersaba, where the Holy Land
> Borders on Aegypt and the Arabian shore:
> So wide the opening seemed, where bounds were set
> To darkness, such as bound the ocean wave.
>
> [III.528–39]

The point where Satan stops to rest is also the passage that Milton's muse takes down over Sion. It provides access to a wider, less constricted influence of power than Spenser had allowed himself in his upward glimpse; it explains in part, I think, the huge expansiveness and freedom associated with Satan's flight across the buoyant void of Milton's cosmos. And while the dialogue in heaven is audacious, the poetry of Satan's flight is a fictive analogue to the bard's flights beyond the Aeonian mount, above previous attempts at heroic quest—those quests to which Milton alludes in the simile for Satan's vision: as of a scout seeing new land or some shining metropolis. This is the sort of language to which Edward Said doubtless refers when he says that "Milton's verse seems to have overpowered the void within his epic."[17]

> then from pole to pole
> He views in breadth, and without longer pause
> Down right into the world's first region throws
> His flight precipitant, and winds with ease
> Through the pure marble air his oblique way
> Amongst innumerable stars, that shone
> Stars distant, but nigh hand seemed other worlds,
> Or other worlds they seemed, or happy isles,
> Like those Hesperian gardens famed of old,
> Fortunate fields, and groves and flowery vales,
> Thrice happy isles, but who dwelt happy there
> He stayed not to inquire;
>   [III.561-71]

The language of this flight contains a beautiful indeterminacy, for the terms that spring most naturally to mind to describe Satan's voyage come from pagan fable. In the same way, whether Satan flew by "centre, or eccentric," it is "hard to tell." Putting aside Milton's scrupulous indecision about the exact structure of the solar system, we see again that merely following Satan's flight is a

17. Edward Said, *Beginnings: Intention and Method* (New York: Basic Books, 1975), p. 280. To sense the impact of Milton's insistence on the reality of this journey here, compare its description with Spenser's questions—so similar verbally—at the outset of Guyon's epic quest in the Proem to Book II of *The Faerie Queene:* "Why then should witlesse man so much misweene / That nothing is, but that which he hath seene? / What if within the Moones faire shining spheare? / What if in euery other starre vnseene / Of other worldes he happily should heare? / He wonder would much more: yet such to some appeare."

study in potentially false surmise, just as it is itself a parody of epic quest, the full heroism of which will be, in due time, denied. Yet, insofar as Satan stands looking down on earth from the lower stair, he stands at a very privileged spot for Milton. It is this passageway that allows God to bend his "eye with choice regard" downward on his creatures, and so in this poem Satan, God, the privileged narrator (and reader) can share the same physical perspective. Close to Sion, the passage is at least neighbor to the named place of Milton's meeting his muse in the invocation to Book III. The boundaries of this passage are important as well—and subtly indicate the rhetorical relationship that Milton expects his muse to have to his reader.

The opening itself, "so wide," is like the bracketed vision of the ineffable godhead presented in Book III, bracketed, as Milton explains, "where bounds were set to darkness." The boundaries of the vision itself are those two moments of a very Spenserian kind of allegory, through the mediate landscapes of which (Chaos, the Paradise of Fools) Satan's parodic flight of heroism moves. Isabel MacCaffrey notes that the Paradise of Fools is there "to provide an interlude where Book III's two planes of narrative can intersect."[18] Yet what intersect in Book III are not so much heavenly and earthly locations for action, but truth and fiction. The passage that Milton locates as the space of intersection insists upon the union of his rhetoric—aimed at his earthly reader—and his art—directly derived from the Heavenly Muse. The boundaries set to darkness, if they be sensed as limits to the quite personal conduit for Milton's voluntarily moved numbers, are also limits "such as bound the ocean wave." While the first meaning of this "ocean" is doubtless the original creation itself, the geographical context of this "passage" calls up another typologically related moment in history: the miraculous binding back of the waters of the Red Sea when Moses led his chosen people across to the promised land—across that border between Egypt and the Holy Land which God eyes with "choice regard" in the immediately preceding lines—a wide and momentous passageway. Moses' passing was, of course, the passing about which Dante's souls are singing when they are ferried by angels'

18. MacCaffrey, in *New Essays*, p. 77.

wings across the wide water in the second canto of *Purgatorio,* for their psalm recalls the typological moment in the Old Testament which exactly prefigures their passage into purgatory.[19] If this analogy is to be read, and it is analogy ("such as"), then the passage of Milton's muse may function as Moses' did, to lead his faithful readers to the promised land (within). It is not so much that Milton claims to be another Moses, or that *Paradise Lost* is another book of sacred scripture, but that the poem may function, by virtue of its divine inspiration, in ways analogous to Scripture. It will serve the same purpose for the reader.

In offering back up to God the darkness of his fiction, its limiting frame as well as the truth and light it aims to contain, Milton arrogates to himself a remarkable humility. An age too late, or too cold a climate might damp his "intended wing . . . if all be mine / Not hers who brings it nightly to my ear." The longer one ponders that proposition, the more one sees that Milton claims less and less of the poem for himself. In a sense, the easiest way around the problem of ineffability is to let divine agency take over one's language; if one's own words will never be able to reach up to God, the Logos himself will surely come down to redeem the very limitations of that verbal struggle. Insofar as he claims in the poem to have been directly and literally inspired by Christ, Milton need not apologize for or even alert his readers to the mediacy of his muse. Milton's claims for direct, literal inspiration—as if the poem were some kind of automatic writing—are everywhere in the text. They transform much of the self-conscious references to his own artistry—as in his indication of the Muse's passageway—into a signal to the reader to consider the option that the poet was literally able to dismiss the need for allegory in his approach to the ineffable being of God, because, with what appears to be absolute certainty about his inspiration, he did not need a language in which the divine presence was other, or *allos.*

19. For discussions of Dante's typology, see Erich Auerbach, *Mimesis: The Representation of Reality in Western Literature,* trans. Willard Trask (1953; rpt. New York: Doubleday, 1957), pp. 169–73; A. C. Charity, *Events and Their After-Life: The Dialectics of Christian Typology in the Bible and Dante* (Cambridge: Cambridge University Press, 1966).

The Problem of Prophecy: The Reader's Part

Milton's stance toward his inspiration has been called "prophetic." William Kerrigan, among others, has forcefully argued that Milton's statements in the poem about its divine agency are to be taken as literally and thoroughly true. Thus the invocations "present the requests of the poet and introduce the answer of God."[20] In this view, Milton means not only to share in Moses' revelations, and to share in the sacred effect of Scripture, but to provide a version truer than Genesis:

> if the poet claims higher inspiration than Moses, it seems distressingly easy to conclude (let rude ears be absent) that the epic intends to be a document superior to a portion of Holy Scripture. . . . Attempting the unattempted, the poet will sing an adventurous song of the "beginning" more perfect than Genesis.[21]

Whether or not Milton intended this conclusion—and Kerrigan is right to insist that it seems inescapable—it is not exactly clear how acknowledging it would affect the way we read the poem other than to shrink the interpretive act into mere assent. The greater "perfection" of the account in *Paradise Lost* is, after all, a result of history, of God's continued revelation to man through history. Milton's version has the benefit of Gospel revelations, of the fulfillments of Moses' merely shadowed account. It is more perfect because it is more perfected; we know the story's end.

Yet Milton's relation to his muse claims more than merely this greater knowledge of New Testament history—a matter, finally, of public record. While he does not claim to have seen God, for that "no Creature can behold," we do in the poem see Christ in heaven: "In whose conspicuous countenance, without cloud / Made visible, the almighty Father shines" (III.385–86).

As we shall see, this is to see much more than Spenser ever allowed himself. But again, Milton's vision is here enfolded within

20. William Kerrigan, *The Prophetic Milton* (Charlottesville: University of Virginia Press, 1974), p. 7.
21. Ibid., p. 129.

the song the angels sing in Book III; his song therefore takes its ambiguous position within the choir. Does he merely record the song as heard, or does he actually see the characters to whom it is addressed, those personages invisible to mortal sight? In this ambiguity is protection against trespass.

There is, however, another moment when Milton grants himself no such saving ambivalences, where it appears that Kerrigan is right to say that Milton believes he is directly recording the Holy Spirit's voice, giving details of the story that no one but this source could possibly possess. Such, for instance, is the extremely bizarre remark Milton lets drop about Satan's flight through Chaos in Book II:

> all unawares
> Flutt'ring his pennons vain plumb down he drops
> Ten thousand fathom deep, and *to this hour*
> *Down had been falling,* had not by ill chance
> The strong rebuff of some tumultuous cloud
> Instinct with fire and nitre hurried him
> As many miles aloft:
> [III.932–38; emphasis added]

An amazing potential erasure of story, this remark about Satan's falling opens for a moment a huge indeterminacy in the plot. The fate of all human history appears to hang here on the hinge of "ill chance." What is "this hour"? The hour in which Milton wrote? Or, more probably (and more interestingly), the hour in which the reader reads? If the latter, we are invited momentarily to imagine ourselves unfallen in Satan's fall. The effect of the remark on the reader—its rhetorical function—is useful and typical. It engenders a jolt of recognition: one is reading in "this hour" the story that explains the inexorability of all our hours, each one leading to the next, ending finally in our death.[22] But we may in the midst of our

---

22. Fowler notes that at other points the plot appears to depend on similar contingencies, such as the moment when Satan finds Eve "accidentally" separate from Adam. None of these moments, however, has the specific address to the reader (as in "this" hour) and all of them are finally contingencies made necessary by the original version. Satan's fall is unique in being so unnecessary.

readerly self-consciousness still ask: by what authority does Milton know this plummeting took place?

One may sympathize with Milton's predicament: the story was well known; it was canonical. He has, in fact, very little room in which to interpolate new fictions; Satan's unrecorded journey across Chaos is one place where the poet would be less likely to incur blame. It is the place for the stuff left over from God's own creation, and therefore, we could say, another creator may feel freer to extemporize there. We may say too that the place is filled with "'mere'" personifications, and so carries its signature as fiction. The ontological status of Chaos being different from heaven's, the poet need not be so careful. But the very form of the remark insists upon the real and temporal profundity of Chaos—it is so deep that Satan could be falling at this very moment, an eternity of depth. Our own confused sense of temporal and spatial coordinates, so nicely handled in our precipitous drop into hell in the opening lines, is the more poignant here. An abyss opens between our own ignorance and the singer's incredible knowledge. It is an abyss to be closed by the intimacy of the personal details revealed in the invocation to light a hundred or so lines later, and thus prepares the necessary ground for that revelation: in the invocation Milton explains the immediacy of his relations to the source of knowledge about such unknowable events.

William Blake had early recognized the remarkable literalness of Milton's relations to his muse; though some of Blake's other remarks about Milton's inspiration in *Paradise Lost* may make us suspect the authority with which he speaks, he is right to emphasize Milton's crediting the poem to its source:

> And tho' I call them Mine, I know they are not Mine, being of the same opinion with Milton when he says that the Muse visits his Slumbers & awakes & governs his Song when Morn purples the East.[23]

Milton would doubtless have called his certainty "faith" rather than "opinion." Yet Blake is also right to call this problem the "predicament of the prophet who says: I cannot go beyond the com-

23. Joseph A. Wittreich, Jr., ed., *The Romantics on Milton: Formal Essays and Critical Asides* (Cleveland: Case Western Reserve University Press, 1970), p. 92.

mand of the Lord, to speak good or bad." There is an inescapable
risk involved in prophecy, not merely the risk haunting the question
"May I express thee unblamed?" but a consequent confrontation
of limitations. Is there any space for "fiction" in a poem authored
directly by divine agency? If not, we might as well give up criti-
cizing Milton and concern ourselves directly with the skills of the
Holy Spirit.[24]

It is, however, necessary to recognize the reality of the temptation
to treat the poem as automatic writing, for it emphasizes the large
distinction between Milton's mode of "prophecy" and Spenser's.
Of the many critics who argue that Spenser is the beginning of the
prophetic line in English literature, after whom Milton follows (or,
conversely, who prepares Milton's way), Kathleen Williams has
this very Spenserian definition of prophecy to offer:

> The trust of the prophetic poet is . . . in visions, and his work is to
> articulate vision into a fiction that contains its own lesson in inter-
> pretation, so that the reader may in reading learn how to read, how
> to see the fiction in the light of those epiphanies and visions which
> from time to time irradiate it.[25]

24. A reviewer of James Merrill's *Divine Cantos* did just this when he took the
fiction for the author's truth and, bypassing Merrill's authorship, impugned the
taste of the spiritual agencies who had transmitted the poems through the Ouija
board. Robert B. Shaw, "James Merrill and the Ouija Board," *New York Times Book
Review* (April 29, 1979).

25. Kathleen Williams, "Vision and Rhetoric: The Poet's Voice in *The Faerie
Queene,*" *Journal of English Literary History* 36 (1969), 32; see also Kathleen Williams,
"Milton, Greatest Spenserian," in *Milton and the Line of Vision,* ed. J. A. Wittreich,
Jr. (Madison: University of Wisconsin Press, 1975), pp. 25–55; J. A. Wittreich, Jr.,
"'A Poet Amongst Poets': Milton and the Tradition of Prophecy," in *Milton and the
Line of Vision,* pp. 97–142; J. A. Wittreich, Jr., *Visionary Poetics: Milton's Tradition and
His Legacy* (San Marino, Calif.: Huntington Library, 1979); rightly stressing differences, Wittreich remarks that "Spenser . . . could disregard the vast space between
the first and second resurrections, the very space that by Milton had to be filled with
a political vision. . . . while Spenser and Milton both join prophecy to epic, Milton
effects a merger different from and more complete than Spenser's . . . Milton em-
braces what Spenser represses, restoring the hieratic relationship between epic and
prophecy fostered by the Bible" (p. 57). While "repression" may not be the aptest
term to describe Spenser's poetics—especially in terms of his yearning for ultimate
visions—or apolitical a true assessment of his history, Wittreich's stress on Milton's
prophetic immediacy states a crucial distinction. See also A. Bartlett Giamatti,
"Spenser: Root of the Visionary Line," review of MacCaffrey, *Spenser's Allegory,* in
Yale Review 62 (1977), 124–28.

Leaving aside for a moment the crucial distinction between Spenser's visual manner of "vision" and Milton's auditory experiences of what was brought nightly to his "ear," we may notice that there are two stages of responsibility for the "prophetic" poet: first, the trust in vision, that is, the acceptance of it as truth; and second, the "articulation" of it into something that may profit a reader. Because Williams is commenting on Spenser, we need experience no nervousness in her use of the term "fiction." The problem, however, becomes crucial (and virtually insurmountable) when we apply this definition to Milton. Milton manages the problem of ineffability by insisting on the already accommodated directness of divine agency for his language. His inspiration is such that he can claim the poem works only insofar as it can be ceded to the Muse. Milton may "sing" of doings in very high places indeed; his only sacrifice is his own authorship. Spenser, not sacrificing so much, is confronted with his own limits: the song remains his and so cannot aspire so highly.

Another way of noting this crucial difference is to realize that while Milton may be said to pick up his harp and sing in Book III directly to Christ—"Hail Son of God, Saviour of men, thy name / Shall be the copious matter of my song"—Spenser never mentions Christ directly in *The Faerie Queene.* His usual indirection in this matter instructs us in his allegory; thus a reference to Christ's sacrificed blood comes in the terms of the book the Redcrosse Knight exchanges with Arthur in canto ix of Book I: Christ's presence in the world of Book I is indistinguishable from the action of right reading.

In the *Mutability Cantos* Spenser uniquely refers to an event in Christ's human history other than the Passion; the context again insists upon the humility of the poet's aspirations, and again Christ is associated with a text: it is a text, moreover, that crucially signals the readable textuality of Spenser's own verse, so very different from the auditory terms (singing, hearing) in which Milton expresses his relation to the sacred source and subject of his poem.

Spenser is confronted with the need to describe Nature's veil, a garment that hides her entire face and figure. The terms Spenser uses for this veil are themselves indistinguishable from the terms he uses for his allegory, and so the description that Spenser does not give of this veil confronts the limits of his language with the ineffability of vision; Spenser tells us what others have said about this veil:

> That well may seemen true: for well I weene
>> That this same day, when she on *Arlo* sat,
>> Her garment was so bright and wondrous sheene,
>> That my fraile wit cannot devise to what
>> It to compare, nor find like stuffe to that,
>> As those three sacred *Saints,* though else most wise,
>> Yet on Mount *Thabor* quite their wits forgat,
>> When they their glorious Lord in strange disguise
> Transfigured sawe; his garments so did daze their eyes.
>> [VII.vii.7]

In the first account the veil purports to protect human sight from an uncouth vision, a traditional definition of allegory. In the second account, even the veil itself comes to be seeable only by the mediated vision as of an image in a glass. That it is the veil itself that is so bright (and not Nature's unseeable face) only appears after careful scrutiny of the ambiguous grammatical referent for the "it" of line 6: the next stanza makes it clear that Spenser describes the garment:

> That well may seemen true: for well I weene
>> That this same day, when she on *Arlo* sat,
>> Her garment was so bright and wondrous sheene,
>> That my fraile wit cannot devise to what
>> It to compare, nor find like stuffe to that,
>> As those three sacred *Saints,* though else most wise,
>> Yet on Mount *Thabor* quite their wits forgat,
>> When they their glorious Lord in strange disguise
> Transfigured sawe; his garments so did daze their eyes.
>> [VII.vii.7]

Discussing this passage as an example of a "bright conceit" that illuminates "nothing but itself, as though both interior and exterior disappeared in the brilliance of pure surface," John Guillory rea-

sons that the impenetrability of the garment derives from its identification with Christ's:

> Stanza 7 "compares" this veil to the garment of Christ at the
> Transfiguration, but of course there is no difference between these
> two garments and therefore no comparison. Figuration is itself
> transfigured.[26]

In hesitating to call the reference a "comparison," Guillory is
surely wise; yet we may question that Spenser in fact equates the
two garments. To do so would claim a scriptural numinousness for
Nature's veil and therefore for his own text which Spenser is careful
to disclaim elsewhere. What is being compared are not the garments or their brightnesses, but the ineffability of human response
to these two moments of vision. They are not merely beyond the
reach of human speech, but beyond, it appears, human apprehen-
sion altogether. Spenser introduces the transfigured Christ into his
poem to reveal the limits of human speech, to show what his poetic
language cannot do, though it may come close. The saints, "else
most wise," experience the same incapacity as Spenser. Or, as Guillory rightly puts it, "Spenser's choice of the text on transfiguration
quite explicitly demarcates an upper boundary of the inexpressible
in art."

We might pause to compare for a moment Milton's language in
the angels' song in Book III which glimpses the Father's brilliance
before turning to His expression in the Son's more visible glory:

> thee author of all being,
> Fountain of light, thy self invisible
> Amidst the glorious brightness where thou sit'st
> Throned inaccessible, but when thou shadest
> The full blaze of thy beams, and through a cloud
> Drawn round about thee like a radiant shrine,
> Dark with excessive bright thy skirts appear,
> Yet dazzle heaven, that brightest seraphim
> Approach not, but with both wings veil their eyes.

26. John Guillory, *Poetic Authority: Spenser, Milton, and Literary History* (New York:
Columbia University Press, 1983), pp. 59–60.

> Thee next they sang of all creation first,
> Begotten Son, divine similitude,
> In whose conspicuous countenance, without cloud
> Made visible, the almighty Father shines,
> Whom else no creature can behold;
>
> [III.374–85]

Robert Crosman has shown how Milton, if he has made "darkness visible" in Book I, also manages to give us a sense of "light invisible" in Book III;[27] in this passage we can see the legerdemain at work. We "see" the angels not being able to look when they "veil" their eyes; the Son's conspicuous face makes all clear, yet we cannot say that we have been told what Christ looks like. The only physical detail offered is finally Spenser's: the word "skirts" leaps out at the reader, blazing from the offered particular of a feminine human garment into a divine masculine presence of spatiality. If the outskirts of this vision are so bright, what must the center be? God is invisible, but not beyond the powers of language to express.

Lest we miss the point that Spenser, unlike Milton, is insisting on his vision's inexpressibility, the poet provides for us two further comparisons to elucidate his struggle with ineffability:

> So hard it is for any liuing wight,
>   All her array and vestiments to tell,
>   That old *Dan Geffrey* (in whose gentle spright)
>   The pure well head of Poesie did dwell)
>   In his *Foules parley* durst not with it mel,
>   But it transferd to *Alane,* who he thought
>   Had in his *Plaint of Kindes* describ'd it well:
>   Which who will read set forth so as it ought,
> Go seek he out that *Alane* where he may be sought.
>
> [VII.vii.9]

Guillory for one sees this movement to the secular tradition of literary history as a movement away from sacred vision ("a pretence to the authority of sacred revelation . . . is certainly rejected"); it is a

27. Robert Crosman, *Reading Paradise Lost* (Bloomington: Indiana University Press, 1980), chap. 2.

rejection similar to the implicit discontinuity Spenser has indicated in the list of visionary mountaintops in Book I. Poesie may fly high, above the lunar sphere, and the *Mutability Cantos* do take us to the physically highest point of vision in the poem, but unlike Milton's verse, the actual doings of the Christian God remain "too high a ditty" for Spenser's simple song.

Spenser's reference to Alain has been a puzzle for many readers of the *Mutability Cantos;* the latest editor of the *Cantos* has even suggested that Spenser never read Alain.[28] Thus Guillory has reasoned that in Spenser's reference to Alain,

> the quest for ultimate textual origins . . . is amusingly frustrated in a reference to pure textuality. The text is greater than the sum of its words, and it is the idea of the text within the community of authors that constitutes authority. Whatever Alanus may have had to say about the veil of Nature matters less than the authority his name has accumulated, the name of the text. It is that authority (continuity) to which Spenser defers.[29]

It is only to change this argument slightly to say that what is important for Spenser about Alain's work is that it is a text within a community of readers. That this reference to his tradition comes in one of Spenser's most direct addresses to his reader as an active participant in that tradition ("go seek . . . out") is crucially central to the veil's rhetorical function and to Spenser's sacred effects. To insist, as I would like to do, on the actual continuity between Spenser and one of his named sources is not only to save the source, it is also to understand the pivotal function of the reader in the tradition of narrative allegory. If the origin of a poem's composition is not itself sacred, the work of reading it may be. To see a real link here may save the "prophetic" purposes of Spenser's epic, if not its "prophetic" divine agency.

28. S. P. Zitner, ed., *The Mutabilitie Cantos* (London: Thomas Nelson and Sons, 1968), p. 133.

29. I quote an earlier version of the argument from Guillory's dissertation ("Poetry and Authority: Spenser, Milton, and Literary History," Yale University, 1979), p. 97; in the book the argument has been somewhat recast, *Poetic Authority*, p. 64.

Because it is important that we understand how Spenser did, in fact, read Alain, a brief bibliographical note will be useful. The editor who dismissed Alain from Spenser's reading argued as he did because there were no printed editions of the *De planctu* available to him. Rosemond Tuve has, however, usefully reminded us that we need not limit Spenser's reading to printed editions, as he had access to and used manuscript texts (he read them just as if they were books). Spenser had demonstrable access to at least nine extant manuscript copies of the *De planctu* and possibly to a greater number now lost.[30] The note of discontinuity—"Go seek ye out that Alane where he may be sought"—bespeaks at least a search, and if it was one frustrated at the time of Spenser's composing the *Cantos* (probably in Ireland), that does not make it necessarily a search never rewarded with success.

What Spenser would have found in seeking out Alain (and what any reader, taking Spenser's command seriously, finds) is a twelfth-century Latin allegory that deals directly with the relation of Christian revelation to classical myth, that is, to a secular tradition of poetry that vied with revelation. Spenser's mention of Alain in the *Mutability Cantos* appears, then, to bear directly on his own rewrit-

30. Four of the manuscripts are in the Royal Library collection in the British Library: MS Royal 7.C.i, MS Royal 12.E.xi, MS Royal 13.A.xviii, MS Royal 15.C.xvi. Royal 7.C.i and Royal 13.A.xviii are listed in the 1542 catalogue and so were in the collection when Spenser, as the Earl of Leicester's secretary, would have had easiest access to the royal books. The other two entered the collection some time afterward (the collection was not catalogued again until 1666). It is impossible to date the acquisition of the MS currently in the Cambridge University Library; it appears on no sixteenth-century shelflist. Dr. John Dee did own a copy of the *De planctu* at the time Spenser could have known him through Sidney. Robert Cotton and the Earl of Southampton both owned copies; Sidney's sister, the Countess of Pembroke, had a famous library of books at Wilton, but it and presumably the catalogue of its contents burned with the house in 1667. What we must not assume is that simply because the work was not printed, Spenser would have been unable to read it. For Tuve's arguments about Spenser's use of his aristocratic friends' manuscripts, see "Spenserus," and "Spenser and Some Pictorial Conventions," in *Essays by Rosemond Tuve*, ed. Thomas P. Roche, Jr. (Princeton: Princeton University Press, 1970). For further discussion of the relevant manuscripts of the *De planctu*, see the Appendix to my "Words and Sex: The Language of Allegory in the *De planctu naturae, Le Roman de la Rose,* and Book III of *The Faerie Queene,*" *Allegorica* 1 (1977), 214–16.

ing of Ovid's *Metamorphoses*, and so on the problems of reading the fictions of the pagan pantheon in relation to Christian truth. If we view Alain's text as a consideration of the burdens involved in right reading of literature, we may see what remains continuous not only between Spenser and his tradition, but between Milton and his.

In the *Complaint of Nature*, Lady Natura arrives in a vision to castigate the poet—specifically for perverted poetry in the service of perverted love. The burden of her complaint is that human beings indulge in unnatural sexual practices, but the terms in which she couches this complaint indicate her overriding concern with the language of poetry. Complaints about sexual perversions thus take the form of complaints about bad grammar; or, as C. S. Lewis put it, Alain was tempted to write about the problems of perverted love because they offered "endless opportunities for fantastical grammatical metaphor about the proper relations of masculine and feminine, or subject and predicate in the grammar of Venus."[31]

More important, Lady Natura corrects the poet's way of reading Ovidian fable. In the fourth prose section of the work, Lady Natura laments her manufacture of such creatures as Pasiphae, Myrrha, Medea, and Narcissus, all of whom reflect the widespread corruption of chastity she has come to lament. In defense of himself and of mankind in general, the poet reminds her that in "the compositions of the poets," the gods themselves have fallen prey to similar inordinant appetites, and he mentions in particular Jupiter and Ganymede. The literary personages that concern both the poet and Lady Natura are drawn, for the most part, from the tenth book of Ovid's *Metamorphoses*. At this objection from the poet, Lady Natura becomes angered, and her response is a ringing declaration of the principles of allegorical reading:

An ignoras . . . in superficiali litterae cortice falsum resonet lyra poetica, interius vero auditoribus secretum intelligentiae altioris

31. C. S. Lewis, *Allegory of Love* (1936; rpt. Oxford: Oxford University Press, 1957), p. 106.

eloquitur, ut exterioris falsitatis abjecto putamine, dulciorem nu-
cleum veritatis secrete intus lector inveniat.

Can it be thou dost not know . . . that in the shallow exterior of
literature the poetic lyre sounds a false note, but within speaks to
its hearers of the mystery of loftier understanding, so that, the
waste of utter falsity cast aside, the reader finds, in secret within,
the sweeter kernel of truth?[32]

What Natura describes here is one means by which the continuity
between pagan and Christian literature may be saved. When the
poet's next question concerns the tear in Natura's gown just at the
place where man was to have been figured, we may see a connection
between the issue of right reading and the very garment the goddess
wears. The tear in the gown may be read to mean that men are
violently unnatural, an abuse that has meaning both in sexual
terms and in the terms of rhetoric:

> [men] themselves tear apart my garments piece by piece, and, as
> far as in them lies, force me, stripped of dress, whom they ought
> to clothe with reverential honor, to come to shame like a harlot.
> [Moffat, p. 41]

Following Alice Miskimin, John Guillory stresses Spenser's
omission of this tear in the gown and his further failure to make use
of the "symbols" on it. Such absences, he argues, alert us to Spenser's interest in the "authority of textuality itself, conceived apart
from the hubris of the message."[33] In these omissions, Spenser is, in
fact, following Chaucer, who before him had transplanted the em-
blematic birds (appearing as fine embroidery on the gown of
Alain's Natura) into the physical landscape. There he had made
them speak in a parliament, thus literalizing by dramatizing
Alain's ekphrastic and allegorical *concilium* (Wright, p. 437). In do-

---

32. Alain de Lille, *De planctu naturae*, ed. Thomas Wright, in *Anglo-Latin Satirical Poets and Epigrammatists of the Twelfth Century*, 2 vols. (Rolls Series, London, 1872), II, 465; translations are from Douglas Moffat, trans., *The Complaint of Nature*, Yale Studies in English, 36 (New York: Henry Holt, 1908).

33. Guillory, "Poetry and Authority," p. 94.

ing so, Chaucer radically de-textualizes his presentation of Nature, at the same time that he "de-allegorizes" the figure, specifically by avoiding the question of how to read her—that is, how to interpret her garment allegorically.[34]

Spenser *re*allegorizes Nature, as it were, by spending so much time on her veil, by re-textualizing her presentation, making her ambiguous appearance something to be read and interpreted. What the name of Alain stands for in Spenser's text is a distinctly non-Chaucerian textuality, but it is a textuality important for its supreme self-awareness of the crucial function performed by the reader of texts, how his or her interpretations (or lack of them) can destroy relations as central as those between man and his natural god-granted sexuality. There are two poetries in Alain's text: Natura's and Orpheus's lyric delirium. There are two Venuses, two Cupids—a persistent doubling of actors. Alain is concerned to distinguish between them in order to heal the rift; that he ultimately fails in his task is not as significant as his attempt.[35]

Alain is important to Spenser, then, not as a name in a poetic canon, but as a poet who had broached an issue crucial to Spenser's own remythologizing in the *Mutability Cantos*. The citation of Alain helps to insist on the potentially sacral character there is in reading works produced by nonsacred inspiration. By giving us his vision of God's eternal order through the mediated characters of Natura and the pagan pantheon, Spenser insists that if the human words of *The Faerie Queene* do not derive directly from a divine origin, they may yet point to a divine end. This is the disjunction—coming in the

34. Chaucer does not in fact say anything about what his goddess wears, or how difficult it is to describe her. It is this information that he rather perfunctorily transfers to Alain: "And right as Aleyn, in the Pleynt of Kynde, / Devyseth Nature of aray and face, / In swich aray men myghte hire there find" (*Parlement of Foules,* 316–18). For further discussion of Chaucer's de-allegorization of Nature, see my "Allegory, Allegoresis, and the De-allegorization of Language: *The Roman de la Rose,* the *De planctu naturae,* and the *Parlement of Foules,*" in *Allegory, Myth, and Symbol,* ed. Morton Bloomfield, Harvard Studies in English, 9 (Cambridge, Mass.: Harvard University Press, 1981), 163–86.

35. Winthrop Wetherbee, *Platonism and Poetry in the Twelfth Century* (Princeton: Princeton University Press, 1972), p. 195, summarizes that Natura's "account of poetry does not explain how true and false myths are to be distinguished."

midst of a desire for conjunction—that Spenser aims to elucidate in the Faunus story and in the story on which it comments, the challenge of Mutabilitie.

Interestingly, Spenser does not rewrite Ovid's tale of Actaeon in the received allegorical manner; instead, he suggests that Actaeon was not transformed into a deer. Thus Faunus is placed to view Diana:

> That neuer any saw, saue onely one;
> Who, for his hire to so foole-hardy dew,
> Was of his hounds devour'd in Hunters hew.
> [VII.vi.45]

If we take the meaning of "hew" in Spenser's usual usage, Actaeon is destroyed while still dressed in hunter's garb—a serious rewriting of Ovid indeed, of the sort we more normally associate with Milton and his sense of the demonic errancy of pagan fable. "Hew" may also mean, however, "destruction," a usage that tends to preserve the notion of metamorphosis; yet because Spenser does not transform Faunus in his own version of the story, but merely disguises him in a superfluous animal hide, Spenser makes clear his insistence on the lack of metamorphosis.[36] While Spenser thus disallows Diana the power to transform Faunus, he yet insists that what Faunus had desired to see was a goddess at her bath. Spenser avoids the usual allegorical reading that secularizes the tale by rendering Diana merely an image of female sexual allure, no goddess at all. The Spenserian metamorphosis of the story itself moves it from tragedy to comedy; Faunus is hardly punished as he ends by eluding his pursuers in a parodic chase. The bathos of the Faunus episode—an antisublime—is comic counterpart to the more divine comedy celebrated in the great calendar at the close of Mutabilitie's story. Still, however, corrected in the specifics of Spenser's rewriting of the Actaeon story, the Ovidian genre informs the close of Faunus's tale, where the fable turns into an etiological myth. While

---

36. Richard N. Ringler, "The Faunus Episode," in *Essential Articles for the Study of Edmund Spenser*, ed. A. C. Hamilton (Hamden, Conn.: Archon Books, 1972), pp. 289–98.

Faunus's story ends with no tragic metamorphosis of the dramatis personae (Molanna is "whelmed" with stones, meaning merely that the river passes through a rapids before it joins the Fanchin), Diana's absence does, however, leave tragedy behind:

> Thence-forth she left; and parting from the place,
> There-on an heauy haplesse curse did lay,
> To weet, that Wolues, where she was wont to space,
> Should harbour'd be, and all those Woods deface,
> And Thieues should rob and spoile that Coast around.
> Since which, those Woods, and all that goodly Chase,
> Doth to this day with Wolues and Thieues abound:
> Which too-too true that lands in-dwellers since haue found.
> [VII.vi.55]

Ancient fable fades into present truth. As Michael Holohan movingly summarizes:

> The land it is that dies. Only the poet, indweller yet outlander that he is, can see the pity of Cynthia aping Astraea and offer his complaint that an excess of displeasure, in the name of justice, has abandoned a lovely island to waste and corruption.[37]

The waste of Ireland lamented at the close of canto vi finds its more cosmic counterpart in the prayer of the two stanzas of the imperfect canto vii, stanzas that close the *Cantos* and—for us—the poem. Both passages figure the recalcitrant threshold of the "now," beyond the powers of mere poetry to transform—though, at least in the lament for Ireland one sees the residue of a political attitude: Ireland might be mended were a virgin exemplar of justice to decide not to abandon it.

Guillory argues that "if the poet cannot escape the temporality of his medium, there cannot be sacred poetry."[38] Milton may be said to have transcended this temporality—at least in part by the personal immediacy of his inspiration, which claims no difference be-

---

37. Michael N. Holohan, " 'Iamque opus exegi': Ovid's Changes and Spenser's Brief Epic of Mutability," *English Literary Renaissance* 6 (1976), 262.
38. Guillory, *Poetic Authority,* p. 65.

tween Moses' Sinai and Milton's Sion within—while what we have last from Spenser is his acknowledgment that the only escape will come at the true apocalypse.

> Of that same time when no more *Change* shall be,
> But stedfast rest of all things firmely stayd
> Vpon the pillours of Eternity,
> That is contrayr to *Mutabilitie:*
> For, all that moueth, doth in *Change* delight:
> But thenceforth all shall rest eternally
> With Him that is the God of Sabbaoth hight:
> O that great Sabbaoth God, graunt me that Sabaoths sight.
>   [VII.viii.2]

Spenser everywhere insists that his poetry is of the "middest"; the apocalypse that Spenser awaits at the end of the *Mutability Cantos* is the same event postponed at the end of Book I. This postponement of the end—analogous to Milton's deeper incursions into the beginning—insofar as it leaves the reader stranded in the meanderings of the middle, gains for Spenser the atemporal possibilities of myth, which have in Spenser's text a still sacral character. As Michael Murrin argues the relation: "No allegorical tale ever really ends. They remain open not only to interpretation but to further stories."[39] If Spenser's epic may be said to be essentially without beginning (because we never get to its end, which was to have been its narrative beginning), it also, by being an endless work, provides a pattern for a sacral rereading of our lives during the living of them. Implosions of the divine into the lives of Spenser's characters are never definitively transforming. If visions offer glimpses of divinity, Spenser's human (and faery) characters all suffer from the mortal frailty of backsliding.

The *Mutability Cantos,* themselves incomplete, finally give us only the latest version of the Actaeon myth—how a desire to see god leads, potentially, to annihilation. It may be an annihilation devoutly to be wished, but it is a consummation that consumes into

---

39. Michael Murrin, *The Veil of Allegory: Some Notes toward a Theory of Allegorical Rhetoric in the English Renaissance* (Chicago: University of Chicago Press, 1969), p. 101.

silence. An earlier version of the myth subtly adumbrated in the Garden of Adonis episode (which concerns the same problems of things both eternal and mutable) suggests that the divinity of such myth resides for Spenser in the sacral purposes of its so often overloaded sexual content (that content that was so intractably problematic for Alain's Natura). That Spenser can make the Great Mother speak for the God of Nature who never himself speaks within the poem may mark for us the potentialities as well as the limits of Spenser's language.[40]

The potency of his language is nowhere more forceful than in the *Mutability Cantos*. Thus the very terms in which Mutabilitie states her claim to hegemony over the universe provide the argument that Nature marshals against her. When Mutabilitie insists

> Then since within this wide great *Vniuerse*
> Nothing doth firme and permanent appeare,
> But all things tost and turned by tranuerse:
> [VII.vii.56]

Nature need only turn her words against her and, literalizing the etymology of "universe," simply undo the upstart's claim:

> I well consider all that ye haue sayd,
> And find that all things stedfastnes doe hate
> And changed be: yet being rightly wayd
> They are not changed from their first estate;
> But by their change their being doe dilate:
> And turning to themselues at length againe,
> Doe worke their owne perfection so by fate:
> Then ouer them Change doth not rule and raigne:
> But they raigne ouer change, and doe their states maintaine.
> [VII.vii.57]

The vast calendar procession literalizes the same one-turning as Spenser offers in the circular dance another more coherent vision of the Wheel of Fortune with which the *Cantos* open. Persistent play

---

40. For a discussion of Nature and Mutabilitie as "diametrical versions" of Magna Mater, see Peter S. Hawkins, "From Mythography to Myth-making: Spenser and the *Magna Mater* Cybele," *Sixteenth Century Journal* 12 (1981), 63–64.

through the *Cantos* on the root of the titular virtue, "Constancy," (*sto, stare*—with further puns on "star" and in such locutions as "their *sta*tes maintain") reveals Book VII to have been quite aptly named, and proves further that the word magic works in the last fragment much as it does in the first book. Nature's control of this word magic suggests that if the vision of her is itself ineffable— beyond the powers of human language to describe—the sufficing articulation of divine order, turning so pivotally on the magic of that language, may be found hidden within it. Although Spenser's Nature is indescribable, she may, like Alain's Natura, read out of the density of man's language a divine truth.

When in the last two stanzas Spenser finally turns out to be a reader of the conflicting texts of Mutabilitie and Nature, he appears to be no longer content with that magic, but to yearn for a more immediate experience of the divine than that embedded in the polysemy of his words. His final line is a prayer addressed to the Christian God, a prayer for vision—and the only "invocation" so addressed in the poem. That he writes nothing after it suggests that he has prayed for what must be a wordless vision; to see it is finally to be rapt up into silence.

In a sense, *Paradise Lost* is what that same prayer's answer might, in fact, have sounded like; and in this same sense, what we see in Milton's prelapsarian paradise is not the activity of the last Sabbath, but something close to its type—the first week. Milton's escape from temporality is by the route of first beginnings, before time was, and so Adam and Eve may remember their births while still protected from time's devouring mutabilities. Spenser elects to regard the cycle of time not from its beginning, but from the point of view of its end, and from this point of view time seems necessarily inconclusive. So Milton may imagine time not as an experiential state, but as a spatial arrangement; thus Adam rejoices:

> How soon hath thy prediction, seer blest,
> Measured this transient world, the race of time,
> Till time stand fixed: beyond is all abyss,
> Eternity, whose end no eye can reach.
>
> [XII.553–56]

Unlike Spenser's cycles, Milton's linear (if repetitive) time stretches on a continuum; if the eye cannot reach the end of eternity itself, it may still see far enough to see that it can see no farther. Spenser must shut his eyes even to see the beginning.

The Problem of Elizabeth

Unspoken in Spenser's last stanza and its prayer for rest in the Lord is the Hebrew word "Elizabeth"—which means "rest or peace of the Lord." In a sense, Spenser's final prayer is not only for the sight of the Lord, but for the Lord's vicar on earth: Spenser's anointed queen, Elizabeth, Supreme Governor of the English Church. It was she who, as Gloriana, had validated by her divine origin the dual nature of the Redcrosse Knight's quest. This validation has its basis in political fact: as both secular and sacred head of her society Elizabeth did speak for God in Elizabethan society. That she chose not to say very much is to her immediate credit, but her politique reluctance to make windows into men's souls did allow the reforming impulse to gather head: as long as one paid one's tithes it did not matter what one believed. Later people questioned paying tithes for support of a Church in which they did not believe. Still later people felt that God could speak directly to them without the intermediary of a Church at all.

Spenser does not speak Elizabeth's name explicitly in the last stanza and it is well to remind ourselves that we do not know when Spenser wrote the *Mutability Cantos:* however fine an ending they supply the poem, they may not be Spenser's last thoughts on various matters. But the word hovers with real significance over the last stanza's distinctions in Hebrew spelling, Sabbath and Sabaoth. It is as if in its last, most transcendent moment, the poem is still haunted by the desire to speak the name of its most politically powerful contemporary reader.

We do not need to seek far for the presence of Elizabeth within the *Cantos* themselves. The challenge posed Diana by Mutabilitie, and Faunus's comic vision of the naked goddess, both adumbrate comic discourses on Elizabeth's rule as the virgin goddess Diana. The very setting in Ireland, moreover, queries Elizabeth's policy at the point where Spenser was disposed to be most personally critical. Here her constant vacillations made her too much of an adherent of her motto: *Semper eadem,* always the same. This motto can also be found lurking, ironically, within Natura's decisions on the issues of mutability.

There is, however, an even more peculiarly subtle pressuring of female authority within the very nature of the genre Spenser writes in the *Mutability Cantos.* They comprise a more distinctly medieval (Chaucerian, Alainian) type of narrative than the chivalric quests of the earlier books. Medieval allegory is based more typically on the animation of abstract nouns; and these animations, often figures of highest authority, take on a female gender. Thus we have Boethius's Lady *Philosophia,* Chaucer's (and Alain's) *Natura,* Langland's Holy Church (*Ecclesia*). The femininity of these figures is due to grammatical accident, the formation of abstract nouns from verbs requiring a noun feminine in gender classification. To take a significant instance: Sapientia comes from *sapiens*—to know (by tasting). Thus in Spenser's "An Hymne of Heauenly Beavtie," Sapience sits within the bosom of the ineffable Almighty, "The Soueraine dearling of the *Deity,* / Clad like a Queene in royall robes" (184–85). As one who "rules the house of God on hy, / And menageth the euer-mouing sky," Sapience is a recognizable sister to other Spenserian abstractions in places of high authority, especially Mutabilitie and Nature. Of course, Mutabilitie takes on a female gender not simply because the grammatical classification of her name; her "sex" has to do as well with the tradition of Lady Fortuna and with Ovidian myth. But it is convenient that Spenser uses a subgenre of allegory which relies for the sex of its dramatis personae on the inherent femininity of figures of authority when he both compliments and criticizes his royal reader. He does not mention her name Elizabeth, but desires its meaning at the end (rest of the Lord). And it is she who as virgin goddess may also mean, beyond that devoutly desired consummation, the restless mutability of the moon. If the problems of female authority are inherent in the linguistic basis for allegory, these problems become crucially acute in the peculiar political situation of *The Faerie Queene*.

Milton has no similar excuse for ceding his own authority, insofar as he does, to the Heavenly Muse—which he identifies at a crucial juncture as female. He calls upon Urania, the meaning not the name (which is necessarily female); doing so he calls upon a pagan figure that may in more ways than one be an outmoded image for his inspiration. Sister to Sapientia, Urania inhabits an interesting place of authority in Milton's cosmos. When we remember that Sin prophesies to Satan that she will sit at his right hand, "thy daughter and thy darling without end," we may hear Milton's rewriting of Spenser's Sapience's place as the Almighty's "dearling" (Sin's "darling" is one of only two uses of the word in Milton's works).[41] Duplicitous, errant, biform fiction is female (like Sin), the direct "other" from the male Logos. But also female, it appears, is truth. Or such, at least, is implied by Milton's surrender of the poem's writing to Urania; much may he fail "if all be mine, / Not hers who brings it nightly to my ear" (IX.46–47).

Milton's most careful adjudication of relations between male and female powers within the poem is nowhere more evident than in his transformation of the reader's generic (inherited) sense of masculine, epic, heroism. Satan's first stance in the poem exhibits it early:

> To bow and sue for grace
> With suppliant knee, and deify his power,
> Who from the terror of this arm so late
> Doubted his empire, that were low indeed,
> That were an ignominy and shame beneath
> This downfall;
>
> [I.111–16]

(That Satan delivers this speech while lying prostrate is one of Milton's wry witticisms at the expense of evil; if we laugh, our laughter is a derisive snigger, akin to God's unattractive humor.)

---

41. I wish to thank Balachandra Rajan for the point about Sapience as the Deity's darling and its connection to Milton's Sin.

To notice that the first character in the poem who does take this supplicatory posture rejected by Satan is Eve forces us to recognize the enormity of the redefinition of heroism which Milton undertakes in *Paradise Lost*. It is a redefinition that not only substitutes a feminine posture of supplication for a masculine stance of heroic defiance, it is one that removes the moment of heroism from the field of battle and lodges it in that most intimate (and humdrum) of domestic dialogues, a husband and wife making up after a quarrel. Milton rightly realized that his redefinition would not find universal applause: his audience would be fit and few.

If we turn now to look at that audience and compare it with Spenser's, we will not be leaving the question of inspiration or sacred purpose behind. The troublesome femaleness of Milton's muse as of Spenser's sovereign reader is intricately bound up with each poet's rhetorical address of the reader's reading. It is especially bound up with each epic's confrontation with and redefinition of the heroic in its culture.

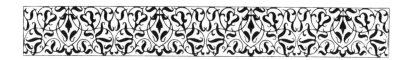

CHAPTER *4*

The Gender of the Reader
and the Problem of Sexuality

IF one of the first rules of rhetoric is to find an argument that suits the particular audience at hand, then a necessary step in defining a politics of reading is to describe the readers posited by the argument. Spenser and Milton were both faced with the problems posed by their attempts to create fiction out of the conflict between sacred history and a tradition of secular literature for which the Renaissance had named itself. It is a problem they shared, although their two epics were written seven decades apart, and although those decades experienced some of the most radical upheavals English culture has known. By virtue of this intervening history, the audiences of the two poems were necessarily very different, and however much Milton and Spenser may have shared in their need to find a rhetoric suitable to the conflicts between pagan fiction and sacred truth, the vast difference in their audiences dictated two very different solutions.

It is vital to remember that both these men were politically engaged artists. Spenser was, however briefly, closely attached to two of his monarch's favorites—first, Robert Dudley, the earl of Leicester, and later, Sir Walter Ralegh, two of the most powerful men in the realm—and he was an ardent propagandist for them within Elizabeth's regime; one should even say that at least at the beginning of his career, he was an ardent propagandist for her regime itself.[1] Milton's own position as paid propagandist—for which, he tells us, he sacrificed his very eyes—was, of course, for a political cause diametrically opposed to Spenser's. That fact alone suggests that any treatment of the two poets which hopes to speak to their rhetorics (and rhetoric's necessary political considerations) must be founded in an explication of differences, not in a search for similarities, and is therefore best served by separate argument when political poetics are at issue.

To pose questions about each epic's treatment of the problem of sexuality may seem to be sidestepping the larger political issues of history—for the gender of the reader and the problems of sexuality have at first glance little to do with British imperialism after the Armada or with the aftermath of the civil war. But the particular questions about sexuality we shall be considering in this chapter are more profoundly political than the accidents of history, and indeed they are often the same—as when the historical accident of the sex of Henry VIII's successors determined the details of British history in the last half of the sixteenth century. Control over sexual relations between men and women is control over the basic unit of society— the family—and over the basic process of social reproduction. Sexuality itself is deeply religious as well, being, since the scriptural imprimatur of the Song of Songs at least, an apt analogue for the spiritual raptures of union with the deity. The Renaissance epics, *Paradise Lost* and *The Faerie Queene,* are about sexuality in ways more fundamentally political than most other works of comparable stature before or after (*War and Peace* comes to mind: but its very disjunctive title insists on the lack of interconnections between sexual intimacy and political destiny—interconnections that are causal in the two Renaissance poems).

Why this should be so has perhaps many reasons, but I would like to offer a bit of historical theorizing in order to make apparent at least one potential link connecting politics and sexuality in the two

---

1. Stephen Greenblatt, *Renaissance Self-Fashioning: From More to Shakespeare* (Chicago: University of Chicago Press, 1980), chap. 4, argues that Spenser propagandizes for Elizabeth in Book II of *The Faerie Queene;* while it is true that Spenser celebrates Elizabeth in the early *Shepheardes Calendar,* the 1590 *Faerie Queene* insinuates criticism within praise. See below, pp. 189–90.

Renaissance epics. Since Max Weber's *Protestant Ethic and the Spirit of Capitalism,* it has been thought useful to argue a connection between the rise of Protestantism and of capitalism. And ever since Marx, it has been felt useful to scrutinize the difference between feudalism and capitalism in terms of its reorganization of labor. More recently, social historian Lawrence Stone has chronicled the rise of a new kind of family structure concurrent with the "rises" of Protestantism and of capitalism with its free-market ideologies. It is easy to sense without going into detail that these historically concurrent developments were not only simultaneous but interactive, each helping to bring about and change the others. These three interacting forces, I suggest, find expression in the Renaissance epics at the point where they intersect most pivotally: in the Protestant redefinition of the family and in its understanding of the sexually differentiating work done within it. Woman's work is to be no longer physically productive for the new marketplace—or even preeminently reproductive—but psychologically and spiritually supportive of another's work.[2] This crucial shift in the definition of the work done by women—an economic fact developing throughout the period bounded by *The Faerie Queene* and *Paradise Lost*—is a crucial epic theme shared by both poems.

Queen Elizabeth's unique and anomalous existence poses special problems for Spenser's Protestant epic—and in these problems we see how her unique sexual status causes him great trouble because he writes in service of a specific sexual program. The queen's virginity conflicts with the broad sweep of the Protestant redefinition of the family—and therefore of women and of sexuality itself. Spenser's service of the sociology of his religion conflicts with the service of his virgin queen. He needs to celebrate his virgin patroness in a poem that elevates human sexuality to a sacred level and ennobles wedded love, while elevating the social and yet depressing the psy-

2. For a suggestive analysis of the interconnections between capitalism and women's work in the Renaissance from a Marxian-feminist perspective, see Roberta Hamilton, *The Liberation of Women: A Study of Patriarchy and Capitalism* (London: Allen and Unwin, 1978). For a discussion of the relations between a Marxian and Weberian analysis of capitalism, see Jean Baechler, *The Origins of Capitalism,* trans. Barry Cooper (Oxford: Basil Blackwell, 1975).

chological status of the wife. *Paradise Lost* addresses the behavior of
the family at the end of this major shift in its historical development.
More directly than Spenser's poem, but in a line of evolution from
it, Milton's epic confronts the change of women's work.

Such theorizing would remain the basis of mere *allegoresis*—a political "allegorization" of the two poems—were it not for the fact
that such issues, as they are contained within the two works, are
addressed to the readership of the epics in its basic political (and
biological) organization. To pose questions about the gender of the
reader is to pose questions that open the texts' relations to the political arrangement of their audiences—an arrangement that has remained fairly constant up to now. (Biology will not change; politics
may.)

The best method for posing such new questions about the politics
of reading is to ask at the outset the clearest and most concrete
questions about the two different poems' address of their audiences.
Did Spenser or Milton specifically consider the two genders within
their audience? Did either distinguish between male and female
readers when he broached issues of central concern to them both?
Can we as twentieth-century readers usefully distinguish between
arguments addressed to male and to female readers? Strange as
such questions may at first seem, they are not utterly foreign to
recent critical theory, centered as it has been of late on the various
ways readers are asked to fictionalize themselves as they respond to
the specifics of the texts they read, and by so doing (re)create the
meaning of those texts. To pose questions about the gender of the
reader addressed by a text is to ask about response less purely controlled by a text's rhetoric, gender being tied to a more thoroughly
inculcated set of values (connected as they are to certain irreducible
biological facts), than other sorts of institutionally or culturally in-
duced forms of interpretive behavior. It is to pose questions about
the reader's behavior which are inescapably political.[3] But to do so
does not require that we become terrorists of the text, radically rein-

3. Questions about the political implications of reading are broached by Jane P.
Tompkins, ed., *Reader Response Criticism: From Formalism to Post-Structuralism* (Baltimore: Johns Hopkins University Press, 1980); Tompkins remarks in her introduction that "when discourse is responsible for reality and not merely a reflection of it,

venting its significance against the intentionality of its surface. The issue of woman was a historical concern of the Renaissance; Spenser overtly and Milton covertly address the female reader directly: and their political intentions are clear.

Spenser's Audience

The proliferation of sonnet cycles in the last decade of the sixteenth century may act as a gross indicator that women were a notable, distinct, and publicly marked class of readers within Spenser's aristocratic audience during the reign of Elizabeth. To be sure, not all of these sonnets are addressed to women, even fictively; in "My mistress's eyes are nothing like the sun"—to take an easy and obvious example—the reader is not imagined as female at all, but as male. Fully 80 of the 108 sonnets in *Astrophel and Stella* are not addressed to Stella, but to other men—to friends, detractors, other poets, wise counselors—who would dissuade Astrophel from loving; or addressed to rhetoricized pieces of Astrophel's own psyche, torn between those characters out of old allegories—Reason, Desire, Hope, and Despair. But in the twenty or so poems that do address Stella directly, and in the five or so that immediately follow "My mistress's eyes" in Shakespeare's cycle, the lady is the first reader, in whose place all subsequent readers must, for the moment

---

then whose discourse prevails makes all the difference" (p. xxv). In a conclusion she elaborates on the political implications of poststructuralist literary theory, which, she argues, in claiming that reality is language-based, moves closer to classical and Renaissance theory. For both, "language is a form of power": "The questions that propose themselves within this critical framework therefore concern, broadly, the relations of discourse and power. What makes one set of perceptual strategies or literary conventions win out over another? If the world is the product of interpretation, then who or what determines which interpretive system will prevail?" (p. 226). One senses that the power in question here is primarily that residing in the academic institutions of literary studies—not what one would call political power at large. To introduce questions of gender is to make the jump into society a bit more directly, and to query relations which, if they have only recently been perceived as being "political," have always formed the basic unit of social organization—an organization that has remained remarkably constant throughout the centuries. That fact itself seems to insist upon the critical usefulness of such questions in the study of all literary periods.

of the poem's reading, in part fictionalize themselves. Doubtless we tend not to be conscious of reading lyric this way, unaware of the need to recognize the gender specificity of a poem's readership. But, it appears, Sidney himself did. In the *Apology for Poetry*, for instance, he rates English lyric low by saying, "But truly many of such writings as come under the banner of unresistible love, *if I were a mistress*, would never persuade me they were in love; so coldly they apply fiery speeches, as men that had rather read lovers' writings and so caught up certain swelling phrases . . . than that in truth they feel those passions."[4] Here of course Sidney assumes the purpose of lyric to be persuasion, and—if only for the purposes of his own rhetoric in the *Apology*—can appear easily to fictionalize himself in the role of the female reader, as if that were the right role from which to judge the success of the lyric.[5] (Kin to this flexibility in role playing is the comic cross-dressing of the Old Arcadia, a text notable as well for the lyric experiments aimed at elevating English verse; to read as a woman was to read from a position of some power.)

Compared with the sonnets Milton wrote and (save for the Cavalier tradition) most verse in the later seventeenth century—again seen in very general terms—the sheer number of earlier sonnet cycles imply that women later lost a marked spot in public readership. One reason for their markedness in the late sixteenth century is preeminently obvious—all who wrote Elizabethan literature wrote under the sway of a woman, and a woman, moreover, for whom the

    4. Sir Philip Sidney, *An Apology for Poetry*, ed. Geoffrey Shepherd (London: Thomas Nelson, 1965), pp. 137–38; emphasis added.
    5. Hallet Smith, *Elizabethan Poetry: A Study in Conventions, Meaning, and Expression* (Cambridge, Mass.: Harvard University Press, 1952), pp. 145–52, discusses the "double readership" of such cycles as *Astrophel and Stella*, where the reader "must partly share Stella's position." Clark Hulse discusses the function of Penelope Rich as the critically privileged reader of *Astrophel and Stella* in "Stella's Wit: Penelope Rich as Reader of Sidney's Sonnets," a paper delivered at the conference "Renaissance Woman/Renaissance Man: Studies in the Creation of Culture and Society," Yale University, March 12–14, 1982. For a demonstration of the extent of female literacy in the Renaissance in England, based on the number of books specifically addressed to a female readership, see Suzanne W. Hull, *Chaste, Silent, and Obedient: English Books for Women, 1475–1640* (San Marino, Calif.: Huntington Library, 1982). Hull counts Sidney's *Arcadia* and *The Faerie Queene* among the books aimed at a female book-buying public, p. 14.

courtly Petrarchan literary conventions, which the English Renaissance had inherited from the continent, were ideally suited, politically. In the late sixteenth century under Elizabeth, Petrarchan poetic convention elides into politics.[6] As I have suggested in the first chapter, *The Faerie Queene* is aimed at a distinctly double-gendered readership; and so Spenser explains in the Letter to Ralegh (himself a redoubtable practitioner of politically motivated Petrarchism): "The generall end therefore of all the booke is to fashion a gentleman or noble person in vertuous and gentle discipline." The redundancy of moral qualities—gentle, noble, virtuous, gentle—is hard to keep straight, and appears at first to be another example of what Ben Jonson objected to when he said that Spenser "writ no language." But this redundancy is not otiose and makes careful distinctions between a male and a paradigmatic, royal, female readership. "Virtuous and gentle" distinguish male and female values, for embedded within the notion of "gentle" as a marker purely of social rank is a feminine Christian quality opposed to but also complementary to "virtue," which, deriving from *vir*, *virtus*, has its roots in classical notions of manly valor. The apparent redundancy reinforces a distinction without, however, making the parallel phrasing absolutely divisive. Spenser was manifestly not aiming to make only his male readers valorous or his female readers "gentle." His genius is to call each gender to experience the heroism of the other.

As the letter's further analysis of Elizabeth's own double personhood makes clear, Spenser through his chivalric metaphor is analyzing the behavior of men held in the sway of a female's power. All quests are organized (in the "Letter" at least, Britomart being a conspicuous exception) from the reference point of Gloriana's court, and Gloriana is only one manifestation of Elizabeth's power:

6. Greenblatt, *Renaissance Self-Fashioning*, p. 166, cites Bacon's observation that Elizabeth's "dalliances detracted but little from her fame and nothing at all from her majesty, and neither weakened her power nor sensibly hindered her business." In fact, her power was immeasurably strengthened by such "dalliances"; they were a way of giving a traditional literary form to her troublesome female sovereignty. Without such strengthening fictions, Henry VIII's worst fears about his successors' female weaknesses might have come true.

her princely sway. Belphoebe, yet another character, is of course there to define the queen's erotic power as unpossessable woman. Elizabeth, both as first reader and as goddess-muse, has a global effect on the production of Spenser's text; and the crux of her gender as female prince is central. The poem is named for it.[7]

That it was culturally wrong for a woman to be on the throne in the sixteenth century is of paramount importance for understanding the strange blend of medieval and Petrarchan convention that marks late Tudor court ceremony.[8] The fact of Elizabeth's elder sister Mary's gender, we need to remember, was the motivating force for the Henrican reformation, at least in its initial stages. (Elizabeth's own sex was the cause of her mother's downfall.) In the political theory of the Renaissance, women were not supposed to rule. To take only the most notorious caveat against this problematic state of affairs, we have John Knox's *First Blast of the Trumpet against the Monstrous Regiment of Women,* published—unhappily for Knox—in the year of Elizabeth's accession, 1558. In it he had argued that for a "woman to beare rule, superiorite, dominion or empire above any realme, nation, or cite is repugnant to nature, contumelie to God, a thing most contrarious to his revealed will and approved ordinance, and finally it is the subversion of good order, of all equite, and justice."[9] There was no second blast to this trum-

7. Jonathan Goldberg, *Endlesse Worke: Spenser and the Structures of Discourse* (Baltimore: Johns Hopkins University Press, 1981), discusses the impact of Elizabeth's power on the "social production" of *The Faerie Queene* in chap. 3, "The Authority of the Other," pp. 122–65.

8. In ibid., p. 127, Goldberg argues: "the reality of the courtly fictions that surrounded Queen Elizabeth . . . had to be . . . in the text if the poet was ever to find favor with his monarch."

9. John Knox, *The First Blast of the Trumpet against the Monstrous Regiment of Women,* ed. Edward Arber (London: English Scholar's Library, 1878), p. 11; of the many arguments Knox marshals, the one from the notion of the body politic had bearing on Elizabeth's parliament's restrictions on her styling herself "Head of the Church": "And no lesse monstrous is the bodie of that common welth, where a woman beareth empire. For ether doth it lack a laufull heade (as in very ded it doth) or els there is an idol exalted in the place of a true head" (p. 27). Arber also prints Knox's letters of apology and explication to Elizabeth, pp. 57–62.

pet, while Knox spent the rest of his life trying to convince Elizabeth that he had not meant her by his criticism; she for her part never let him back in England. Knox's silence suggests the success Elizabeth had in overcoming her liabilities as a woman on the throne."[10] Yet her situation was constantly more precarious than her huge historical success may allow us to recall. Even very late in the queen's reign, Essex was convinced he could effect her overthrow. In great part English stability under Elizabeth was managed by astute propaganda—in which court poets and would-be court poets played willing and eager roles.

As Marie Axton has fascinatingly shown, even such ineluctible unliterary productions as the Inns of Court Revels fed the literary machine of accommodating the disturbing fact of Elizabeth's gender.[11] Tracing the various goddesses chosen throughout the realm to present an acceptable face to Elizabeth's rule (and to argue for different positions on the problem of the succession, a continual vexing—and sexual—question), Axton (among others) shows the penultimate phase of the Cynthia-Diana-Astraea identifications, where the Cynthia/Diana myth allows poets to "explore the discrepancy between the two bodies of the monarch."[12] The final phase, employing Elizabeth's own motto, *Semper eadem,* is managed by a gender switch: the phoenix, usually male, is transformed into a female, so that out of her ashes may arise a new (male) monarch.[13]

While Book V of *The Faerie Queene* gestures in the direction of the

10. John Aylmer, *An Harborowe for Faithfull and Trewe Subiectes agaynst the laste blowne Blaste, concerninge the Gouernment of Wemen* (1559), was the first book to have been dedicated to Elizabeth's favorite, Robert Dudley, as patron. See Eleanor Rosenberg, *Leicester: Patron of Letters* (New York: Columbia University Press, 1955), pp. 27–30.

11. Marie Axton, *The Queen's Two Bodies: Drama and the Elizabethan Succession* (London: Royal Historical Society, 1977), pp. 38–72. Frances A. Yates, *Astraea: The Imperial Theme in the Sixteenth Century* (London: Routledge and Kegan Paul, 1975), cites the arguments of such texts as John Foxe's *Book of Martyrs* and John Dee's *General and rare memorials pertaining to the Perfect Arte of Navigation* (1577) as propaganda for Elizabeth's imperial virgin court mythology, p. 50.

12. Axton, *Queen's Two Bodies,* p. 71.

13. See ibid., pp. 116–32.

Astraea myth, Spenser primarily exploits the Phoebe/Diana phase—as the character of Belphoebe proves (named after Ralegh's excellent "conceipt" of Cynthia).[14] Diana's Astraea-like departure from Ireland in the *Mutability Cantos* is only Spenser's latest reference to the mythic-political material he exploits throughout the entire epic. The politically weighted virginity of the queen—whereby she was not only associated with the imperial themes of Astraea as other male monarchs of the period were, but actually became Astraea-Diana and was worshiped as such—posed peculiar problems to a protestant poet who wished to celebrate married love, not to mention the dilemma in which it placed poets who would necessarily have been interested in preserving the powerful structures of patriarchy.[15] How to celebrate sexuality in a mythic universe dominated by Diana's (or Astraea's) chastity is one of the Elizabethan poets' peculiar problems; how to make a Knoxian argument for traditional male political dominance is another.

Spenser's answer to the problem posed by Elizabeth's double personhood—as woman and as prince—is the doubling of the characters of virgin huntress Belphoebe and imperial Gloriana. But this doubling invites a further one which may figure the erotic allure of Elizabeth's power: so Spenser supplies the virgin Belphoebe with a twin sister, Amoret, thus producing another version of the double image used by many other Elizabethan poets trying to cope with the erotic element in the Cynthia/Diana myth.[16] Spenser's production

14. Thomas H. Cain, *Praise in The Faerie Queene* (Lincoln: University of Nebraska Press, 1978), p. 149, notes the odd "failure to make connections" to the Astraea cult in Book V, where Astraea gives Artegall his sword.

15. For Charles V and his use of Astraea themes, see Roy Strong, *Splendor at Court: Renaissance Spectacle and the Theatre of Power* (Boston: Houghton Mifflin, 1973), p. 81 (and fig. 65); for Henry IV, see Yates, *Astraea,* pp. 208–10 (and figs. 42b, c); Yates stresses the similarity between French and English uses of the image of the imperial virgin (p. 211), but Strong notes that "the double nature of Elizabeth" as sovereign and romantic heroine "intensified" the imperialist mythology into a "cult" (p. 115). It is important to remember that Elizabeth's imperialist mythology relied for its power on a physical fact, that she was a virgin, and that this was a sexual role (as well as an actual physical state) made necessary (and useful) by hard political realities.

16. Axton, *Queen's Two Bodies,* p. 72, describes Lily's double images, citing the precedent of Gascoigne's Kenilworth shows.

of the double image—the literal birth of the two twins—bears careful scrutiny for the ways it distinguishes between a male and a female readership for his poem.

Book III and the Gender of the Reader

Titled "The Legend of Chastity," Book III directly addresses the problem of the queen's politically powerful virginity and the dynamics of its erotic allure. More importantly, it addresses these questions to overtly inscribed female readers. But before we can go on to see the immediacy and specificity of Spenser's appeal to a female reader, it is necessary to consider for a moment the possible differences between male and female responses to Book III. I take it that it is useful and legitimate to say that, in the main, men and women find the "other" sexually attractive, and that, unlike men, women (with some notable exceptions) bear children. Beyond that it may not be safe to go, neither is it necessary for the purposes of the present argument. The Renaissance had, of course, another much more elaborate set of terms for defining the differences: Ruth Kelso has massively and meticulously documented the entire doctrine for the lady of the Renaissance as it was written down in theory. The major component of the doctrine is not surprisingly the concept of chastity, which Kelso takes in the main to be a sexual continence of a sort not important for men.[17] Spenser's treatment of chastity in Book III of *The Faerie Queene* suggests that it is, however, something more than a mere physical negative. Milton's appropriation of the theme in *Comus* insists upon the potential there is to see in Spenser's treatment of it, a shaping of the self—an embracing of personal destiny that includes on Britomart's part an active confrontation of the misshaping power of the labyrinth in which she wanders.

If any of Spenser's books is organized with a gender-specific set of responses in mind, evidence is doubtless clearest in Book III.

17. Ruth Kelso, *Doctrine for the Lady of the Renaissance* (Urbana: University of Illinois Press, 1956), pp. 24–25.

What can we say about the reader inscribed by its rhetoric? First, the homology between reading and action, whereby the reader is made to take on the perspective of the protagonist/reader of the landscape, establishes a female vantage point. Spenser further insists on Britomart's own responses as gender-specific. The troublesome beginning to the book makes absolute sense if and when we realize that with it Spenser is asking the reader to notice its female perspective. The opening scene, when Britomart unhorses Guyon, sets up the female's greater power: this opposition between Temperance and Chastity not only ranks their respective virtues, it also ranks, at least for the moment, female and male sexual values in a hierarchy. The second movement of the narrative establishes this perspective even more narrowly. When Florimell flies across the landscape, Spenser proceeds to bracket out the male experience of the labyrinth. As a damsel in distress, Florimell is notable for two characteristics: first, her extreme, cosmic beauty, and second, her fear, the latter easily understood because Spenser shows us a grisly forester riding after her in a manner most impressive in its phallic goal orientation. The three male knights who have been accompanying Britomart immediately take off after Florimell and her pursuer, in a way that the narrator describes as "full of great enuie and fell gealosie." This statement has given readers pause, especially because it seems to invite condemnatory moral judgments of the heroes Arthur, Guyon, and Timias. Thomas Roche first suggested that the mad rush after Florimell is there merely to insist that Britomart is female. Unlike the male knights, "she would not so lightly follow beauties chace / Ne reckt of Ladies loue." Roche remarks:

> With the disappearance of the others, the point of view changes. We cannot suppose that Spenser intends the reader to think ill of Arthur and Guyon. . . . The motivation attributed to Britomart is one way of emphasizing the fact that she is a woman, which is the subject Spenser is about to undertake.[18]

18. Thomas P. Roche, *Kindly Flame: A Study of the Third and Fourth Books of Spenser's Faerie Queene* (Princeton: Princeton University Press, 1964), p. 14.

This is eminently sensible and a much better way to read Spenser's text than to translate the action into "allegorical" labels—which is always to end in a tangle in midspace, above the text. Thus, if we are meant to see that Magnificence and Temperance must attempt to save Beauty from Lust, why then doesn't Chastity also come to the aid of Beauty—surely a much more practical solution to the problem? A much better way of reading Spenser's text, attentive to its carefully constructed surface, is to take seriously the pun on *chase* here, which is not a bad one, or even merely witty, but a profound structuring principle at work throughout the book.[19] Thus Florimell remains "chaste" even though she is "chased" by every character she meets—save for Britomart. The pun coordinates Florimell's flight with the nature of two virgin hunts of singular importance in Book III—Diana's and Belphoebe's—and with another hunt that does not take place because it is written out of the myth of Adonis by Spenser's peculiar topography of the garden in canto vi. When the narrative proceeds to follow Britomart not on her "chace," but in her measured pace through the parlous place, we have no choice but to proceed in a manner distinctly different from the hot-footed race of the male knights.

A similar differentiation of male and female points of view may be said to occur as well at the opening of Book II; a brief glance at that episode will make Spenser's procedures clearer. At the beginning of his quest, Guyon witnesses a grisly scene: the death of two parents, Mordant and Amavia, the latter a suicide. As a result, he becomes responsible for the care of their baby boy, Ruddymane— so named because his hands are stained with his dying mother's blood. Finding he cannot wash the baby's hands, Guyon takes him to Medina and leaves him with her. We might read this extremely tricky episode (having to do with the original sin we all inherit at our physical engendering and birth) by suggesting from our gender-oriented stance that Guyon assumes the burden of articulating principles of order from which the idea of female nurturance (such

19. Angus Fletcher, *Prophetic Moment: An Essay on Spenser* (Chicago: University of Chicago Press, 1971), pp. 99–101, argues for the significance of such "bad" puns.

as that which revives the Redcrosse Knight in the House of Ho-
linesse) has been distinctly bracketed out—just as the male point of
view is bracketed out of the narrative at the beginning of Book III by
the precipitous departure of the three male knights. So Phaedria's
appropriation of scriptural terms for peace are threatening to Guyon's laborious, pedestrian progress (terms themselves not threatening but reassuring when voiced by Cambina in Book IV), and his
experience in the Bower of Bliss is a distinctly male version of the
pornographic lure of the labyrinth's leisure.

Spenser's direct addresses to female readers are far more numerous in Book III than elsewhere throughout the poem. Here, too, he
addresses the queen directly within the body of the narrative rather
more often than in other books, because Britomart is presented as
the founder of Elizabeth's line, the one in whom she is to see the
warlike puissance of antique women, while, Spenser tells her directly, "of all wisdome be thou precedent." When it finds expression, the male perspective on the experiences of Book III's narrative
is radically censured; such, for instance, is Spenser's judgment of
that view in the opening stanzas to canto ii:

> Here haue I cause, in men iust blame to find,
>> That in their proper prayse too partiall bee,
>> And not indifferent to woman kind,
>> To whom no share in armes and cheualrie
>> They do impart, ne maken memorie
>> Of their braue gestes and prowesse martiall;
>> Scarce do they spare to one or two or three,
>> Rowme in their writs; yet the same writing small
> Does all their deeds deface, and dims their glories all.
>
> But by the record of antique times I find,
>> That women wont in warres to beare most sway,
>> And to all great exploits them selues inclind:
>> Of which they still the girlond bore away,
>> Till enuious Men fearing their rules decay,
>> Gan coyne streight lawes to curb their liberty;
>> Yet sith they warlike armes haue layd away:
>> They haue exceld in artes and pollicy,
> That now we foolish men that prayse gin eke t'enuy.
>
> [III.ii.1–2]

The candor in the collapse of rhetorical distance between the narrator and one segment of his (double-gendered) audience is striking: that Spenser goes on to criticize at the same time he celebrates Elizabeth in a later canto reveals how real his confessed "envy" is. In canto v, in one of his most extended direct addresses to his women readers, he praises Belphoebe's chastity. Using terms drawn out of the *Roman de la rose,* Spenser rewrites that text of deflowered virginity into a paean for Elizabeth's chastity—with, however, an undercutting twist at its end. In justifying Belphoebe's denial of the "soveraigne salve, in secret store," she might have granted to Timias, Spenser sings, "That dainty Rose, the daughter of her Morne, / More dear than life she tendered" (III.v.51), and traces the flower of chastity to God who implanted it in flesh as an example, which Spenser exhorts his women readers to copy:

> Faire ympes of beautie, whose bright shining beames
> Adorne the world with like to heauenly light,
> And to your willes both royalties and Realmes
> Subdew, through conquest of your wondrous might,
> With this faire flowre your goodly girlonds dight,
> . . . .
> To youre faire selues a faire ensample frame,
> Of this faire virgin, this *Belphoebe* faire,
> To whom in perfect loue, and spotlesse fame
> Of chastitie, none liuing may compaire:
> Ne poysnous Enuy iustly can empaire
> The prayse of her flesh flowring Maidenhead;
> For thy she standeth on the highest staire
> Of th'honorable stage of womanhead,
> That Ladies all may follow her ensample dead.
>
> [III.v.53–54]

The OED gives a 1561 citation of "dead" meaning "utmost." Here, then, Spenser is praising Belphoebe's utmost example of absolute virginity. But he is also saying that it is dead. Isabel MacCaffrey argues that "she is dead only in the sense that she was visible in Fairy Land, far away and long ago."[20] It is true that Spenser often

<hr/>

20. Isabel G. MacCaffrey, *Spenser's Allegory: The Anatomy of Imagination* (Princeton: Princeton University Press, 1976), p. 275.

distinguishes the degeneracy of his time from the purity of the ancient past, but Belphoebe is, in the sense announced in the Letter, Elizabeth herself; to preserve the compliment to Elizabeth—dead meaning "perfect"—is also to see the simultaneous criticism of such perfection. In the next canto Spenser neglects to fulfill the narrative expectations he arouses by turning from the dead example of Belphoebe's chastity to the life-breeding forces of the place where her twin sister, Amoret, is reared.

The canto in which the Garden of Adonis is described is addressed at its outset to women readers, as if to answer a question such readers might have about the breeding of Belphoebe:

> Well may I weene, faire Ladies, all this while
> Ye wonder, how this noble Damozell
> So great perfections did in her compile,
> Sith that in saluage forests she did dwell,
> So farre from court and royall Citadell.
> [III.vi.1]

While we hear of Belphoebe's birth, we do not hear of her training, save that she is taken off by Diana while Amoret is taken off by Venus. The story of the birth of the twins, given to explain the genesis of the elder Belphoebe's character, swerves to emphasize instead twin Amoret's nature. The birth itself is one of "strange accident"—it is a wondrous virgin birth:

> For not as other wemens commune brood,
> They were enwombed in the sacred throne
> Of her chaste bodie, nor with commune food,
> As other wemens babes, they sucked vitall blood.
> [III.vi.5]

Belphoebe is born free of the loathly crime "that is ingenerate in fleshly slime." In correcting a specifically male reader—"him that reads / So straunge ensample of conception"—Spenser takes care to explain that the birth is reasonable: for it is like the process whereby, after the Nile's flood, "Infinite shapes of creatures men

do fynd, / Informed in the mud, on which the Sunne hath shynd"
(III.vi.8). By this correction of a specifically male vision of the action, Spenser rewrites his own first use of the spontaneous generation of the flooding Nile, which in Book I he had used to demonstrate the extreme sliminess of Errour's progeny (who are in
themselves hermaphroditic, controlled moreover by an archetype
of the devouring mother). In Book III he places this same image in
the service of innocent, virginal impregnation and birth, as if the
only slime (that from which Belphoebe escapes) were a mortal, human fatherhood (as "father of generation," the sun shares his celestial operations with his "fair sister" who "for creation ministreth
matter fit" [III.vi.9]).

Our entry into the garden proper, by way of Venus's trespass on
Diana's territory, provides another instrument for fine-tuning the
perspective from which we are to view events in the garden; if I am
correct, it is the subtlest of Spenser's bracketing procedures. When
Venus finds Diana, the virgin goddess of the hunt has just taken off
her clothes from the heat of the chase: she is at her bath. In the last
chapter we considered Spenser's explicit rewrite of the Actaeon
myth in the *Mutability Cantos*. Spenser does not explicitly call up the
same myth in this passage, yet it would doubtless have been a rare
reader of Renaissance literature who would not have remembered
Actaeon's tragic dismemberment as punishment for his vision of
Diana at her bath.

> she found the Goddesse with her crew,
> After late chace of their embrewed game,
> Sitting beside a fountaine in a rew,
> Some of them washing with the liquid dew
> From off their dainty limbes the dustie sweat,
> And soyle which did deforme their liuely hew;
> Others lay shaded from the scorching heat;
> The rest vpon her person gaue attendance great.
>
> She hauing hong vpon a bough on high
> Her bow and painted quiuer, had vnlaste
> Her siluer buskins from her nimble thigh,
> And her lancke loynes vngirt, and brests vnbraste,

> After her heat the breathing cold to taste;
> Her golden lockes, that late in tresses bright
> Embreaded were for hindring of her haste,
> Now loose about her shoulders hong vndight,
> And were with sweet *Ambrosia* all besprinkeld light.
>
> [III.vi.17–18]

In Ovid's version Diana cannot reach her quiver to shoot Actaeon, so she sprinkles water on him, and from these cursed drops the metamorphosis begins. The clustering movement of the nymphs who try to shield Diana in Spenser's rendition is similar to the movement in Ovid; yet Spenser's Diana is only half wroth:

> Soone her garments loose
> Vpgath'ring, in her bosome she comprized,
> Well as she might, and to the Goddesse rose,
> Wiles all her Nymphes did like a girlond her enclose.
>
> [III.vi.19]

The great difference, of course, is that "Goodly she gan faire Cytherea greet" (III.vi.20); this is not a mortal male's trespass on the sacred ground of the virgin goddess, but rather a meeting between two goddesses who share between them (and between their foster daughters) the definition of womanhood. The garden remains a completely female place.[21]

Here the potential male viewpoint, the point from which a male might view these events—"Look!" as Ovid tells his readers—is quietly elided; it is a viewpoint that needs first correction and then silent elision, as being a perspective not so much dangerous to, but

21. The femaleness of the process of generation and culture imaged here finds an analogue in Titania's view of maternal generation in *Midsummer Night's Dream,* in which, as Louis Adrian Montrose describes it: "a biological genitor and social father play no role in the making of a child," ("The Cult of Elizabeth and the Sexual Politics of *Midsummer Night's Dream,*" a paper delivered at the conference "Renaissance Woman/Renaissance Man," Yale University, March 12–14, 1982). See Edgar Wind, *Pagan Mysteries in the Renaissance* (1958; rpt. Harmondsworth, Middlesex: Penguin Books, 1967), pp. 77–78, for a discussion of the cult of the virgin Elizabeth as a "cult of Venus in disguise."

potentially endangered by, the vision about to ensue. (An analogue
is the way Calidore's trespass on Colin's vision in Book VI causes
the evanescence of the vision of the Graces and the "hundred naked
maidens lily white / All raunged in a ring, and dauncing in delight"; it is something which Calidore finally admits, "I mote not
see.") Likewise, Chrysogone's mollifying bath, prefatory to her
impregnation, takes place "In a fresh fountaine, farre from all
mens vew"(III.vi.6).[22]

The unmentioned Actaeon myth subtly insinuates a warning
that the safest vantage point for viewing the cycles of death and
creation, and of the cosmic act of sexual intercourse played out in
the landscape of the garden, is that of Venus herself—that is, the
female perspective. From such a position there is no discomfort in
acknowledging Venus's awesome power over Adonis, by which she
makes safe his perpetual fatherhood. The vision of the garden's
landscape is a vision of the female body, focused specifically on the
"somewhat" that, in the *Mutability Cantos,* Faunus had seen and
sniggered at. Here the image of the Mount of Venus is offered not
merely to be translated into female genitalia—rather the genitalia
are features within the garden's landscape to metonymize the
power in which they participate—cosmic regeneration. Shakespeare's *Venus and Adonis* may offer an instructive contrast to Spenser's use of the anatomical landscape. In Shakespeare's version
Venus herself offers the garden as metaphor for her own body:

"Fondling," she said, "since I have hemm'd thee here
Within the circuit of this ivory pale,

22. While the phrase "farre from all mens vew" is, of course, formulaic, the
distinctly feminine context of the goddesses' meeting and the garden itself make the
phrase function as if gender-specific. Childbirth was not, in any event, something
males witnessed in the sixteenth century. In *Midwives and Medical Men* (New York:
Schocken Books, 1977), Jean Dennison describes the ruses men-midwives had to
resort to in order to enter the lying-in room undetected (men-midwives became
recognized in the early seventeenth century); Percival Willughby crawled into the
room on all fours in order to assist his daughter-midwife in a problem delivery (p.
11).

> I'll be a park, and thou shalt be my deer:
> Feed where thou wilt, on mountain or in dale;
>   Graze on my lips; and if those hills be dry,
>   Stray lower, where the pleasant fountains lie.
> "Within this limit is relief enough
> Sweet bottom-grass and high delightful plain,
> Round rising hillocks, brakes obscure and rough,
> To shelter thee from tempest and from rain;[23]

The salacious allure of this innuendo is posed by its invitation to translate different elements of the landscape into specific parts of the female body. Conversely, Spenser's landscape resists immediate one-for-one paraphrase:

> Right in the middest of that Paradise,
>   There stood a stately Mount, on whose round top
> A gloomy groue of mirtle trees did rise,
>   Whose shadie boughes sharpe steele did neuer lop,
>   Nor wicked beasts their tender buds did crop,
> But like a girlond compassed the hight,
>   And from their fruitfull sides sweet gum did drop,
> That all the ground with precious deaw bedight,
> Threw forth most dainty odours, and most sweet delight.
>   [III.vi.43]

As Isabel MacCaffrey notes, "this stanza is among other things a description of the Mount of Venus; but the erotic anatomical suggestion is undergirded by still deeper instincts and impulses." These impulses are served by Spenser's organizing the bower so that we do not have a sensation of "moving *up*" but "of coming into a small, protected, intimately enclosed space"; this movement, MacCaffrey explains, "probably satisfies an atavistic urge in all of us."[24]

> There wont faire *Venus* often to enjoy
>   Her dear *Adonis* ioyous company,
>   To reape sweet pleasure of the wanton boy;

---

23. *The Complete Plays and Poems of Shakespeare,* ed. William A. Nelson and Charles J. Hill (Boston: Houghton Mifflin, 1942), "Venus and Adonis," 229–40; p. 136.
    24. MacCaffrey, *Spenser's Allegory,* pp. 261–62.

> There yet, some say, in secret he does ly,
> Lapped in flowres and pretious spycery,
> By her hid from the world, and from the skill
> Of *Stygian* Gods, which doe her loue enuy;
> But she her selfe, when euer that she will,
> Possesseth him, and of his sweetnesse takes her fill.
> [III.vi.46]

The deepest and most atavistic urges satisfied by this landscape have, doubtless, to do with the desires involved in Venus's immense power, here essentially female—for her protection of Adonis is effected specifically by her power over the deepest point of this landscape, almost as if the cave beneath the mount were yet another image of the secret recess where Adonis lies "lapped" in spicery.[25] Venus provides Adonis his illogical subjection to mortality—while yet being "eterne in mutabilitie"—by means of her entrapment of the boar within the cave:

> There now he liueth in eternall blis,
> Ioying his goddesse, and of her enioyed:
> Ne feareth he henceforth that foe of his,
> Which with his cruell tuske him deadly cloyd:
> For that wild Bore, the which him once annoyd,
> She firmely hath emprisoned for ay,
> That her sweet loue his malice mote auoyd,
> In a strong rocky Caue, which is they say,
> Hewen vnderneath that Mount, that none him losen may.
>
> There now he liues in euerlasting ioy . . .
> [III.vi.48-49]

The location of the cave, along with confusions over who is everlastingly happy where (confusions caused by the ambiguous pronouns of the transition between stanzas), suggest that the anatomical allegory plays out in the landscape a female control over everlasting

---

25. Lauren Silberman describes the cave directly as the "vagina dentata, ultimate expression of Venus' fearsome power," in "Singing Unsung Heroines: Androgynous Discourse in Book II of *The Faerie Queene*," a paper delivered at the conference "Renaissance Woman/Renaissance Man," Yale University, March 12–14, 1982.

sexual communion. Of course, the boar "is" death: but, as Mac-Caffrey puts it, "the meekness and health of Adonis turn aside the wrath of fallen bestiality."[26] The boar therefore is a metonymy for fallen bestiality, which by its very name—"bore"—suggests the power of the male phallus. The boar's position within the land-scape, functioning now as if it were a synechdoche, connects it to the threatened dismemberment of Actaeon, passed over in the era-sure of that myth's presence from the text. Again, the most com-fortable and unthreatened viewpoint for reading the events of the garden is female. Thus the garden's eroticism should not be read as dismemberment, but as the mythic displacement of desire and as a vision of male sexuality brought safely and creatively under the control of an awesome female power. (In a sense, Adonis's position is merely Verdant's passivity seen from a different perspective—one that insists on the cosmic legitimacy of the female Eros's tri-umph over a male Thanatos.)

We should remember, too, that the forester who had threatened Florimell at the outset of Book III was threatening precisely because he wielded a "bore speare":

> Lo where a griesly Foster forth did rush
> Breathing out beastly lust her to defile:
> His tyreling iade he fiercely forth did push,
> Through thicke and thin, both ouer banke and bush
> In hope her to attaine by hooke or crooke,
> That from his gories sides the bloud did gush:
> Large were his limbes, and terrible his looke,
> And in his clownish hand *a sharp bore speare he shooke.*
> [III.i.17; emphasis added]

In the center of the book, this threatening force is controlled by being contained, not destroyed. Out of its containment come the creations of chaste love, of the perpetual successions imaged by Adonis's fatherhood in his rewritten myth, and of the generations

---

26. Greenblatt, *Renaissance Self-Fashioning,* p. 171, notes that the Garden of Adonis "has almost no erotic appeal." MacCaffrey also notes the greater "sen-sual" excitement of the Bower of Bliss episode—with its "mindless somatic responses"—over the garden's appeal (*Spenser's Allegory,* p. 258).

who, Merlin prophesies, will rise from Britomart's womb.[27] The
end of this prophecy is, of course, the birth of the royal virgin Elizabeth, whose chastity Book III praises. That the female power the
book does finally celebrate in the garden is a female power in conjunction with male sexuality (however disconnected from its social
role of dominance) suggests not only the compelling importance of
sexuality itself in Spenser's mythology, but the need to reintegrate
female sexual power into a structure that includes male potency.
Spenser may counsel his female readers to follow Belphoebe's example of virginity, but the chastity he truly extols is Amoret's: it is
the chastity not of a virgin queen, but of a wedded wife.

If the allegorical core to Book III, the Garden of Adonis, is a look
at female power from a peculiarly female perspective, the scene of
Britomart's rescue of Amoret is a scrutiny of female sexual fear,
seen again from a female vantage point. Spenser hints at the ex-
change of power for vulnerability when he says of Amoret at the end
of the Garden of Adonis canto that she was so well brought up there
that many a man found "His feeble hart wide launched with love's
cruell wound." It is, of course, not a male knight's but Amoret's
own heart that suffers the widely gaping, hideously sadistic wound
in Busyrane's masque in canto xii. In listing the dramatis personae
of this masque Spenser includes a signal remark:

> There were full many moe like maladies,
>   Whose names and natures I note reden well;
> So many moe, as there be phantasies
> In wauering wemens wit, that none can tell,
> Or paines in loue, or punishments in hell;
> All which disguized marcht in masking wise,
> About the chamber with that Damozell,
>   [III.xii.26]

The "fantasies" that Spenser does not read for us doubtless derive
from the figure of Danger in the *Roman de la rose*—a resource for
most of the rest of the masque—and image therefore a legitimate
female fear of sexuality, of the sort less easily dismissed in the first

27. For further discussion of the close connection between Britomart's sexuality
and the garden's, see my "Words and Sex," pp. 208-9.

vision of Florimell pursued by the forester. The sadomasochism of
the masque is troublesome because it is so relentless; if the twelfth
canto of Book II images a male pornographic fantasy (and response
to that fantasy), then canto xii of Book III may well be Spenser's
version of a female pornographic fantasy—such, at least, is suggested by the line about "wavering wemens wit." But Britomart's
response to this fantasy is not destruction, such as Guyon wreaks on
Acrasia's bower at the end of Book III. Instead we see a typical
response by female power to male violence very similar to that given
in the Garden of Adonis: containment. Busyrane's instrument of
torture is his lyric *pen,* and a profoundly reverberating pun on this
word insists on the sterile, prisonlike effect of his art. Thus when
Scudamour wails, "Why then is *Busirane* with wicked hand / Suffered, these seuen monethes day in secret den / My lady and my
loue so cruelly to *pen*" (III.xi.10), we see that the sadistic sonneteer
has written Amoret into an art that halts the flow of time, inscribing
it within an ecphrastic paralysis, an ever-dying, but never really
dead, death. In great part Spenser manages to correct this (male)
art by viewing it from the opposite perspective of the lady, who
usually merely peruses the lines of the poem. In the end, Britomart
makes Busyrane reverse his verses; but, restrained by Amoret, she
does not destroy him. Like the containment of the boar within the
cave beneath Venus's mount, Britomart's forcing Busyrane to rewrite his verses reveals female control over the phallic power punningly metonymized by these instruments of male aggression. But
here control is not, as it is at the close of Book II, pitiless oblitera-
tion. Amoret's wound is healed when Busyrane is made to chant his
backward spells:

> The cruell steele, which thrild her dying hart,
>   Fell softly forth, as of his owne accord,
>   And the wyde wound, which lately did dispart
>   Her bleeding brest, and riuen bowels gor'd,
>   Was closed vp, as it had not bene *bor'd,*
>   And euery part to safety full sound,
>   As she were neuer hurt, was soone restor'd:
>   Tho when she felt her selfe to be vnbound,
> And perfect *hole,* prostrate she fell vnto the ground.
>   [III.xii.38; emphasis added]

As Jonathan Goldberg points out, the problematic pun insists on the "full ambiguity of being rendered 'perfect hole.'"[28] The wound is healed but remains still the wound of desire—which Britomart shares with Amoret in her own double-wounding, first by Gardante and then by Busyrane. A final pun in the 1590 version of the close of Book III makes the paradox of the wound of love clearer. Britomart regards Amoret's and Scudamour's final embrace:

> Had ye them seene, ye would haue surely thought,
>   That they had beene that faire *Hermaphrodite,*
> Which that rich *Romane* of white marble wrought,
> And in his costly Bath caused to bee site:
> So seemd those two, as growne together quite,
>   That *Britomart* halfe enuying their *blesse,*
> Was much empassioned in her gentle sprite,
> And to her selfe oft wisht like happinesse,
> In vaine she wisht, that fate n'ould let her yet possesse.
>   [III.xii.46a]

Blesser, in French, is to wound; such wounding, a real anatomical event in sexual consummation, is bliss.

Book IV and the Failure of Orpheus

This vision of ultimate sexual consummation ending Book III—addressed in the plural "ye" to an audience fashioned in gentle discipline by having empathetically shared in the sexual experience of the "other"—stood for six years, only to be canceled by the appearance of the 1596 installment of *The Faerie Queene.* The necessity for this had doubtless many causes—the sheer need to generate more story one of them. The cancellation witnesses allegory's generic tendency toward constant revision of threshold texts and pretexts.[29] But because dropping the vision of the hermaphrodite embrace is one of the most radical revisings in the poem, we would do well to question Spenser's rationale for so complete an excision.

28. Goldberg, *Endlesse Worke,* p. 78.
29. See my *Language of Allegory,* pp. 45–47, 81–85.

Surely one reason for the cancellation has something to do with the response the poem had received during the six years between publication of the first and second installments. And it is the negative reaction of certain readers that Spenser specifically addresses in the proem to Book IV. There we see something odd occur: a change in Spenser's own stated view of his audience. The proem to Book IV turns into Spenser's statement about his fit audience though few:

> The rugged forhead that with graue foresight
>   Welds kingdomes causes, and affaires of state,
>   My looser rimes (I wote) doth sharply wite,
>   For praising loue, as I haue done of late,
>   And magnifying louers deare debate.
>   [IV.Proem.1]

This critical statesman is almost assuredly Burleigh, as many have suggested;[30] the character painted here accords well with the nature of the man Spenser had addressed in his dedicatory sonnet to Burleigh appended to the 1590 *Faerie Queene* (where "graue" also predominates). Even then Spenser was worrying about Burleigh's "censure graue" and offering as protection against it the traditional defense of allegory:

> Yet if their deeper sence be inly wayd,
>   And the dim vele, with which from commune vew
>   Their fairer parts are hid, aside be layd.
>   Perhaps not vaine they may appeare to you.

But the reader whom Spenser censures in the proem to IV is not one who has failed to understand the nature of the allegory—it is one who is incapable of feeling love: "Such ones ill iudge of loue, that cannot loue, / Ne in their frosen hearts feele kindly flame." Perhaps more significantly, the censured reader is a traditionalist who appears to have argued that love is not a fit subject for an imperial epic:

---

30. See Paul J. Alpers, *The Poetry of The Faerie Queene* (Princeton: Princeton University Press, 1967), pp. 281–82; Cain, *Praise in The Faerie Queene,* p. 104.

Which who so list looke backe to former ages,
And call to count the things that then were donne,
Shall find, that all the workes of those wise sages,
And braue exploits which great Heroes wonne,
In loue were either ended or begonne.

[IV.Proem.3]

Defiantly, Spenser dismisses this censuring reader and chooses
another:

To such therefore I do not sing at all,
But to that sacred Saint my soueraigne Queene,
. . . .
To her I singe of loue, that loueth best,
And best is lou'd of all aliue I weene:
To her this song most fitly is addrest,
The Queene of loue, and Prince of peace from heauen blest.

[IV.Proem.4]

In fact, what Spenser does in this proem is to dismiss a male reader,
select a paradigmatic female one, and then reconstitute the canceled full-gendered readership (as imaged in the closing embrace of
Amoret and Scudamour) within the "androgynous" queen—who
is both queen of love and prince of peace.[31] The argument of the
proem suggests that Book III was the cause of the negative response
that the first installment received; only there is lovers' dear debate
magnified.[32] Spenser's censure of a male reader's reading of Book
III suggests the real risk he took in writing for his female reader as
he had in Book III. The only solution available to him appears to be
to privilege that readership again, explicitly.

However, the position of the queen in this proem is radically altered from her place in the first three proems of the first installment.

31. I am indebted to Barbara Roche Rico for first suggesting this point to me.
32. Cain notes, p. 104, that many assumed Burleigh took the hermaphrodite
image to be pornographic. Cain interestingly argues for a political rather than sexual objection (if the two are to be distinguished in Elizabethan diplomacy). Thus the
Busyrane episode shadows and criticizes the Alençon match, which Burleigh had
supported. That the fracas over the Alençon match was a good ten years old by the
time Book III was published may not detract from this thesis entirely, especially in
view of our ignorance of Spenser's chronology of composition.

There she functions much as a muse inspiring the poet (Book I), or as a poetic subject (Book II), or as sovereign queen (Book III). In all these proems, moreover, the queen is addressed directly in the second person. Strikingly, in the proem to Book IV she has been moved back into the third person; the poet tells another reader that he sings to the queen. Elizabeth now is uniquely a reader, not a muse or poetic subject, and the poet's request for inspiration is not that he may sing her praises (so far beyond his afflicted style); instead, he prays to Cupid to make her an inspired reader:

> Which that she may the better deigne to heare,
>   Do thou dred infant, *Venus* dearling doue,
>   From her high spirit chase imperious feare,
>   And vse of awfull Maiestie remoue:
>   In sted thereof with drops of melting loue,
>   Deawd with ambrosiall kisses, by thee gotten
>   From thy sweete smyling mother from aboue,
>   Sprinckle her heart, and haughtie courage soften,
> That she may hearke to loue, and reade this lesson often.
>   [IV.Proem.5]

There could be no better indication of how important the reader's inspiration is in reading an allegory than this prayer to Cupid not to inspire the poet to write, but to inspire the queen to read. Doubtless the historical cause of the abyss we see opened here between the poet and his patroness has something to do with Ralegh—Spenser's presenter at court in 1590, himself a poet who shares the honors of the proem to Book III, and the shadow behind the Timias-Belphoebe misunderstandings played out in cantos vii and viii of Book IV (where a turtledove—like Venus's darling dove of the proem—effects a reconciliation). But whatever the causes, we see Spenser's later verse (especially *Colin Clouts Come Home Againe,* written in 1591 and dedicated to Ralegh, but not published until 1595) marked by increasing criticism of the mystifications of court mythology.

The virtues under scrutiny in the last three books of *The Faerie Queene* are not the "private" ones of the first installment but "public." And in the fifth book in particular we see Spenser's critical appraisal of contemporary English politics, more explicitly present in the poem than they have been before. This distinction between "private" and "public" virtues is Spenser's own, of course, part of his plan from the first, as described in the "Letter to Ralegh" (though the public virtues were to have been a separate twelve-book epic unto themselves). But the publicness of the second installment may be not so much an anticipation of the original plan as a result of the poem's own recent publicness, that is, its publication—the intrapsychic dynamics of the first installment's narrative become overtly political, as Spenser responds to the response the poem received.

We have just seen the subtle shift in the way the poem locates itself in relationship to its first reader—the queen—now insistently divorced from (but thereby placed within) an explicit political context (the realm of he who wields "affairs of state"). The "Letter to Ralegh" was canceled. And the cancellation of the hermaphrodite image would also suggest that the gynandromorphic flexibility that Spenser had asked of his readers in Book III would be canceled as well. The methods of the allegory in IV–VI are very different: the density of wordplay, so important to Spenser's accretion of meaning, thins out in the later installments (though it is, to be sure, still present). Indeed, Spenser's entire allegorical program suffers a subtle sea-change. This should not, however, be surprising. A poem aimed so directly at its readers would need to change its rhetoric had the desired response not been forthcoming—as the tone of the proem to IV so strongly insists did in fact happen.

We may sense the nature of the revisionary gestures of Book IV by noticing that Amoret's story begins, in Book III, in a rewritten text of Orpheus's, for it is Orpheus who sings the story of Venus and Adonis in the *Metamorphoses*. Rewriting Orpheus's story to his own purposes, Spenser denies the metamorphosis of Adonis (just as he denies Actaeon's transformation in the *Mutability Cantos*). As we saw, Spenser began his epic with a subtle indication that he hoped to be a different kind of poet from Orpheus, one who would successfully lead his reader out of the hellish wood of Errour. The process would not be simple, but given the grace of revelation, it would succeed. By canto x of Book IV, however, we find Spenser's narrative suffering a failure like Orpheus's. There Scudamour tells of his own capture of Amoret, prior to Busyrane's kidnapping of her on their wedding day. (This was new information, lacking during the six years between the two installments.) The knight ends his story of conquest by making a very dubious comparison—dubious because it tends to throw his whole discourse into doubt.

> No less did *Daunger* threaten me with dread,
>   When as he saw me, maugre all his powre,
>   That glorious spoyle of beautie with me lead,
>   Then *Cerberus*, when *Orpheus* did recoure
>   His Leman from the Stygian Princes boure.
>   But euermore my shield did me defend,
>   Against the storme of euery dreadfull stoure:
>   Thus safely with my loue I thence did wend.
> So ended he his tale, where I this Canto end.
>   [IV.x.58]

Here in the one perfect, closed ending to a canto among the otherwise loose and open-ended closings of all (save one) of the other cantos in the book, Spenser appears to conflate his own voice with Scudamour's; yet if Scudamour is unaware of the irony of this reference to Orpheus, Spenser is not. The irony seems designed to deflate Scudamour's claim about being a good husband—and serves to remind us of his former incapacity to penetrate the flames surrounding Busyrane's palace (Orpheus's failure had been read as an excess of passion). Wishing to disarm the irony of the reference to Orpheus, MacCaffrey argues that in Book IV, Orpheus is "connected with another range of meanings, the power of Concord and her human instruments"; therefore, the reference to Orpheus notwithstanding, Scudamour's triumph at the Temple takes its place alongside the unions of Britomart and Artegall, Belphoebe and Timias, Florimell and Marinell, and the wedding of the Thames and Medway.[33] The problem with this equation is that we do in fact see the other unions brought to successful (if, in the case of Florimell

33. MacCaffrey, *Spenser's Allegory*, pp. 327–28.

and Marinell, belated) conclusions; the union of Scudamour and Amoret would indeed be like these were we allowed to forget Scudamour's loss of her. But we are not. Scudamour's comparison of Orpheus's lack of dread to his own insists upon that loss most particularly, for Cerberus is not mentioned in the *Metamorphoses* until after Orpheus has already lost Eurydice.

> The double death
> Stunned Orpheus, like the man who turned to stone
> At sight of Cerberus, or the couple of rock,
> Oleonos and Letheaea, hearts so joined
> One shared the other's guilt, and Ida's mountain,
> Where rivers run, still holds them, both together.[34]

Spenser himself has just lost Amoret moments before Scudamour begins his narration in one of the more frustrating narrative dissolves in the whole poem. Thus at stanza 17 of canto ix, Prince Arthur has Amoret well in hand—"safe as in a Sanctuary" (ix.19); yet at stanza 36 when he composes the strife among Britomart, Scudamour, and four attacking knights, Amoret has unaccountably disappeared: Scudamour and Britomart vie in lamenting her loss (38). Amoret's story has been rewritten in Book IV to mark an absolute loss. From having begun her story by rewriting Orpheus's story of Venus and Adonis in Book III, Spenser ends it by confessing a shared failure with the pagan poet. Amoret will always be lost, never brought out from the peculiar hells of sexual desire, from which at the end of Book III she had been momentarily extricated. If, in fact, Spenser did intend the tree catalogue in the Wood of Errour in Book I to be a challenge to Orphic poetry, then we must see how far short of the mark he judges himself to have come. Orpheus may indeed share with David and Meneius Agrippa the "godlike" powers of taming passion (IV.ii.2). Yet in rewriting his own text of the canceled hermaphrodite (reconstituted yet again in the narrative as the statue of Venus in canto ix), Spenser resubjects

34. Ovid, *Metamorphoses,* trans. Rolfe Humphries (Bloomington: Indiana University Press, 1955), p. 236.

Amoret to loss.[35] His voice, insofar as it elides into Scudamour's (and Orpheus's) cannot save her. Spenser cannot sing "With other notes than to the Orphean lyre."

Because Orpheus is a poet of such marked interest for Milton as well as for Spenser, it will be useful to consider for a moment the particular sexual dynamic that the mythic poet's career embodies. For both English poets his story figures the female threat to male poetic inspiration. After having lost Eurydice in a second death, Orpheus, Ovid tells us, turns to the love of boys; he then sings and summons the trees. The content of that singing is given in the tales of the rest of Book X of the *Metamorphoses:* Cyparissus, Ganymede, Apollo and Hyacinth, Pygmalion, Cinyras and Myrrha, and Venus and Adonis—in the middle of which is interpolated the story of Atalanta, told by Venus. Book XI then opens with the story of Orpheus's murder by the crazed maenads whose clamor drowns out the sounds of his magical, metamorphosing music. The maenads then dismember him. Finally Bacchus punishes these Thracian women by transforming them into rooted trees.

In the context of his entire career as recounted in the *Metamorphoses,* Orpheus becomes less the poet of concord—that power he demonstrates by swaying all the underworld to grant his request of Eurydice—than of husbandly love poetry, bizarrely at odds with the forces within ecstatic female worship. In this, he is as germane to Milton as to Spenser. In the tension between husbandly love and its implicit antagonism to women (as played out in Ovid's text), we can see a conflict present in the context of Scudamour's narration. Moments before Scudamour launches into his story of conquest, Arthur lectures the assembled knights on the chivalric franchise granted to women "that of their loues choice they might freedom clame / And in that right should by all knights be shielded" (IV.xi.37). Yet Scudamour tells his tale to assert his own right: "Certes her losse ought me to sorrow most / Whose right she is,

35. For another discussion of the differences between III and IV and the refiguring of the loss of Amoret, see Goldberg, *Endlesse Worke,* p. 79: "The crucial difference is the removal of the concept of singularity which seemed central to III. . . . Otherness is, with book IV, before us."

where euer she be straide" (IV.xi.38). Freedom's rights are in conflict:

> She often prayd, and often me besought,
>   Sometimes with tender teares to let her goe,
>   Sometimes with witching smyles: but yet for nought,
>   That euer she to me could say or doe,
>   Could she her wished freedome fro me wooe;
>   [IV.x.57]

There is much to be said in explication of Amoret's coy, reluctant, amorous delay here; it is proper and fitting virginal behavior; neither, doubtless, is Scudamour's exertion of gentle power wrong. What seems to be at issue is the conflict within the terms of chivalric love—those pronounced by Arthur about ladies' undeniable rights, and those rights granted by conquest. (They have persistently dogged the comedy of Amoret's travels with the disguised Britomart.) In this we may be being asked to consider how well Scudamour has understood the first part of the text he reads so carefully at the outset of his adventure in the Temple of Venus:

> *Blessed the man that well can vse his blis:*
> *Whose euer be the shield, faire Amoret be his.*
>   [IV.x.8]

There is something more to love than the lady's faithful chastity (of which Scudamour finally has no doubts). Love fails and Amoret is lost in a fatal misuse of bliss.[36]

What we are left with is a desire for the canceled text of the 1590 ending, a desire that Spenser satisfies with illusory substitutions. The narrative unfolds as before with massive inventiveness but with less and less faith that conclusions can be reached. Like the cancellation of the happy ending to Amoret's story, the cancellation

---

36. Alice S. Miskimin, *The Renaissance Chaucer* (New Haven: Yale University Press, 1975), p. 153, discusses Boethius's use of the Orpheus myth as an investigation into the "antithetical necessity" of love's power for cosmic harmony: "the devouring passion and self-destroying power latent in creation itself."

of the "Letter to Ralegh" suggests an entire reorientation of Spenser's initial program in the face of hard political realities. (The hardest being, no doubt, that Spenser did not win the privileged place at court to which he aspired.) The way the second installment incorporates these political realities into its texts demonstrates Spenser's abiding interest in his audience. The response of that audience becomes, in fact, part of the poem's subject, not merely in the proem to Book IV but at certain key moments throughout the narrative. One thinks of the position of the poet at Mercilla's palace, with his tongue nailed to a post. A more subtle moment is Calidore's trespass on Colin's vision of the graces on Mount Acidale in Book VI. As I have argued elsewhere, allegory more than most genres needs to posit its ideal readers; in the scene staging the poet's vision of his own inspiration, Spenser anatomizes the processes of bad reading, and of the political forces that cause it. Calidore finally admits that the vision of the Graces is something "I mote not see"—and in his misvision, he participates in the invidious detractions that will become forces so powerful, Spenser fears they will rend his own poem. The position of the queen, so closely tied to the position of the reader in the canceled "Letter," is to be displaced even further from her location at the center—removed explicitly in Colin's praise of his own country lass. So displaced is she that Thomas Cain argues that Spenser has nearly executed "an about-face" toward her as an encomiastic subject, turning praise of Elizabeth into blame.[37] If Cain is right in associating the figure of Orpheus in particular with the program of encomium which Spenser undertook in the poem, he is surely right to insist on the remarkable "self mutilation" of the last lines of the poem, where Spenser counsels his epic merely to please, no more to attempt to fashion his reader. In a sense, Spenser had already mutilated *The Faerie Queene* by rewriting the ending of Book III. Spenser as Orpheus fails, however, not because he could not lead his Eurydice out of hell, but because some of his readers would not leave the Wood of Errour.

37. Cain, *Praise*, p. 185.

Book III of *The Faerie Queene* and Milton's *Comus*

Milton also rewrote canto xii of The Legend of Chastity, and it is one of the neater paradoxes of the relations between these two poets that in *Comus,* Spenser's voice *is* able to save the heroine. Busyrane had tortured Amoret not only by forcing her to serve as the centerpiece in the masque (viewed by Britomart on her first day in the palace), he had chained her to a brazen pillar while he wrote "strange characters" with her heart's blood.

A thousand charmes he formerly did proue;
Yet thousand charmes could not her stedfast heart remoue.
[III.xii.31]

Although he had literally removed her heart from her chest cavity, Busyrane could not enforce a more internal transformation. So, too, when Comus threatens to paralyze the Lady in *Comus,* she specifies the limits of his magic transformations:

Comus. Nay lady sit; if I but wave this wand,
Your nerves are all chained up in alabaster,
And you a statue, or as Daphne was
Root-bound, that fled Apollo,
Lady. Fool do not boast,
Thou canst not touch the freedom of my mind
With all thy charms, although this corporal rind
Thou hast immanacled, while heaven sees good.
[658-664][38]

As the Lady is speaking these lines, she is immanacled, paralyzed in her seat, glued to it "with gums of glutinous heat."

Milton's disputants soon reach an impasse when the Lady's rhetoric rises to a climax just as the dramatic climax (the entry of the brothers and Attendant Spirit) approaches. In burning indignation

---

38. *Milton: Complete Shorter Poems,* ed. John Carey (London: Longman, 1971); hereafter cited in the text.

the Lady claims that were she to call on it, she has the power to free herself:

> Thou art not fit to hear thyself convinced;
> Yet should I try, the uncontrolled worth
> Of this pure cause would kindle my rapt spirits
> To such a flame of sacred vehemence,
> That dumb things would be moved to sympathize,
> And the brute Earth would lend her nerves, and shake,
> Till all thy magic structures reared so high,
> Were shattered into heaps o'er thy false head.
>
> [791–98]

Just so, Britomart had felt Busyrane's palace shake and the brazen pillar break "in pieces small" and had seen the opulent anterooms vanished; yet this happens only after the unsaying of Busyrane's charms: Comus fears a magic greater than the mere undoing of his own.

> *Comus.* She fables not, I feel that I do fear
> Her words set off by some superior power;
> And though not mortal, yet a cold shuddering dew
> Dips me all o'er, as when the wrath of Jove
> Speaks thunder, and the chains of Erebus
> To some of Saturn's crew. I must dissemble,
>
> [799–804]

Dismissing her real claim to a real power with one of Milton's most wonderfully bathetic lines—"Come, no more, / This is mere moral babble"—Comus finally tempts the Lady with the words Satan will later use to a very different heroine: "Be wise and taste. . . ." Immediately the brothers rush in "with swords drawn," and Comus and his crew are routed.

The Lady is unique in Milton's canon in being a female who could potentially call upon the higher power that so frightens Comus; she threatens an eloquence so inspired with divine fury that it could simply erase Comus's magic. The reference to Jove's thunder and the imprisonment of the Titans, though protected by the pagan vocabulary, clearly indicates the sacred source. Were she to unleash it, her power of eloquence would have more potency than that of Orpheus—for he could only tame the spirits of the underworld, and of beasts and trees (such as that into which Daphne was transformed), while her language would not only call down the superior power, it would be that power. But she does not speak. She says not another word throughout the rest of the masque. Instead, Spenserian voices sweep in to rescue the Lady, who is now powerless to save herself. In Milton's deferral of the voice of "some superior power" and his substitution of Spenser's voice for it, we see how Spenser is made to serve the same purpose of protection which he later serves in *Paradise Lost*. [39] Here Spenser's presence provides limit markers, transitional characters, which hold together the human artistry too easily shattered by the divine power. Thus when the Attendant Spirit enters, he enters to suggest two Spenserian solutions to the problem which will have the effect of freeing the Lady without recourse to the power she herself felt she could call upon. He explains that the brothers erred when they let the "enchanter" escape, for they failed to confiscate his magic wand.

> O ye mistook, ye should have snatched his wand
> And bound him fast; without his rod reversed,
> And backward mutters of dissevering power,
> We cannot free the Lady that sits here
> In stony fetters fixed, and motionless:
>
> [814–18]

The "reversal" of the rod is not merely Spenser's gesture, for in Book XIV of the *Metamorphoses,* Acaemenides explains how he was released from Circe's metamorphosis when she reversed her rod and tapped his head. Britomart, of course, forces Busyrane to reverse his charms, to "rehearse" the bloody lines he had written with Amoret's heart's blood (stressing this connection, Milton's earlier Trinity manuscript version has "art" for "rod"). Failing this method, the Attendant Spirit elects an even more explicitly Spen-

---

39. For a different argument about Spenser's relation to the Lady's silence, to which my own is deeply indebted, see Guillory's illuminating exposition in *Poetic Authority,* pp. 133–35.

serian manner of rescue, alluding to him in the person of Meli-
boeus, and retelling the story of Sabrina which Spenser tells in Book
II, with a further reprise (significantly altered) of the Garden of
Adonis.

In order to understand the kind of service Spenser provides
Milton in *Comus*'s sexual mythology, we need to consider briefly the
other Elizabethan voice present in the masque. As Angus Fletcher
argues:

> Although much has been made in literary histories of the link be-
> tween Milton and Spenser, we need to insist on the relative unim-
> portance of this link. Milton was not unduly perturbed, surely, by
> the example of *The Faerie Queene*. Milton perceived the problem of
> being Milton: it was that he came after Shakespeare.[40]

Seeing an antithesis between the twin influences of Spenser and
Shakespeare, Fletcher concludes that "if Spenser embodies the allegorical mode and Shakespeare the mimetic, the merging of these
two modalities in a single large work like *Paradise Lost* will have both
the transcendentalism of texture that we expect of allegory and the
containment of this-worldly things that we expect in mimesis" (p.
143). As useful as this summation is, its positing a dichotomy between Spenser's allegory and Shakespeare's mimesis should not be
allowed to obscure our view of their common function for Milton.
What they have in common is that they were both *Elizabethan* poets;
in being so, they both necessarily address not merely the question of
married chastity, but the politically loaded issue of virginity—an
issue that was, of course, of great interest to Milton.

The Shakespeare play that stands most squarely behind *Comus* is
A Midsummer Night's Dream—a play that was, in fact, transformed
by Dryden and Purcell into *The Fairy Queen*. As this metamorphosis
neatly hints, *Midsummer Night's Dream* has close affinities to Spenser's *Faerie Queene*, not because they share relations of source, but
because of their similar social and political situation. Both play and
epic speak to the problematic power of Queen Elizabeth's virginity.
The queen is culturally omnipresent in both texts.

40. Angus Fletcher, *The Transcendental Masque: An Essay on Milton's Comus* (Ithaca, N.Y.: Cornell University Press, 1971), pp. 142–43.

Elizabeth I's virginity was a political act. By means of it she retained her rule; as she said early in her reign, she would have "no master." It was also the basis of her diplomatic maneuvering in the early decades of her reign, as she notoriously played the international marriage market for all it was worth. Her virginity was a crucial political fact in the later decades of the reign because she had produced no heir: the succession was unclear. Her masterful manipulation of her status as virgin transformed her absolutist political power into the socially more acceptable myth of chivalric love: if she belonged to no man, she was free to be wooed by all and no man need call his scramble for political preferment by its real name because it could be called love. The queen profited by this mystification, for she need not call her rule political domination, but loving care of her people. And so she did, in speech after speech, throughout her reign.[41]

The intricacies of the manipulation of this mythology (and its impact on the literature of the period) may be sensed in the brief example of the entertainment provided Elizabeth at Sudely in 1591: in it the queen's virginity is a source of magical potency (much like Sabrina's in *Comus*). Fleeing Apollo, Daphne runs to the queen, who overrules Apollo and gives the chaste nymph sanctuary. As Louis Adrian Montrose remarks, "The Queen's virtuous magic derives from a kind of matriarchal virginity."[42] Nicely revealing the kind of court mythology among which *The Faerie Queene* was to have taken its place, the entertainment illuminates the reversal of the queen's magic in *Midsummer Night's Dream,* when Oberon rights the imbalance of things caused by Helena's pursuit of Demetrius: "Now Apollo flies, and Daphne holds the chase." This is not to suggest that the entertainment—published after the event and so in the public domain—influenced Shakespeare (or Milton) directly,

41. Perry Anderson, *Lineages of the Absolutist State* (London: NLB Press, 1974), p. 128, notes that even without any institutional changes, the absolutist authority of the sovereign increased under Elizabeth as a result of her "personal popularity"; he does not query the underlying manipulations of sexual ideology that formed the basis of her appeal, the notion of sexuality as a political issue being absent from his theoretical categories.

42. Louis Adrian Montrose, " 'Eliza, Queene of Shepheardes,' and the Pastoral of Power," *English Literary Renaissance* 10 (1980), 172–73.

but that it reveals the dynamics of power implicit in Elizabeth's "magical" chastity, which itself left its trace on the texts produced during her reign.

Fletcher argues that Milton appropriates the complexities of *Measure for Measure* in a single word (the word is "viewless"); and this play too may have been marked by the (now) absent virgin queen.[43] But because *Midsummer Night's Dream* makes more overt use of Elizabethan court mythology, it is the more useful text in which to look for that treatment of Elizabeth's presence which may have affected Milton's own mythologizing of the Elizabethans.[44]

The direct reference to Elizabeth in *Midsummer Night's Dream* is Oberon's description of the "imperial vot'ress" he once saw when he beheld (in a neat reversal of Spenser's prayer to Cupid to "sprinckle" "drops of melting loue" on Elizabeth's "imperious" and "awfull Maiestie"):

> Flying between the cold moon and the earth
> Cupid all arm'd. A certain aim he took
> At a fair vestal, throned by the west,
> And loos'd his love-shaft smartly from his bow
> As it should pierce a hundred thousand hearts.
> But I might see young Cupid's fiery shaft
> Quench'd in the chaste beams of the watery moon:
> And the imperial vot'ress passed on,
> In maiden meditation, fancy free.
> Yet mark'd I where the bolt of Cupid fell.
> It fell upon a little western flower,
> Before milk-white, now purple with love's wound.
> [II.i.156–67]

Deflected from the imperial votaress, the shaft of Cupid falling upon the flower gives it the wound of erotic violence which the imperial virgin escapes, but which the other women in the play (and

43. Fletcher, *Transcendental Masque*, pp. 204–9.

44. Montrose usefully argues that Elizabeth need not have been physically present at the play's performance in order for her cultural "presence" to have made itself felt in the play's production ("The Cult of Elizabeth and the Sexual Politics of *A Midsummer Night's Dream*," a paper delivered at the conference on "Renaissance Woman/Renaissance Man," Yale University, March 12–14, 1982).

Britomart and Amoret before them) suffer so profoundly. Free in her royal impregnability, the votaress yet ironically allows Oberon the power to manipulate the flower's magic. As Montrose puts it, "The vestal's freedom from fancy guarantees the subjection of others. She is at once excluded from the erotic world of the play and its efficient cause." Elizabeth's virgin power is thus complimented by putting it in a position that continues to ratify the sexual hierarchy of the patriarchy.

What is perhaps more pertinent to Milton's interest in virginity in *Comus,* however, is the passage immediately preceding Oberon's description of the votaress. He reminds Puck of the time in which he saw this vision by recalling the moment when a maiden sat upon a dolphin's back and sang:

> Uttering such dulcet and harmonious breath
> That the rude sea grew civil at her song,
> And certain stars shot madly from their spheres,
> To hear the sea-maid's music . . .
>
> [II.i.151–54]

A female Arion, this maiden's song has the same cosmic power with which Milton's Lady threatens Comus. These two visions of maiden potency—the votaress's freedom in meditation and the mermaid's powerful song—Oberon calls up to explain the revenge he will take on Titania (smearing her eyes with the flower's juice and making her go mad with love), revenge that will allow him to snatch back the changeling boy and reassert the prerogatives of patrimony. These visions of female power and Oberon's response to them are indications of the larger cultural conflicts played out in the structure of the drama: Theseus's conquest of the Amazon Hippolyta, Oberon's "pacification" of Titania, and the proper rearrangement of the love pursuits by the young people in the forest, not female pursuing male, but the reverse. A reassertion of patriarchal relations.

Theseus's appropriation of paradigmatic princeliness owes much to Elizabeth's example; thus when he explains how to exercise noblesse oblige to Hippolyta, he recalls a famous episode of Elizabeth's early career when she had managed a fearful schoolmaster by telling him before he began: "Be not afrayde," hushing three French diplomats and assorted English lords, and complimenting him afterward: "It is the best that ever I heard."[45] The play that the mechanicals perform is one that obliging Theseus selects from a list that offers other, extremely interesting, candidates, among which is:

"The riot of the tipsy Bacchanals,
Tearing the Thracian singer in their rage."
[V.i.48–49]

This Theuseus rejects as "An old device," and, surprisingly enough, it had been considered an appropriate subject for an epithalamium.[46] The play finally performed by Bottom's crew, if only through inadvertency, has more appropriate bearing on the reorientation of sexual power in the play than Orpheus's dismemberment would have. Thus Pyramus laments not the death of Thisby, but her sexual initiation: "O wherefore, Nature, didst thou lions frame? / Since lion vile hath here deflow'red my dear." Hilarious as this is, it is also apt.

When Milton sounds his final echo of *Midsummer Night's Dream* in the epilogue to *Comus,* he remembers the moment of conflict between Oberon and Titania, fairy patriarch and would-be fairy matriarch. In the epilogue the Spirit sings:

Where young Adonis oft reposes,
Waxing well of his deep wound
In slumber soft, and on the ground
Sadly sits the Assyrian queen;
But far above in spangled sheen
Celestial Cupid her famed son advanced,
Holds his dear Psyche sweet entranced
After her wandering labours long,
[998–1004]

45. John Nichols, *The Progresses and Public Processions of Queen Elizabeth,* 3 vols. (1823; rpt. New York: Burt Franklin, n.d., II, 155–59.
46. Elizabeth Basset Welles argues that Poliziano's *Orpheo* (1480) was written for a betrothal (unpublished essay); see B. G. Picotti, "Sulla data dell' Orpheo e delle Stanze," *Ricerche umanistiche* (Florence: La Nuova Italia, 1955).

Milton's "spangled sheen" remembers Puck's description of the
conflicts between Titania and Oberon:

> And now they never meet in grove or green,
> By fountain clear, or spangled starlight sheen,
> But they do square.
>
> [II.i.28-30]

It has been remarked that the reference to Venus and Adonis is
a reference to another "failed" seduction—but it is, of course, a
seduction of a man by a woman. We might well ask why Milton's Venus sits sadly, when Adonis appears in fact to be, as in Spenser's rewriting of the Ovidian myth, waxing well of his wound?
Psyche's entrancement by Cupid, if it is a legitimate reprise of
the Lady's seduction, here is translated to a stellar sphere where
a female's submission to a male lover is ratified by higher power
than we find in the earthly place where the Assyrian queen sadly
sits. The epilogue gently reverses the sexual powers played out in
the masque proper; the Lady's virginity would give her the power
to destroy Comus were she to speak, but she does not. The songs
that are sung at the end imply that the Lady's virginity is not a final
state; she will lose her virginity and thus her power to sing.

Virginity was for Milton a compelling state in which to figure
forth the power of direct inspiration from God.[47] Chastity being a
traditional female virtue (though Milton, rather uniquely of
course, thought it even more praiseworthy in men), and the occa-
sion of the masque itself dictating the sex of his protagonists, it is
only logical that the hero of the masque be a female virgin. But in
the last analysis she is a troublesome character in which to figure
forth Milton's own ability to be inspired by "some superior

47. Christopher Kendrick, "Milton: A Study in Ideology and Form" (Ph.D.
diss., Yale University, 1981), suggests the implications of virginity for Milton's
inspiration: "The myth, latent in Milton's early chastity fetish, of organic poetry, of
a poetry attached to the poet's bodily state as if by an umbilical cord, is primarily an
Arminian, willful myth, a poetic of total responsibility and control" (p. 17). This
overstates, I think, Milton's sense of his control—*God* chooses *him*—but it does
admirably connect the issues of physical sexuality and poetic inspiration evident in
the poetry and the life.

power." The paradox of his sweeping aside the Lady's voice in favor of Spenser's virgin's song is that this move leads him to select another song sung to a powerful virgin and a plot situation (though not the details, which, if taken from a Spenserian text, are from Book II of *The Faerie Queene*) that insists upon a female's power over demonic magic—but of course, in being Spenserian, that power is framed within the limits of fiction. As a virgin the Lady will suit perfectly the situation of Milton's inspiration; but as female she is wrong. This is not to suggest that Milton did not in fact believe women capable of inspired singing—his sonnets to Leonora Baroni are proof against such a simplified stance—but that the Lady's gender made her profoundly inappropriate for figuring his own poetic powers. As the echo of Shakespeare's "spangled starlight sheen" subtly indicates, Milton needs to rectify the relations between the sexes before he will be able to sing the true song, in which his words will be "set off by some superior power."

The Gender of Milton's Muse and the Problem of the Fit Reader

If we turn now to that superior song and look at one of Milton's invocations in *Paradise Lost,* we shall see how he confronts the problems of the gender of inspiration and the concomitant problem of his reader's gender. In Book VII Milton invokes his muse for the first time by a specific name—Urania—and for the first time explicitly indicates that the Muse can be figured forth as female in gender.[48] Embedded within this invocation is Milton's most famous remark about his readership; it is important to look closely at the interconnections between the source of his inspiration and his fears about his audience. After naming Urania, he makes a request:

48. In Book I, Milton invokes a double-gendered Spirit, who "with mighty wings outspread / Dove-like sat'st brooding on the vast abyss / And madest it pregnant" (I.20–22). The Invocation to III, insofar as it associates the Holy Light with the Son/sun (potentially distinct from the Muse), would appear to address a more specifically masculine source of inspiration. However, guessing the genders to the first two invocations is not as important as sensing the peculiar impact of Milton's directly assigning one in Book VII.

Return me to my native element:
Lest from this flying steed unreined, (as once
Bellerophon, though from a lower clime)
Dismounted, on the Aleian field I fall
Erroneous there to wander and forlorn.
Half yet remains unsung, but narrower bound
Within the visible diurnal sphere;
Standing on earth, not rapt above the pole,
More safe I sing with mortal voice, unchanged
To hoarse or mute, though fallen on evil days,
On evil days though fallen, and evil tongues;
In darkness, and with dangers compassed round,
And solitude; yet not alone, while thou
Visit'st my slumbers nightly, or when morn
Purples the east: still govern thou my song,
Urania, and fit audience find, though few.
[VII.16–31]

There is a special relevance to the gender of the Muse in Book VII, for the book sings the story of creation, of the birth of the earth, the poet's "native" element, in terms of a cosmic femaleness: the earth is female, the light itself is female, the waters themselves a womb, and out of earth's womb come all the other creatures—so that on the sixth day "earth in her rich attire / Consummate lovely smiled" (501–2).[49] Out of a female entity comes a male creature and then a female: thus the female light is born before the male sun, whose light is refracted by the female moon, and the female earth gives birth to the two gendered animals. Only with the creation of Adam is this pattern reversed:

Male he created thee, but thy consort
Female for race;
[VII.529–30]

In the first two invocations, the poet asks for aid in singing his song and for protection against the dangerous ineffabilities he courts in its very singing; in Book VII Milton turns to consider the dangers

49. J. H. Summers, *Muse's Method: An Introduction to Paradise Lost* (Cambridge, Mass.: Harvard University Press, 1970), p. 88, notes that "Milton 'realized' his divine and all-embracing subject more often by sexual than merely sensuous metaphor and allusion."

posed him by his audience. The danger is posed by a force that is, like the inspirational source, peculiarly female:

> But drive far off the barbarous dissonance
> Of Bacchus and his revellers, the race
> Of that wild rout that tore the Thracian bard
> In Rhodope, where woods and rocks had ears
> To rapture, till the savage clamour drowned
> Both harp and voice; nor could the Muse defend
> Her son. So fail not thou, who thee implores:
> For thou art heavenly, she an empty dream.
>
> [VII.32–39]

Of course those who tore Orpheus limb from limb were women, maenads who in the midst of their frenzied worship of Dionysus were themselves inspired by a god. As Ovid tells the story, the women attack Orpheus because they think that he despises them:

> So with his singing Orpheus drew the trees,
> The beasts, the stones, to follow, when, behold!
> The mad Ciconian women, fleeces flung
> Across their maddened breasts, caught sight of him
> From a near hill-top, as he joined his song
> To the lyre's music. One of them, her tresses
> Streaming in the light air, cried out: "Look there!
> There is our despiser!" and she flung a spear
> Straight at the singing mouth, but the leafy wand
> Made only a mark and did no harm. Another
> Let fly a stone, which, even as it flew
> Was conquered by the sweet harmonious music,
> Fell at his feet, as if to ask for pardon.
>
> [Humphries, trans., XI.1–13]

Orpheus's music might have made him safe, but the maenads' own cacophanous music drowns Orpheus's in "savage clamour," and the woods and rocks, at first his worshipers, become the weapons of his death.

This compelling story obviously bothered Milton profoundly; he refers to it in "L'Allegro"—where Eurydice is only half-won and another music may please Pluto more; he refers to it again in "Lycidas," where Milton first asks the question he answers in *Paradise Lost* by calling Calliope an "empty dream":

> What could the muse herself that Orpheus bore,
> The muse for her enchanting son
> Whom universal nature did lament,
> When by the rout that made the hideous roar,
> His gory visage down the stream was sent,
> Down the swift Hebrus to the Lesbian shore.
> [58–63]

The fear of dismemberment so startling in these passages (like the dismemberment written out of *The Faerie Queene* by Spenser's revisions of Ovid), stresses the very vulnerability of the poet in his inspiration. The maenads not only destroyed a great and inspired poet, they destroyed an exemplary husband, who had descended to hell to retrieve his dead wife; as such they are incalculably central to Milton's own problems in writing *Paradise Lost*. The barbarous dissonance of Bacchus and his revelers stand for any readers who read without the proper inspiration that is implied by Urania's rendering them "fit" (though few). Yet we should not dismember the poem's relationship to its Ovidian text here and ignore the undeniable sexual conflict played out in its verses.

To image inspiration itself as female is no threat to Milton: his own muse is a protectress. But the inspiration *of* females—themselves inspired votaries of a god—is; we would do well to ask why. Milton would have known that Dionysus/Bacchus was not merely a wine-besotted drunkard, but a Comus-like god of the earth's fertility and therefore an especially appropriate pagan god to call up and cast out of his account of Hebrew creation. Insofar as the maenads share, however parodically and demonically, in the intimacy of relations between divine power and human song, Milton casts out a type of inspiration at the same time that he casts out a type of reader. His casting-out is, finally, crucially political, and we should consider for a moment how unfashionable and politically suspect the kind of inspiration Milton claimed for himself was in mid-seventeenth-century England.[50]

The anonymous author of *An Answer* to the *Doctrine and Discipline of Divorce* had taxed Milton with antinomianism:

> We answer: this is a wilde, mad, and frantick divinitie, just like to the opinions of the Maids of Algate; Oh say they, we live in Christ, and Christ doth all for us; we are Christed with Christ and Godded with God, and at the same time we sin here, we joyned to Christ do justice in him, for our life is hid with God in Christ.[51]

Milton's answer to this point in *Colasterion* was a witheringly gallant, "the Maids of Algate, whom he flouts, are likely to have more witt then the Servingman at Addlegate" (*CPW*.II.750). The principles on which Milton wrote the divorce tracts are not so free as the principles upon which he wrote *The Christian Doctrine* (where individual inspiration is to be trusted before the letter of Scripture); but that the anonymous author could tax him with a frenzied female antinomianism suggests the real intellectual danger posed by his own understanding of divine inspiration.

Another famous seventeenth-century antinomian, Anne Hutchinson, had not understood the mediate position in which she had been placed simply by being born a woman. If the soul before God had no sex, then why should not women—like maenads—have direct inspired relations with the divinity and be listened to in their

---

50. O. B. Hardison argues for the aesthetic/theological risk Milton takes in making the poem's verse unrhymed iambic pentameter. Citing Hobbes's censure of the notion of inspiration by which the poet, "enabled to speak wisely from principles of Nature and his own meditation, chooses rather to be thought to speak by inspiration like a Bagpipe," Hardison outlines the rationalist attack "on everything that Milton felt sacred in epic style." Of particular import is the need for rhyme as Dryden, for one, described it: "Imagination in a poet is a faculty so wild and lawless, that like a high-ranging spaniel, it must have clogs tied to it lest it outrun the judgment" (Preface to *The Indian Queen*, 1664). (The political implications of this Restoration poetic are obvious.) O. B. Hardison, "A Note on the Note on the Verse of Paradise Lost," a paper delivered at the annual convention of the Modern Language Association, Houston, Texas, December 1980.

51. Cited in *Complete Prose Works*, ed. Douglas Bush et al., 8 vols. (New Haven: Yale University Press, 1953), II, 750n.

interpretations of Scripture, equally with their husbands?[52] In 1666 Quaker Margaret Fell had written and published an argument in favor of the ministry of women, titled *Women Speaking Justified, Proved, and Allowed of by the Scriptures.*[53] Christopher Hill quotes two contradictory remarks by her fellow Quaker George Fox about the subjection of women. In the earlier remark, Fox flatly states that he would "suffer not a woman to teach nor usurp authority over the man, but to be silent. . . . If they will learn anything, let them ask their husbands at home." The later remark in 1680 shows qualified support of women: "Neither did God set the man over the woman whilst they kept the image of God and obeyed his voice." As Hill remarks, "between the two statements I have quoted, Fox had himself married."[54] (It was Margaret Fell whom he married.)

As the example of Anne Hutchinson suggests, the history of Protestantism is in part the history of controlling the expectations it raised in women.[55] A telling point made by the anonymous *Answer*

52. Daniel D. Hall, *The Antinomian Controversy, 1636–38: A Documentary History* (Middletown, Conn.: Wesleyan University Press, 1968), p. 311, explains that "Hutchinson's dramatic statement that she received divine revelations became the pretext for her banishment." As one of the judges remarks in the riveting transcript of her trial, "It is the most desperate enthusiasm in the world" (p. 342). She was condemned not merely for desiring to be "a greate Prophites" (p. 381), but because of the danger her "fluent Tongue & forwardness of Expression" posed "simple weomen of her own sex" (p. 365). Another judge summarizes: "You have stept out of your place, you haue rather bine a Husband than a Wife and a preacher than a Hearer; and a Magistrate than a Subject" (p. 383). News of the New England controversy made its way back to England immediately, forming the basis of the Presbyterian attack on Congregationalism in Robert Baillie's *A Discourse against the Errours of the Time* (1648).

53. Cited by Doris Mary Stenton, *The English Woman in History* (1957; rpt. New York: Schocken Books, 1977), p. 179.

54. Christopher Hill, *Milton and the English Revolution* (New York: Viking Press, 1977), p. 118.

55. Keith Thomas, *Religion and the Decline of Magic* (London: Weidenfeld and Nicholson, 1971), p. 138, remarks: "The prominence of women among the religious prophecy of this period is partly explained by the fact that the best hope of gaining an ear for female utterances was to represent them as the result of divine revelation." See also Natalie Zemon Davis, "City Women and Religious Change," in *Society and Culture in Early Modern France* (Stanford, Calif.: Stanford University Press, 1975), pp. 65–95.

to Milton's first divorce tract was that Milton's position allowed
women the same freedom as men had to divorce for incompatibility.
In the later *Tetrachordon* Milton even went so far as to allow the
woman to rule the man, if she were in fact his natural superior: for
then "a superior and more natural law comes in, that the wiser
should govern the less wise, whether male or female"
(*CPW*.II.589).

Against these startling and sweeping freedoms, Milton places the
originary law:

> He for God only, she for God in him.

What is perhaps less immediately striking, but more profoundly
interesting (in the context of Milton's sense of his inspiration) is that
in this arrangement of the wife's subjection to her husband there is
established not only a sexual hierarchy, but a mediated position for
the woman with respect to the divine source. *It negates a direct relationship between God and woman.* She is "covered" by her husband, the
male, and it is only through him that she may experience the divine.
The purpose of her existence is to know divinity, but only mediately,
through the darkened glass of her husband's divinity within.

The reasons for this choice (Fox at least had taken a different
stand on Eve's status in paradise) are understandable in terms of
the social history of seventeenth-century England. If each believer
had become his own priest, and was no longer a member of an
institutionally visible church, this priest found his congregation
shrunk to the literal foundation upon which Paul had based his
metaphoric description of Christ's relationship to his church: the
love of a husband for his wife. The monarchial state had also dis-
solved, to be reconstituted anew but without the divine sanctions so
successfully promulgated by Elizabeth and so unsuccessfully by the
Stuarts. Radical Protestants were thrown back on the one social
unit that might still stand—the nuclear family. The intense pressures on this unit required new political emphases, and the stress of
Puritan theology, while it looks like a fostering of woman's status,
actually puts her—as Milton does—in a more mediated position.

As Lawrence Stone points out, "one of the first results of the doctrine of holy matrimony was a strengthening of the authority of the husband over the wife, and an increased readiness of the latter to submit herself to the dictates of the former. . . . This is similar to the paradox by which the first result of an increased concern for children was a greater determination to crush their sinful wills by whipping them."[56]

Such is the chicken-and-egg problem of social change that it is also a distinct possibility that the need to reorient the family along stricter hierarchical lines was a cause of the doctrine of holy matrimony, not merely its result. Increasing the authority of the husband over the wife is a conservative social move designed to act as a safety valve on the revolutionary energies unleashed by the Reformation: if there were to be no more bishops and no more kings, there were still to be, finally and irrevocably, patriarchs. Smaller their kingdoms than before, but patriarchies nonetheless.

For a woman to have inspiration directly from God would be to threaten the last hierarchical relationship left; she would thereby have the authority to challenge her husband. By purging his audience of bacchantic revelers Milton purges the disordered unreason of anyone who would not be a fit reader. But taken in its Ovidian context, Milton is purging the maenad female reader who insists on a more direct relationship of her own to divine inspiration.[57] This may seem needlessly to narrow the definition of the unfit—doubtless many more readers than frenzied Protestant prophetesses actually belong in that number. But it usefully indicates the place where Milton draws the line between his traditional, masculine po-

56. Lawrence Stone, *The Family, Sex, and Marriage in England, 1500–1800* (1977; abridged ed., New York: Harper and Row, 1979), p. 142.

57. In the context of this negation of direct female inspiration from God, Sandra Gilbert and Susan Gubar print a very interesting female "revision" of Milton's Eve in Book V; in *Shirley*, Charlotte Brontë's heroine imagines a "woman-Titan. . . . she reclines her bosom on the ridge of Stilbro' Moor; her mighty hands are joined beneath it. *So kneeling, face to face she speaks with God.* That Eve is Jehovah's daughter, as Adam was his son" (*The Madwoman in the Attic: The Woman Writer and the Nineteenth-Century Literary Imagination* [New Haven: Yale University Press, 1979], p. 194; emphasis added). That Brontë keeps the kneeling posture may perhaps suggest her sympathetic response to Milton's underargument for female heroism.

etic inspiration—at the end of a long line of both pagan and Hebrew prophets—and the newer enthusiasms in which women could legitimately participate (and for which Milton has some Protestant political sympathies). It distinguishes the works of inspiration—some are true vocations, others are not.

The casting out of the maenad reader also usefully suggests where Milton's female reader, reading as a female, must place herself. To be a fit reader, the woman must accept a mediated, covered position, must freely choose to conform to the hierarchy. The hierarchical arrangement is flatly stated; it is not something Milton argues. The arrangement holds by divine fiat (rather like "die he or justice must"); and to "justify" God's ways to woman is not to explain the situation, but to make her choose to accept it. The entire pressure of the argument of *Paradise Lost* as directed at this "covered" female reader is for her freely to choose the mediated position and to accept its rewards with gratitude. And the poem most persuasively holds that there are rewards, rewards as great, in fact, as the rewards held out for man's acceptance of Christ to which they have from the time of Paul been an analogue. Adam chooses to die for love of Eve. Christ chooses to die for love of man. The first choice is wrong and the second is right: but they are both based in love. And one may heretically suspect that Adam's offered sacrifice derives from the divinity within him for which Eve was made.

Eve as Reader

Eve's mediate creation puts her in a distinctly more difficult interpretive situation than Adam; in a sense, Eve's position shares the mediateness of the fallen reader's perspective from the very inception of her prelapsarian creation. Just as Adam will need to be taught how to find the metaphorical "paradise within" after he has lost the literal paradise without, Eve has from her origin been enjoined to find a divinity within—moreover not within herself, but within another (or to put it even more narrowly, within a relationship with another). The indirectness of her position with respect to divine power informs the smallest but most telling details of her description of her own creation; if we contrast that description with the scene in which Adam remembers his own creation we shall see just how natural and proper her mediate position is—and again, what dangers it potentially poses.

When Adam tells Raphael in Book VIII how he awoke to find himself created he explains that:

> Straight toward heaven my wondering eyes I turned,
> And gazed a while the ample sky, till raised
> By quick instinctive motion up I sprung,
> . . . .
> Thou sun, said I, fair light,
> And thou enlightened earth, so fresh and gay,
> . . . .
> Tell, if ye saw, how came I thus, how here?
> Not of myself; by some great maker then,
> In goodness and in power pre-eminent.
>
> [VIII.257–79]

Adam knows instinctively and immediately what Satan so crucially forgets. Compare Eve's memory of her creation in Book IV as she describes it to Adam:

> I first awaked and found myself reposed
> Under a shade of flowers, much wondering where
> And what I was, whence thither brought, and how.
> Not distant far from thence a murmuring sound
> Of waters issued from a cave and spread
> Into a liquid plain, then stood unmoved
> Pure as the expanse of heaven; I thither went
> With unexperienced thought, and laid me down
> On the green bank, to look into the clear
> Smooth lake, that to me seemed another sky.
>
> [IV.450–59]

Where Adam looks up at the true sky and then springs up, immediately to intuit his maker, Eve bends down to look into "another sky"—a secondary, mediated, reflective sky: a mirror, in more ways than one, of her own being. In exchanging a vision of her own image in the "other sky" of the pool's mirror, for Adam, "whose image thou art," she ceases to look into a mirror, to know herself to be, in a sense, one herself. To say that Eve inhabits a mirror world of successively mediated figurations of divinity is to suggest the sheer difficulty of her interpretive situation. Because her first look at Adam does not tell her instantly that he is her superior, she needs to learn to see in a way necessarily more sophisticated than does Adam, who immediately knows in his vision that "one came, methought, of shape divine." Where Adam can see a true and present God, Eve must "see" moral abstractions:

> I yielded, and from that time see
> How beauty is excelled by manly grace
> And wisdom, which alone is truly fair.
> [IV.489–91]

Such interpretive experiences ought to have made her proof against the tempter's ploy: "Look on me, / Me who have touched and tasted" (IX.686–90); but in having learned to interpret her first responses as wrong (and her first responses in the temptation scene are right), Eve's prelapsarian experiences do not serve her well. She errs in assuming that the injunction against eating the apple is open to interpretation. She has already learned that her ignorance can be turned to wisdom by mediating advice, from Adam. And so rightly in her dream she mistakes the demonic voice she hears for Adam's. In this dream, too, she experiences an inspiration like the poet's: "Forthwith up to the clouds / With him I flew, and underneath beheld / The earth outstretched immense, a prospect wide" (V.86–88). Such inspiration is, of course, a demonic parody of the true, and her own waking response and Adam's interpretation of it prove it to be so.

Eve is, as she was made to be, a good listener. In having learned to love wisdom by listening to Adam, Eve may the more easily listen

to the tempter; all she finally does in choosing to eat the apple is to
substitute one mediating instrument of wisdom for another:[58]

> Here grows the cure of all, this fruit divine,
> Fair to the eye, inviting to the taste,
> Of virtue to make wise:
>
> [IX.776-78]

Satan chose his victim well.

He also, of course, chooses his time well, seducing Eve when she
is separate from Adam, her proper mediator. The means by which
she becomes separated from her husband—her own desire to labor
separately and hence more efficiently—are crucial to the redefinition of the family which Milton reflects and effects in his poem, and
to the differentiation of the labor of men from the labor of women
within society. In Adam and Eve's conversation on gardening in
Book IX, we see the economic issues of the reorganization of labor
which was being effected in the second half of the seventeenth century debated directly on the surface of the text. Briefly put, Eve
argues for a more efficient division of labor: "Let us divide our
labours." Adam argues against her point. Efficiency in the service
of God is not necessary. Labor is sacred.

> Yet not so strictly hath our Lord imposed
> Labour, as to debar us when we need
> Refreshment, whether food, or talk between,
> Food of the mind,
>
> [IX.235-38]

In Adam's view, this taskmaster God is one to whom he and Eve
owe feudal fealty (262), one who makes no division between labor
and living, or labor and leisure. Eve envisions an entirely different

---

58. For a subtle analysis of Eve's character as it may be understood in relation to
the arguments of the divorce tracts, see Mary Ann Nevins Radzinowicz, "Eve and
Dalila: Renovation and the Hardening of the Heart," in *Reason and Imagination:
Studies in the History of Ideas, 1600-1800* ed. J. A. Mazzeo (New York: Columbia
University Press, 1962), pp. 155-81.

arrangement, in which one "earns" the right to supper. Two different economic organizations find expression here—baldly put, a
feudal arrangement, in which God is lord, and a protocapitalistic
one, in which the laborer hires out his physical exertion and is paid
in terms of how much he has achieved. The ideology of labor
opened up here is not, of course, merely a consideration of
seventeenth-century modes of production; the Gospel parables offer such terms of labor as a way of talking about true service of God.
Yet when Adam prefaces his praise of Eve's eagerness for efficiency,
he interestingly confuses their two positions:

> nothing lovelier can be found
> In woman, than to study household good,
> And good works in her husband to promote.
>   [IX.232–34]

Adam's terms subtly distinguish between Eve's work (household
good) and his own ("good works") even as he maintains that they
must continue doing their identical work together. This distinction
seems to be moot—and would, in any event, not finally exist in a
truly feudal arrangement such as Adam has envisioned, where production and consumption take place together in the same household
unit. Was not the curse of the fall just such a division of labor, where
man must earn his living by the sweat of his brow, woman "laboring" now in pain to produce more laborers?

In Adam's praise of Eve's efficiency, we can see the modern patriarchal division of labor that, paradoxically, Eve's suggestion
about laboring separately would bypass. The narrative logic of the
poem insists that Eve's desire for independent labor is what helps to
make the fall happen; had she remained close to Adam, the fall
(presumably) would not have happened. The curse for the fall is
that men and women labor separately; the contemporaneous economic reality adumbrated by the poem was the great impact on
women of the reorganization of labor under the early capitalist system of seventeenth-century England. As evicted peasants turned
wage-laborers, women could no longer combine their general labor

with their care of their children. Thus by the seventeenth century women were overrepresented in the growing crowds of destitute laborers. Upper-class women, cut off from the imperialist world of capital production, became increasingly useless. Creatures of the salon, bearers of culture in a world where the arts and humanistic discipline had no real relation to politics. The new household, as Roberta Hamilton points out, was no longer

> a place to produce, rather a place to consume; no longer a place to "work" but only a place to "live": a place for private emotions and intimacy, a place for children, a world for women. This was a far different home from the one in which the Protestants had so recently enclosed the woman as good wife. And by a stroke of historical irony, when the world was divided in two, not only women but religion itself was relegated to the home.[59]

The conversation between the first husband and wife about efficient labor is preternaturally in touch with the shape of this ensuing history. The poem warns the reader that in Eve's desire for more efficient, literal labor lies the threat to a sacred vocation; what is true at the level of the poem's plot (and this part of the plot is Milton's creation) is true of history. Adam by his interpretation of what true labor is (it is sacred) would restrain Eve's slide into secularity. But it was a slide, as Max Weber points out, that became inevitable in history. That Eve's daughters lost a viable position in the new economy of secularized (separate) labor is also figured in the poem's concern for her "household good." Eve is pivotal in the poem's refiguration of labor as vocation and labor as work.

---

59. Hamilton, *Liberation of Women*, p. 96. Hamilton sees the greatest social change impinging on women when "Protestantism crossed historical paths and became entwined with capitalism. Its particular form of patriarchal ideology was then itself altered, providing a remarkably successful, at least in terms of its persistence, ideological basis for the bourgeois family" (p. 95). For an illuminating discussion of the impact of economic change on the laboring poor through the early modern period, see Keith Wrightson and David Levine, *Poverty and Piety in an English Village: Terling, 1525–1700* (New York: Academic Press, 1979), esp. chap. 7, "The 'Better Sort' and the Laboring Poor."

Eve's proper, freely chosen work includes listening. Thus rightly
Eve leaves the scene of Raphael's instruction of Adam, preferring
to hear such discourse not from an angel, but from her husband.

> Yet went she not, as not with such discourse
> Delighted, or not capable her ear
> Of what was high; such pleasure she reserved,
> Adam relating, she sole auditress;
> Her husband the relater she preferred
> Before the angel, and of him to ask
> Chose rather;
>
> [VIII.48–54]

The choice is not hard (and, considering Raphael's answer answer-
less about the astronomical organization of the universe, not entirely wrong in any event), and the rewards are compelling:

> he, she knew would intermix
> Grateful digressions, and solve high dispute
> With conjugal caresses, from his lip
> Not words alone pleased her. O when meet now
> Such pairs, in love and mutual honour joined?
>
> [VIII.54–58]

What Eve gains in going away is a topic for the meet and mutual
conversation that Milton had deemed, in the divorce tracts, to be
the sole basis of a fit marriage. As the narrator's outburst about
present loss makes clear, Eve's choice is the crucial foundation for
the perfect bliss of Edenic marriage:

> he that can prove it lawfull and just to claime the performance of a
> fit and matchable conversation, no lesse essentiall to the prime
> scope of marriage then the gift of bodily conjunction, or els to have
> an equall plea of divorce as well as for that corporall deficiency . . .
> shall restore . . . matrimony . . . as much as may be, to the serene
> and blissfull condition it was in at the beginning;
>
> [CPW.II.239–40]

The signal word used here and throughout the divorce tracts to describe a proper marriage bears directly on Milton's sense of his reader's cooperation in *Paradise Lost.* Because most of his direct addresses to the reader in the poem have to do with the problem of prelapsarian sexuality, it will be useful to look at Milton's arguments in the tracts about the means society may use to resurrect that relationship.

Milton persistently uses the word "fit" to describe the proper relations between husband and wife. So he asks in *Tetrachordon,* "Unless there be a love, and that love born of fitness, how can it last?" What "fitness" appears to mean is a union of minds, a likeness of disposition, and—specifically for the wife—an easy and happy conformity to her husband's desires. Milton's scriptural terms for the wife's position is as a "meet help." "Unfitness" is a "contrariety of mind," arising from a cause in "nature unchangeable": and Milton would not allow that any exercise of the will could repair "utter unfitnesse," it being by definition an "utter disconformity not concileable, because not to be amended without miracle" (*CPW*.II.669). Milton's consistent stance throughout the divorce tracts is that sexuality and procreation are lesser ends of marriage than mutual solace and help—the amiable and fit conversation of matrimony—a meet meeting of minds and characters, rather than sheer bodily conjunction. In this, of course, he went far beyond his century, and in defining the wife's work in marriage as being preeminently psychological ("concileable" support), the tracts failed, like *Areopagitica,* to move their immediate audience to action.[60]

What is perhaps most striking about Adam and Eve's marriage in the poem is that, in the context of the tracts' having made so little of sexuality in their arguments, Milton should then go on to cele-

60. Milton went so far as to argue that the wife's adultery should not be considered grounds for divorce—in this outstripping all centuries: "Next adultery does not exclude her other fitnes, her other pleasingnes; she may be otherwise both loving and prevalent, as many adulteresses be; but in this general unfitness or alienation she can be nothing to him that can please. In adultery nothing is given from the husband, which he misses, or enjoyes the less, as it may be suttly giv'n; but this unfitnes defrauds him of the whole contentment which is sought in wedloc" (*CPW*.II.674).

brate prelapsarian sexuality in such detail.[61] We do, of course, hear a "fit" conversation first, just before we witness the first embrace between our first parents: so Eve recounts her birth and its drama of her free acceptance of submission moments before we see the two naked embrace:

> our general mother, and with eyes
> Of conjugal attraction unreproved,
> And meek surrender, half embracing leaned
> On our first father, half her swelling breast
> Naked met his under the flowing gold
> Of her loose tresses hid:
>
> [IV.492–97]

This cannot help but be arousing to readers of both genders: a primal scene is a primal scene whatever the sex of the child. And that we read from a child's point of view is absolutely structured by Milton's constant reference to the pair as "our father," "our mother," and the stress on Eve's "swelling breast" (all infants have experienced nursing).

Though perhaps with less reason than the reader, Satan's response sums up the tumult of emotions such a scene necessarily arouses:

> aside the devil turned
> For envy, yet with jealous leer malign
> Eyed them askance, and to himself thus plained.
>   Sight hateful, sight tormenting! Thus these two
> Imparadised in one another's arms
> The happier Eden, shall enjoy their fill
> Of bliss on bliss, while I to hell am thrust,
> Where neither joy nor love, but fierce desire,
> Among our other torments not the least,
> Still unfulfilled with pain of longing pines;
>
> [IV.502–10]

---

61. John Halkett, *Milton and the Idea of Matrimony* (New Haven: Yale University Press, 1970), p. 115, suggests that Milton is obliged to underplay his heterodox opinions in the poem, it being a different public forum from the pamphlets.

So rhetorically adept a poet as Milton is never unaware of his reader's presence or response—and here he provides terms for what must be a large part of the reader's experience of Adam and Eve's embrace. Milton does not directly label this response as the reader's—it is Satan's. So it is with all the greater emphasis that Milton does explicitly indicate the reader's presence at another moment of Adam and Eve's sexual communion. Perhaps the most signal address to the reader (similar to the less stressed lecture on "shame," just after Milton describes the couple's nakedness at IV.313-18) is the paean to Wedded Love, where Milton defends Adam and Eve's sexual intercourse after they retreat to their "bower" at IV.739-75:

> into their inmost bower
> Handed they went; and eased the putting off
> These troublesome disguises which we wear,
> Straight side by side were laid, nor turned I ween
> Adam from his fair spouse, nor Eve the rites
> Mysterious of connubial love refused:
> Whatever hypocrites austerely talk
> Of purity and place and innocence,
> Defaming as impure what God declares
> Pure, and commands to some, leaves free to all.
> Our maker bids increase, who bids abstain
> But our destroyer, foe to God and man?
> Hail wedded love, mysterious law, true source
> Of human offspring, sole propriety
> In Paradise of all things common else.
> [IV.738-52]

The vocabulary and grammatical construction of this passage are strange. Its sense is, "whatever hypocrites say, this—I believe—happened." The negative constructions are not unmiltonic ("nor turned," "nor refused"), but they do defend against a trespass on privacy which more active constructions might have had; and they limn in little—turning away, refusing love—what happens all too often between fallen couples. The phrase "I ween" is signal: it is, in fact, unique to *Paradise Lost*. It is *hapax logomenon* to Milton's entire canon (at least on the testimony of the concordance). That it is Spenser's typical locution suggests, I think, the great indebtedness Milton has to Spenser in celebrating physical sexuality. Milton's own narrator's knowledge of Adam and Eve's sexual love comes spoken in Spenser's language.

Milton may owe to Spenser as well his defense of his poetic subject, which is here a fully and profoundly sexual, wedded love. Spenser had told us that he did not sing to such who could not feel kindly flame. Milton for his part makes an equally exclusive, radical choice:

> Far be it, that I should write thee sin or blame,
> Or think thee unbefitting holiest place,
> Perpetual fountain of domestic sweets,
> Whose bed is undefiled and chaste pronounced.
>   [IV.758–62]

In arguing against the hypocrites who talk austerely, and who held that Adam and Eve did not enjoy sexual intercourse before the fall, Milton casts out a barbarous dissonance like that made by Bacchus's revelers.[62] The social organization founded in this fully sexual love is, of course, specifically patriarchal: "all charities / Of father, son, and brother first were known" (IV.756–57). The "mysterious" law of wedded love is the "sole propriety" in paradise, that is, the sole instance of property rights ("all things common else"). In a sense, sexual intimacy is the sole continuity between pre- and postlapsarian human experience. While this continuity validates a sexual hierarchy (and the privacy of property vested in sexuality) by establishing it from the very beginning (as Fox's later view denied), Milton also elevates sexuality itself, justifying it by making it so profoundly basic to innocent human experience. Sexuality is political because it is literally the basis of the polis; its political importance defends its rights.

62. Kerrigan, *Prophetic Milton,* p. 136, interestingly argues that Milton's celebration of Love's "revels" purges the word of its association with Bacchus's rout: "As he drives off the fallen connotations of 'revels' Milton quite literally drives far off the savage clamor of 'Bacchus and his revellers.'"

What these daring celebrations of sexuality do in the poem is to enforce the physical reality of relations between Adam and Eve and make sense of, if they do not excuse, the drama of Adam's uxoriousness. What they do for the "covered" female reader is to persuade her of the importance of woman's participation in sexuality, the foundation of human society. Sexual pleasure itself is innocent when wedded to its relations in prelapsarian intimacy. A good marriage is a resurrection of the fall, restoring relations "as may be" to the condition they were in "at the beginning."

The price of so close an approximation of prelapsarian experience is the wife's submission. But Milton insists on its rewards, and although we may no longer need or care socially and theologically to assent to the arguments, it is not just to ignore Milton's attempts at persuasion. Eve's double subjection—for her punishment is not merely to bear children in pain, but to (re)submit to her husband's will—allows her to play a crucial part in the restoration of the couple to God's favor. Her powerlessness becomes the avenue to power in the new dispensation. In her plea, "Forsake me not thus Adam," Eve anticipates the successful supplication of them both before God. If Adam's choice to suffer death for her is not a true imitation of Christ's "heroic martyrdom unsung," but rather a hideous parody of it (though it is so close that Milton needs to correct any possible interpretation of it in this light as soon as it is suggested: IX.993), then Adam's relenting and his forgiveness is the true office of the bridegroom toward his bride:

> She ended weeping, and her lowly plight,
> Immovable till peace obtained from fault
> Acknowledged and deplored, in Adam wrought
> Commiseration; soon his heart relented
> Towards her, his life so late and sole delight,
> Now at his feet submissive in distress,
> Creature so fair his reconcilement seeking,
> His counsel whom she had displeased, his aid;
> As one disarmed, his anger all he lost,
> And thus with peaceful words upraised her soon.
> [X.937–46]

The repetition of the twice-described prostrate postures Adam and Eve take at the end of Book X (X.1085–1105) insists upon the centrality of her submission to the whole series of relations that are clearer after the fall than before. The inferior position Eve complained of just before she fell becomes no mere slot in a hierarchy, but an absolute foundation for repentance and love. Milton argues this series of connections in reverse in *Tetrachordon:*

> if man be the image of God, which consists in holines, and woman ought in the same respect to be the image and companion of man, in such wise to be lov'd, as the Church is belov'd of Christ, and if, as God is the head of Christ, and Christ the head of man, so man is the head of woman.
>
> [*CPW*.II.591]

It is, to be sure, a very complicated set of relations to bring to bear on a hierarchical social relation few people doubted at the time. Yet what we see in this argument is not so much Milton's personal misogyny, as a crucial social conservatism. We see how closely connected matrimonial and sexual relations are to the state of the literal, physical church—an institution that was very much in doubt in Milton's day. If the only replica of the hierarchy of Christ's church left standing—left to Milton, the radical Protestant and regicide—was the relations between husband and wife, those relations are quintessentially important, being the basic social unit. He argues that it is "unprofitable and dangerous to the Commonwealth, when the household estate, out of which must flourish forth the vigor and spirit of all publick enterprises is so ill contented and procur'd at home" (*CPW*.II.247).[63] Usually the matter of comedy, household discontents for Milton are potentially tragic, the matter not at all of mirth, but of imperial failure. Domestic relations become properly heroic and the fit subject for an epic.

Paradise Lost, by setting the politics of the family, the single basic

---

63. *CPW*.II.154–55; in *Bucer,* Milton makes the same argument: "First it will soon be manifest to them who know what wise men should know, that the constitution and reformation of a commonwealth ... is, like a building, to begin orderly from the foundation thereof, which is marriage and the family" (CPW.II.431).

unit of the human commonwealth, within the larger cosmic family of God the Father's government, is in part an extension of the argument of the divorce tracts' extreme care for the right ordering of human society. What is different from the tracts is the poem's address to the "covered" female reader, its efforts to persuade her freely to choose—as Eve learns the fatal consequences of not doing—the mediated position in which she finally exercises so much sway. The rewards she gains for making this choice are not only to have her gesture of submission and supplication become a paradigm for mankind's supplication of God—she also gains the love granted her by her husband, an intimacy of "conversation" both spiritual and physical which Milton celebrates in the epithalamic middle books of *Paradise Lost*.

The equality of labor which Barbara Lewalski sees as so central to Milton's view of women in *Paradise Lost*—"fully shared work in and responsibility for the human world"[64]—is the physical equivalent of their mutual conversation in the garden. Of course, postlapsarian, seventeenth-century English society saw no such equality of labor: economically women were losing ground to new modes of manufacture.[65] But Adam and Eve's shared labor is a powerful part of Milton's persuasive argument to his female reader that she can be placed in a position of helpmeet, which looks at the last like the equal sharing of life's important labors. Because of the sexual intimacy of Milton's focus, Adam and Eve are of equal importance, if not equal to each other.

In the last two books of the epic, Eve drops out almost entirely; it is not by her own choice that she is not given the vision of future history which Michael presents first to Adam's view and then to his hearing. Only recently has the narrative of the last two books of *Paradise Lost* not been felt to be, as C. S. Lewis so quotably put it, an

64. Barbara Kiefer Lewalski, "Milton on Women—Yet Once More," *Milton Studies,* 6 (1974), 7.

65. There was even less equality of labor as the century wore on. "As the workshop was severed from the household, most women became domestic household drudges for their absentee husbands," Christopher Hill, *Some Intellectual Consequences of the English Revolution* (Madison: University of Wisconsin Press, 1980), p. 39.

"untransmuted lump of futurity."[66] What is missed in Books XI and XII is not merely the loss of a densely textured verbal surface, but an intimacy of focus. Stanley Fish has suggested that Milton's technique in the parade of paradigmatic scenes in Michael's history is "reminiscent of *The Faerie Queene* where phrases like 'many a day' or 'meanwhile' or 'it fortuned then' are there only to separate one part of the allegory's total statement from another"—so each successive scene is merely another image of the same reality.[67] It is Milton's lesson in "reading history figuratively."

Insofar as the culminating lesson is Adam's understanding that what he has been given is "A paradise within thee, happier far," we can sense some rationale for Eve's exclusion from such instruction; such figurative reading has been her mode from the beginning, designed as she was for a God within. In any case, of course, she has her own series of "gentle dreams / Portending good" (XII.595–96): another parallel female vision of history, perhaps? We may lament Milton's suppression of this history (he was not loath to recount Eve's earlier dream). And it is not entirely irresponsible to guess that it might have moved along the lines of, say, Merlin's prophecy to Britomart—like Michael's, a Spenserian history: out of her womb would come a race culminating in the birth of another virgin, not Elizabeth, of course, but Mary, Mother of God. In suppressing this history (a suppression we know of only because he explains that there was, in fact, another set of dreams), Milton may finally become the "first of the masculinists"—as Virginia Woolf complained of him. Yet, when Eve recounts what those dreams were like (XII.610–23) she claims—against Michael's language— that *her* dreams came from God. It appears that while Michael recounts the visions of history to Adam, Eve gets hers direct from the divine source, unmediated. Eve's claim is unanswered. In asserting it, she has, literally, the last word in the poem, spoken by a character within it. The suggestion of direct inspiration and the placement of

66. Cited by Stanley E. Fish, *Surprised by Sin: The Reader in Paradise Lost* (Berkeley: University of California Press, 1971), p. 316.

67. Ibid., p. 317; such figuration is a way back to the "literalism we enjoyed before the Fall."

the speech gives Eve's claim great weight and a pivotal character. After the extremely careful theology and ethical discourse extensively given in Michael's prophetic history, we have Eve's assertion that the drama has all been hers:

> though all by me is lost,
> Such favour I unworthy am vouchsafed,
> By me the promised seed shall all restore.
> [XII.621–23]

(We may perhaps guess by this that Eve's dream might have been *Paradise Regained,* where her seed finally crushes her serpent adversary, after which "he unobserved / Home to his mother's house private returned.") What Eve chooses to do on the basis of her dreams, however, is more instructive and more pivotally political than their unknown content. She says to Adam:

> but now lead on;
> In me is no delay; with thee to go,
> Is to stay here; without thee here to stay,
> Is to go hence unwilling; thou to me
> Art all things under heaven, all places thou,
> Who for my willful crime art banished hence.
> [XII.614–19]

She virtually commands Adam to lead, actively choosing to follow and to remain inseparable from her husband. If Adam's paradise has become one "within," Eve's has become being with Adam. He has become her place. She chooses him over the garden she had wanted to manage independently of him.

To say that Milton argued for women's suppression/submission in *Paradise Lost* is to say nothing new; it has recently become a major complaint against Milton's achievement.[68] But to see the poem in terms of its politics of reading, asking if, in fact, we may distinguish

68. Marcia Landy, "Kinship and the Role of Women in *Paradise Lost,*" *Milton Studies,* 4 (1972), 3–18.

arguments made to readers of different genders, is to isolate the rewards offered for such submission. That the rewards are unacceptable does not mean they are not forcefully and alluringly offered. Lewalski rightly says that "few writers of any era—including our own—have taken women so seriously as Milton does."[69] Spenser of course did so before him; and like Spenser's, the seriousness of Milton's consideration of women has necessarily included women readers—with certain crucial political preconditions—within the fit readership of his poem. If it is too much to claim that the fit female reader—she who chooses obedience and submission—is a paradigm for *the* fit reader of the poem, it is still true that Eve's initial interpretive situation is closer to the fallen reader's corrected reading than any other perspective within the poem (Satan's is uncorrectable—though some readers may still choose it). So, too, Eve becomes the first character to choose the supplicant posture that Satan refuses to adopt with such resoundingly "heroic" rhetoric in Book I. That classical, masculine heroism Milton specifically rejects as an epic subject. One may legitimately wonder then, to whom belongs the "heroic martyrdom unsung" that Milton sings.

When Adam and Eve descend from their high garden they come out onto that level plain of human existence across which Una and the Redcrosse Knight, the first pair of Spenser's wanderers, begin, in high silhouette, to make their journey. Dryden, of course, noticing this connection, saw that *Paradise Lost* ends where *The Faerie Queene* begins. And so Spenser's couple, like Milton's, are also journeying toward the resurrected internal and apocalyptic garden of Eden. Dryden weighs together their claims to be true heroic poems:

> Spenser has a better plea for his Faery Queen, had his action been finished, or had been one. And Milton, if the Devil had not been his hero, instead of Adam; if the giant had not foiled the knight, and driven him out of his stronghold, to wander through the world with his lady errant.[70]

69. Lewalski, "Milton on Women," p. 5.
70. John Dryden, *Essays,* ed. W. P. Kerr, 2 vols. (1900; rpt. New York: Russell and Russell, 1961), II, 165.

Dryden is wrong in his judgments of the poems as epics; his censure of *Paradise Lost* reveals how completely his neoclassical reading misses Milton's redefinition of heroism, a misreading all the more remarkable because in recognizing Milton's relations to Spenser, he had before him all the ingredients for a right reading of Milton's poem. Spenser had prepared the way for seeing the politically complicated relations between the sexes as itself a heroic subject. Caught by history in a polis ruled by a woman, Spenser had fulfilled his epic assignment of imperial celebration by scrutinizing the full force of sexual power within his society. If he failed to win that society's approbation (and to finish his epic), the fault was not entirely his own. Following after Spenser, and finding himself in an entirely different political dilemma, Milton like his grand original also scrutinizes the crucial political issue of relations between the sexes and like his teacher argues that faithful love is as heroic a subject, and one as fundamental to empire, as the "tedious havoc" of "battles feigned."

Yet however wrong Dryden is in condemning the poems as epics, he is profoundly right to sense that, at the very end of *Paradise Lost,* Adam and Eve, bringing us with them, come to live in a Spenserian world for good.

> The world was all before them where to choose
> Their place of rest, and Providence their guide:
> They hand in hand with wandering steps and slow,
> Through Eden took their solitary way.
> [XII.646–69]

That the infinity of possibility seems somehow comforted of its fearsome blankness by the promise of providential guidance; that Adam and Eve's solitary, yet hand-in-hand wandering balances loss against saving touch; that this pair, driven out into the desolation away from paradise, is still, finally, coming home—that all this can possibly be true witnesses the subtle balance of emotional power there is in *Paradise Lost,* and testifies to the success with which Milton makes readers take a Sidneyan goodness in hand which without delight they would fly as from a stranger. His achievement is more than an argument for a *felix culpa;* it is also more than the quiet beyond tragedy. It is a miracle of tone, and part of the immense pressure behind the power of the moment, both for Milton and for his reader—together readers of Spenser—flows from its origin in *The Faerie Queene*.

Index

Milton's Spenser

Designed by G. T. Whipple, Jr.
Composed by Emerald Graphic Systems
in 10½ point Baskerville, 3 points leaded,
with display lines in Signet
Roundhand and Baskerville.
Printed offset by Thomson-Shore, Inc.
on Warren's Number 66 text, 50 pound basis.
Bound by John H. Dekker & Sons, Inc.

Library of Congress Cataloging in Publication Data

Quilligan, Maureen.
   Milton's Spenser.
   Includes index.
   1. Milton, John, 1608–1674.   Paradise lost.
   2. Milton, John, 1608–1674.   Areopagitica.   3. Spenser,
   Edmund, 1552?–1599.   Faerie queene.   4. Spenser,
   Edmund, 1552?–1599—Influence—Milton.   5. Politics
   in literature.   I. Title.
   PR3562.Q54   1983   821'.4   83-45149
   ISBN   0-8014-1590-X